The Cooper's Hawk

Breeding Ecology & Natural History of a Winged Huntsman

Robert N. Rosenfield

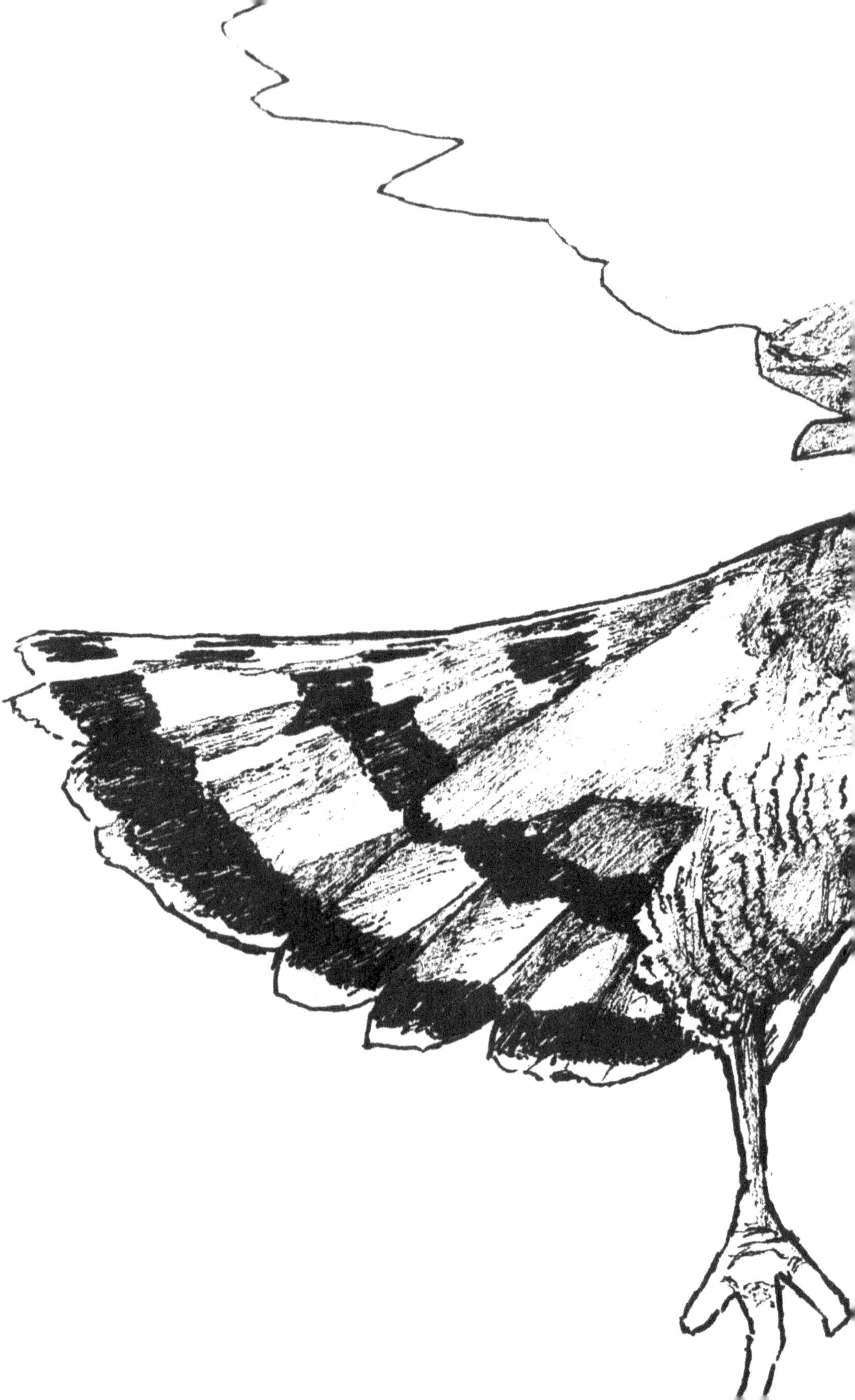

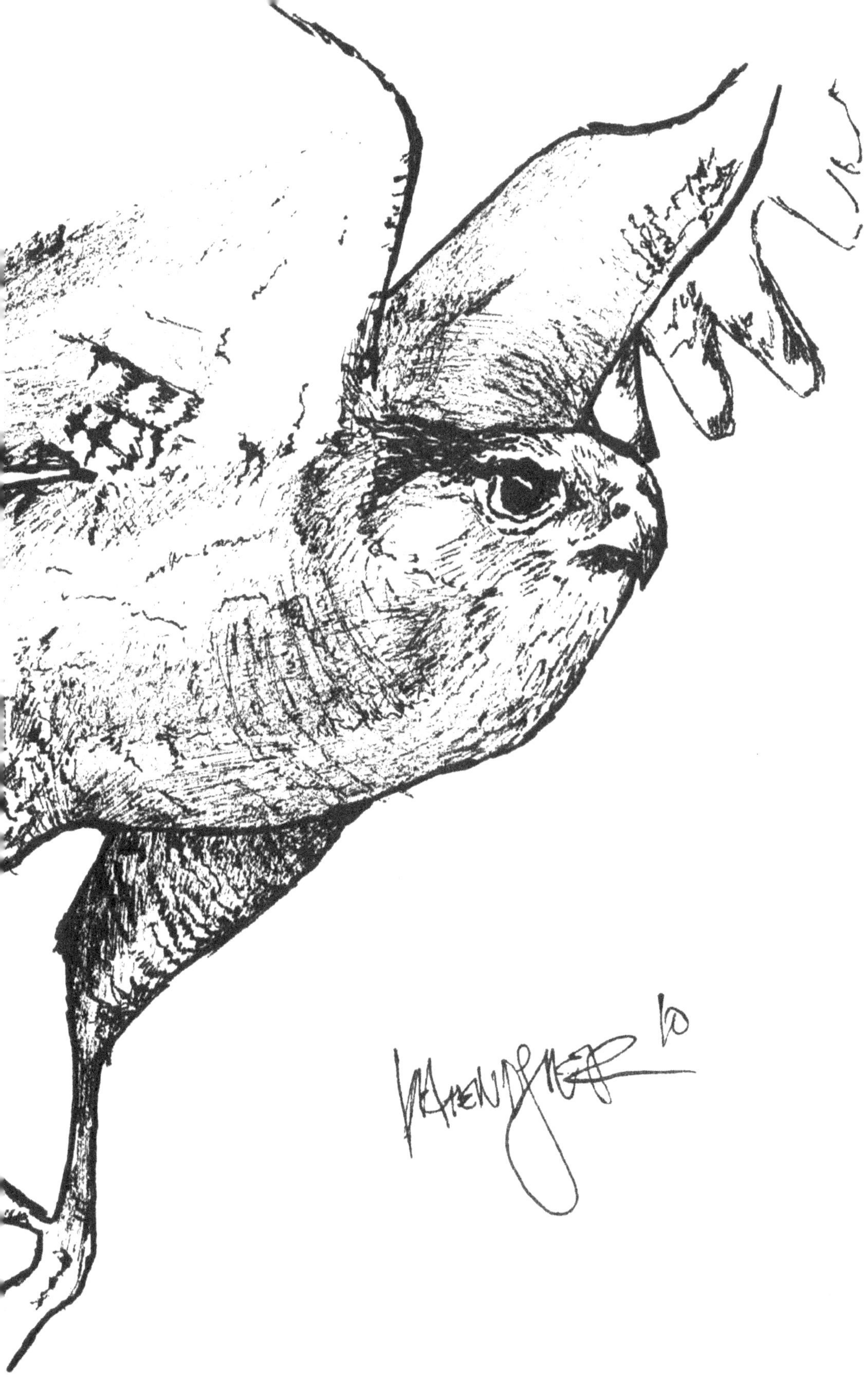

ISBN-13: 978-0-88839-082-0 [trade edition softcover]
ISBN-13: 978-0-88839-116-2 [trade edition hardcover]
Copyright © 2018 Robert N. Rosenfield

Cataloging in Publication Data

Library and Archives Canada Cataloguing in Publication

Rosenfield, Robert Norman, author
The Cooper's hawk : breeding ecology & natural history of a winged huntsman / Robert N. Rosenfield.

Includes bibliographical references and index.
ISBN 978-0-88839-082-0 (softcover)
ISBN 978-0-88839-116-2 (hardcover)

1. Cooper's hawk. I. Title.

QL696.F32R665 2018   598.9'44   C2018-902850-5

All rights reserved. No part of this publication may be reproduced, stored in a retrieval system or transmitted, in any form or by any means, electronic, mechanical, photocopying, recording, or otherwise (except for copying permitted by Sections 107 and 108 of the U.S. Copyright Law and except for book reviews for the public press), without the prior written permission of Hancock House Publishers.

Illustrations and photographs are copyrighted by the artist.

Printed in the USA

PRODUCTION: M. Lamont
TECHNICAL EDITOR: A. Stewart

FRONT COVER: Cooper's Hawk pursuing juvenile American Robin by Bryce Robinson (ornithologi.com)

BACK COVER: Juvenile Cooper's Hawk by Brian Rusnica

Published simultaneously in Canada and the United States by
HANCOCK HOUSE PUBLISHERS LTD.
19313 Zero Avenue, Surrey, BC Canada V3Z 9R9
(604) 538-1114   Fax (604) 538-2262

HANCOCK HOUSE PUBLISHERS
#104-4550 Birch Bay-Lynden Rd, Blaine, WA U.S.A. 98230-9436
(800) 938-1114   Fax (800) 983-2262

www.hancockhouse.com   sales@hancockhouse.com

THE COOPER'S HAWK

Breeding Ecology & Natural History
of a Winged Huntsman

ROBERT N. ROSENFIELD

TABLE OF CONTENTS

Foreword 09
Preface 13

CHAPTER ONE — 18
Introduction

The Species and its Celebrity 18

CHAPTER TWO — 27
You Are What You Eat

Overview 27
Food habits study, diet & foraging behavior 29
Bird feeder use and disease 39
Climate change 47

CHAPTER THREE — 50
Courtship & Nesting Biology

Overview & nest building 50
Courting 58
Vocalizations 64
Extra-pair paternity 68

CHAPTER FOUR — 77
The Breeding Population & Habitat Suitability

Overview 78
Population abundance & finding nests 79
Nesting densities 85

Reproductive output 92
Nest Success 98
Survival of breeding adults 101
Habitat suitability 111

CHAPTER FIVE 119
Individual Traits: The Descriptive Currencies of Natural History Dynamics

Overview 119
Eye color 121
Body Mass 126

CHAPTER SIX 132
The Meaning & Implication of Natural History Variation

Natural history variation among populations of
breeding Cooper's Hawks 133
Variation in breeding natural histories between Cooper's
Hawks and other raptors 137
Final thoughts.. 138

References 142

Index 159

*For David Evans, my first mentor,
Madeline Hardin, my life partner,
Alexandra and Keeley, my daughters,
and for Louella, my mother.*

Foreword

Whenever anyone, be it a raptor biologist or a member of the general public, raises the subject of the Cooper's Hawk with me, four things immediately come to mind: 1) how things have changed for this species over time; 2) dinosaurs; 3) tenacity, and 4) Bob Rosenfield. Let's tackle number one first.

Way back in 1904, Neltje Blanchan, a U.S. scientific historian and nature writer who published several books on wildflowers and birds and was known for synthesizing scientific interest with poetic phrasing, actually penned these words to describe the Cooper's Hawk in her book Birds That Hunt and Are Hunted: "Like the sharp-shinned hawk in habits as in plumage, this, its larger double, lives by devouring birds of so much greater value than itself that the law of the survival of the fittest should be enforced by lead until these villains, from being the commonest of their generally useful tribe, adorn museum cases only…. It is well known to be the most audacious robber the farmer has to contend with in the protection of his poultry … unfortunately it is only too often the case that many of our harmless and really beneficial hawks have to suffer for the depredations of these daring thieves."

To be fair to Ms Blanchan, in those days, and carrying right on into the Dirty Thirties, when countless numbers of eagles, hawks, and falcons were blasted out of the air for sport at fall migration places such as Pennsylvania's Hawk Mountain, almost all raptors were deemed to be "chicken-hawks" that were to be shot on sight. While raptors are now protected by federal, state, and provincial laws to their fullest extent, I was saddened to read in this volume that misguided shootings still occur here and there, particularly in urban areas! But what came next for the Cooper's Hawk was far worse. We almost lost the bird! The insidious overuse of organochlorine pesticides, such as DDT, in our incessant war on insects, coupled with industrial by-products in the form of poly-chlorinated biphenyls (PCBs), caused several bird-eating species, including the Cooper's, to produce abnormally thin-shelled eggs that cracked under the incubating adult. Their numbers plummeted over the years until, thankfully, in 1972 the use of organochlorines was prohibited in the U.S. and soon elsewhere. Cooper's Hawks have not only roared back with a vengeance, but may even surpass their original population size. Like their raptorial cousins, the Peregrine Falcon, the Merlin, and the Bald Eagle, to name but a few species, these speedy hawks have adapted to living in cities and suburbia in a big way! Today, Cooper's Hawks are the most common raptor seen hanging around bird feeders, which means that millions of North Americans are likely to see one in their lifetime. For those who do not get that exquisite pleasure, just take a peek on YouTube. This book will undoubtedly help those lucky folks to better understand and appreciate this marvelous product of nature.

And why do Cooper's Hawks remind me of dinosaurs? Well, if the mighty Golden Eagle represents the Tyrannosaurus Rex of that long-gone reptilian world, surely the Cooper's Hawk is the Velociraptor of the bird world! I have heard numerous stories about their intelligent hunting techniques, including using rooftops of houses as cover to sneak up on an unsuspecting group of Rock Pigeons, only to dash out at the right moment and sink their needle-sharp talons into the back of one of the slowest or dull-witted flock members. It is also common knowledge that Cooper's Hawks are not averse to getting "down and dirty" by hitting the ground to run down prey in the thickest of thickets.

That brings me to the third aspect of this amazing bird—its tenacity. I wish that I could recall where I read it, but all I can conjure up in my aging grey cells is that it was definitely a legitimate anecdote in some book written by one of those icons of wildlife management, such as Cleveland Bent, Joseph Grinnell, or Edward Howe Forbush, back in the good old days. I read it years ago and I have never forgotten it. Now, I am not sure if those reading these words know what a bustle is, but to save you Googling it, it is "a type of framework used to expand the fullness or support the drapery of the back of a woman's dress, occurring predominantly in the mid- to late 19th century." Picture a pioneer woman wearing such a dress and standing in the front yard of her log home and chatting with a neighbor. Now visualize a totally panicked, screaming chicken bolting across the yard toward her with a Cooper's Hawk on foot in hot pursuit! With nowhere to hide, the hen ducks under the woman's huge dress and cowers there, thinking that it has outsmarted its relentless tormentor. But this is no ordinary hawk, and the hunter, not to be deterred, dashes right under the woman's dress to grab the chicken! What a great story!

So, I have saved the best for the last. I cannot remember which it was of the forty or so Raptor Research Foundation meetings where I first laid eyes on Robert Rosenfield, but I do recall that I took an immediate and strong liking to him! Who can forget the very first presentation they witnessed being given by this youthful, energetic man?! He often had his audience in stitches, but at the same time completed what was invariably a class act by basing his talk on solid scientific facts and hypothetical-deductive reasoning. Who would be surprised to learn that Bob has been given a slew of awards for his teaching and his research abilities?! To be truthful, I was sometimes taken aback by his almost over-the-top politeness and complimentary nature in my conversations with Bob, but I soon came to realize that, "Hey, this guy's the real deal—he is just a totally sincere and respectful fellow!" More to the point, I must have done something right in his eyes, because here I am, writing the foreword for his terrific new book on his favorite bird—the Cooper's Hawk. While lots of researchers have studied this species over the years, there is nobody, and I mean nobody, who matches the knowledge and enthusiasm possessed by this remarkable man. Who among us can claim to have climbed into over 1,500 Coop nests over a 38-year period?! He is literally Mister Cooper's Hawk!

As someone who studied American Kestrels as a model for raptor research for four decades, attended more raptor conferences worldwide than I can remember, and published almost 200 peer-reviewed papers on birds of prey, I thought I knew a lot about Cooper's Hawks. Boy, was I wrong!! Using his impressive scientific and narrative skills, incorporating myriad spectacular and well-chosen color photographs, and throwing in a dash of entertaining prose here and there (I loved his stories of mist-netting these hawks and the tail-less male!), Bob expounds on a wide variety of subjects in his story of the Cooper's Hawk, including climate change, extra-pair paternity, ecological traps, divorce, incest, and adjusting sex ratios. And as the consummate professor, he challenges the reader at the very outset of the book and then offers an opportunity to grade oneself at the end. Do not just buy this book and merely admire the photos and peruse the pages, or worse, immediately shove it up on your library shelf to gather dust there—actually sit down and read it! I guarantee you will not be disappointed.

— **David M. Bird, Ph.D**
Emeritus Professor of Wildlife Biology
McGill University

Photo by Tom Muir

Imagine nature constructing a predator that is fast on both foot and wing, fiercely cunning, and has the ability to transform its size beyond its genetic construct to fit its palate. A species that has stretched its niche by nesting abundantly in just about every landscape that humans occupy, alter, or inadvertently create on this carnivore's behalf this, ironically, despite intense human persecution across generations of the organism's breeders. It can adjust its offspring sex ratio at the command of population shifts, and has sewn a social web of reproductive deceit at the expense of its partner. These natural history phenomena accord with the life and times of the blue darter, a winged huntsman.

This is North America's Cooper's Hawk.

Preface & Natural History Challenge

Natural history is a foundational pillar of biology that involves the exciting possibility of discovering, naming, and, most especially, describing a species. Such a description includes its size, color, what sounds it produces, and if it's a bird, an accounting of its nesting habitat among other histories of its life in a natural setting. By doing this, we archive a unique niche of life.

Natural history accounts of species are important to society, as the primary way most people connect or relate to nature (Beehler 2010). In fact, the mandate of natural history is to tell nature's story. As a discipline, natural history helped pave the way for the modern scientific study of genetics, physiology, ecology, and the potential for a species to adapt or evolve within a fast-changing, human-dominated world. Many of these scientific themes led to my life-long connection with the Cooper's Hawk (*Accipiter cooperii*), a sprint-flying ambush-hunter now frequently observed breeding and preying on birds, 'urban fast food' available in residential backyards across much of North America. This surprising, but now common urban phenomenon involving a species once known as a secretive forest hawk represents a wonderful comeback story. As was true for other birds of prey, or raptors, the population of Cooper's Hawks declined precipitously around the mid-20th century due to the ill-effects of pesticide contaminants, persecution through illegal shooting, habitat loss, and other human-induced environmental degradations. Not so long ago, extinction was believed to be a real possibility for the Cooper's Hawk.

The general and depressing opinion of birders and many avian ecologists was that the Cooper's Hawk was no longer breeding, or was nesting in markedly reduced numbers, in many parts of North America during the 1950s into the 1970s. That led to the formal conservation listing of this raptor in several states. It was declared "threatened" in Wisconsin in 1979. This action prompted my undergraduate advisor, Dr. Raymond K. Anderson, at the University of Wisconsin at Stevens Point, who was familiar with my field studies with other raptors, to offer me an M.S. graduate assistantship to work on determining the population status of Wisconsin's nesting Cooper's Hawks. I humbly turned this gracious invitation down several times before finally agreeing to proceed with the project in 1980. Why my declines? Because I had never seen a Cooper's Hawk nest and had no first-hand knowledge about the natural history of its breeding. I was leery about trying to find nests that might not exist! And I didn't know precisely when or where I should search for breeding birds.

Successful efforts to determine the species' status hinged squarely on being able to find nests, which compelled me to quickly learn and apply information about the bird's natural history. For example, learning that a *whaa* call from a female Cooper's Hawk in spring indicates that she's probably within about 50 meters (164 feet) of her nest alerted me to intensify my search effort when I heard this wail.

Thirty-eight years later, I have found and climbed into well over 1,500 nests, most of these in Wisconsin, where, fortunately, our initial work resulted in a recommendation by me and Dr. Anderson in 1983 to remove the apparently thriving statewide breeding population of the Cooper's Hawk from its formal "threatened" listing in the state. I have also conducted research on the status of nesting Cooper's Hawks while teamed with dedicated scientists in North Carolina, North Dakota, British Columbia, and New Mexico. The scope of this research mostly involved population biology and behavior (and always fun!), but it allowed me to continue expanding my knowledge about the natural history of breeding Cooper's Hawks.

Our investigations of Cooper's Hawks, especially urban birds, includes climbing to tree nests in parks and on residential street boulevards to count and band nestlings, and trapping breeding adults with a live, decoy Great Horned Owl (*Bubo virginianus*). Dazzling defensive flying stoops by scolding, seemingly angry adult Cooper's Hawks at this perceived nest predator readily draws public curiosity, puzzlement and concern. Our work has sometimes even provoked emergency 911 calls to the police! We do, of course, have to secure permission to enter private lands to access many urban nests. In turn, we spend considerable time informing the general public about what we are doing and why. Some of these interactions, I am pleased to say, have led to collaborations with the public that produced new natural history discoveries by citizens that were published in the scientific literature with these collaborators as co-authors (e.g., Rosenfield and Sobolik 2014, Rosenfield *et al.* 2011). Explaining our research activities and answering the public's questions is what most prompted the writing of this book. My objective therefore is to provide general readers interested in nature and birds with a narrative and photos that describe the natural history of breeding Cooper's Hawks.

Throughout the book I've strived to use the plain, conversational language that I use with the public at nest sites, along with some 'professional speak' to be fair and respectful of science.   Citizens frequently ask how we find nests and whether our activities jeopardize the welfare of the birds, so I will also explain why and how field studies are done on predatory hawks, as well as convey findings from my collaborations throughout North America, emphasizing both the variations and commonalities in this hawk's biology among different populations of Cooper's Hawks.

I challenge readers to catalog, as completely as reasonably possible, the number of ways I indicate that the natural history of the breeding Cooper's Hawk varies among populations of this species, and how this hawk's natural history varies from that of other nesting raptors. I make this request in part because, too often, I find the general public and even colleagues tend to overly generalize about the natural history of a species, both within the species and across similar groups of birds, in this case, raptors. Many of the things we've learned about this species demonstrate how inappropriate it is to extrapolate that way and thereby minimize or even confuse the natural histories of different populations of that species or to ambiguate the unique, natural history of one species with another (see Bielefeldt and Rosenfield 1997, Meiri and Yom-Tov 2004, Pavón-Jordán *et al.* 2013). Accordingly, I will provide an overview of some of these Cooper's Hawk novelties and other contexts about natural history in my brief conclusion at the end of this book to help you gauge how well your tally aligns with mine. But try not to peek ahead before you do your homework!

My hope is that this text's natural history accounts will aid the curious public in interpreting the behaviors of nesting Cooper's Hawks and allow them to recognize the ecological contexts of their breeding activities. In turn, the book may enhance the public's appreciation of the nesting activities of a predator that was generally long regarded as shy and difficult to observe. This text, however, should also serve academics, including research and agency biologists charged with management of raptors. The current global concern about the loss and conservation of Earth's biodiversity requires comprehensive, factual knowledge of particular species. Yet, unfortunately, organismal biology and the breadth of a species' natural history is often poorly represented in biological education (Greene 2005).

I also hope that college students and others may find this text useful in prompting new questions for study. Accordingly, I will often point out intriguing new ecological questions that our findings, along with those of our colleagues, have generated regarding this awe-inspiring animal that was formerly in population peril. I encourage readers who may want more scientific detail and context, including information outside of the subject of nesting biology, to consult the technical literature in the References section. I have provided a comprehensive list of the scientific literature concerning the biology of the Cooper's Hawk and other pertinent sources from avian ecology overall.

I believe the Cooper's Hawk's broad, continental, and readily observed urban presence gives it the potential to serve as an ambassador to the public on the biology of birds of prey, and highlights its use as a medium for investigating predator-prey dynamics in increasingly human-dominated settings. These roles could enhance conservation and management efforts, which are always dependent in part on public education in science and biology (Miller 2005, Bird *et al.* 2018).

I emphasize that I did not attain these natural history observations and interpretations alone, and thus my writing often alternates between the first and third person. This book represents scores of collaborations, so it's imperative that I thank several parties and co-workers with whom I forged some of my most enriching, colorful, and lasting friendships, both personal and professional.

The following entities provided essential clerical, logistical, and monetary support: Wisconsin Department of Natural Resources (WDNR); U.S. Geological Survey's Fish and Wildlife Service and the Alaska Science Center, Anchorage, Alaska; the Wisconsin, North Dakota, and Great Lake Falconers Associations; Madison Audubon Society; Wisconsin Society for Ornithology; Nongame Wildlife Program of the North Dakota Game and Fish Department; British Columbia Habitat Conservation Trust Fund; British Columbia Ministry of Environment; Saanich Parks Department of Victoria, British Columbia; and the Society for Tympanuchus Cupido Pinnatus, Ltd. Much closer to my academic home, the Biology Department, Personnel Development Committee, Letters and Science Foundation, and the Wisconsin Cooperative Fishery Unit at the University of Wisconsin at Stevens Point (UWSP) provided pivotal support, both monetary and otherwise. Charles and Mary Nelson, Frank Barick, and B. Bastone-Cunningham made generous financial donations. I extend sincere appreciation to the numerous landowners who provided enthusiastic support for our studies and granted us access to their properties.

Raymond Anderson, my undergrad and M.S. advisor (UWSP), Bill Smith (WDNR), and Randle Jurewicz (WDNR) were keenly instrumental in providing impetus to start this research. Mark Fuller (USGS) and renowned raptor research pioneers Fran and Frederick Hamerstrom guided the study's initial design. I also acknowledge the exemplary raptor-trapping and handling training I received from my good friend Dave Evans, my first mentor, and the excellent counsel and scholarship imparted to me by my Ph.D. advisor, Jim Grier, at North Dakota State University. I extend special thanks for the support and assistance provided by my good friends and colleagues, Bill and Norma Allen, Robert Bell, Mike Bozek, Joe and Karen Branch, Jenna Cava, Timothy G. Driscoll, Eric Epstein, Marge Gibson, Matt Giovanni, Dave Grosshuesch, Gene Jacobs, Shelley Jansky, Andrew Kanvick, Larry Kinyon, Ken Lange, Susan Marquenski, Bill Mattox, Brian Millsap, Chris Morasky, Terri Beth Peters, Adam Rosenfield, James Schneider, Larry Sobolik, Steve and Kathleen Taft, Marc Thwaits, Jonathan Wilde, and Chris Yahnke. I am most grateful to my close friends Andy and Irene Stewart (British Columbia) and Robert Murphy (North Dakota/New Mexico), who allowed me to expand collaborative Cooper's Hawk research across western North America. Bill Stout and I forged a multi-decade research effort on nesting Cooper's Hawks, apart from my 38-year efforts on this breeder elsewhere in Wisconsin, regarding the pioneering population in metropolitan Milwaukee, research that has sharpened my view of urban bird ecology. I much admire Bill's work ethic and professionalism in directing field studies across a very large and bustling study area. My friend Joe Papp also displayed remarkable dedication to difficult fieldwork and contributed arduously long hours in tree-blinds (he helped build) documenting prey deliveries to nestling Cooper's Hawks. Former undergraduate students in my lab, Travis Booms and Sarah Sonsthagen, continue decades later to collaborate with me frequently on Cooper's Hawk studies despite their busy and accomplished biological careers, for which I feel most privileged.

Natural historian photographers Madeline Hardin, Rick Page, Tom Muir, Brian Rusnica, John Seibel, Larry Sobolik, Brad Stewart, Janelle Taylor, Steve Taft, and Eric Wagner graciously contributed excellent images that richly enhanced this book's presentation of this hawk's breeding habits for which I am most grateful. I also extend sincere thanks to Katie Huber and Bryce Robinson for their beautiful illustrations. Bryce worked tirelessly to produce both the cover illustration and the bowing display to 'natural history exactness' for which I am particularly thankful.

I offer heartfelt personal gratitude to Colleen Larson and to my mother and father, Louella and Harold Rosenfield, for their unyielding support to my personal and scientific aspirations. I was also most lucky to have some of the most caring, and at one time, youngest field partners, my daughters Alexandra and Keeley Rosenfield, both of whom always, with poise, remind me of what really matters in life. Madeline Hardin provides a warm place for me to work, and she is an invaluable field and family partner of impeccable personal character. This project could not have been completed without Maddie's varied skills and loving support. She, Travis Booms, Grainger and Terry Hunt, and Andy Stewart provided critical reviews of earlier drafts of this work for which I am most grateful. Much appreciation is extended to Doreen Martens, whose sharp editorial skills also improved this work immeasurably, and to Myles Lamont at Hancock House for his sound guidance in the production of this book.

I dedicate this book to the hundreds of UWSP undergraduate students whose displays of enthusiasm and insightful counsel during our field collaborations with Cooper's Hawks were inspiring. I also dedicate this text to my late and dear friend John Bielefeldt for his keen natural history insights, perceptive wisdom, and warm friendship. His field savvy and communicative skills were unparalleled.

Lastly, I alone own any missteps in this book's presentations.

Robert N. Rosenfield
January 2018

CHAPTER ONE

The Species & Its Celebrity

The Cooper's Hawk is a slender-bodied, crow-sized, diurnal raptor that mostly hunts songbirds and doves, but as a 'switch-hitter', also captures small mammals such as chipmunks. It traditionally has been described as a forest raptor, possessing a long tail used as a rudder and relatively short, rounded wings that, along with its rather svelte build, allow remarkable agility in maneuvering through the relatively thick vegetation in which it likely first evolved. Cooper's Hawks, also called 'blue darters' in part for the gray-blue backs and tails seen in adults, are known for their high-speed flights over short distances in surprise attacks on live prey. They also exhibit quick dexterity in occasional foot chases on the ground, as they will pursue prey into dense thickets and even into earthen burrows. They will boldly pursue prey fleeing into buildings. They have taken captive doves from my garage when the door was only inches ajar!

Adults exhibit an orange-brown or rufous, horizontally barred chest, a gray-blue back and a very dark blue, essentially black, cap. Dark orange to striking (I think sexy) blood-red eyes occur in older males. Adult females of the same age as males tend to have lighter-colored, orange or dark orange eyes. In its first year of life, the bird is markedly different from an adult in plumage pattern and color. As a nestling, it has blue-gray eyes that turn yellow during its first summer, a color that persists through the first winter. Vertical brown streaks adorn the chest and belly, and a brown backside and head occur in first-year birds (Wattel 1973, Rosenfield and Bielefeldt 1993a).

The socially monogamous Cooper's Hawk is widely distributed as a breeding bird in temperate North America, ranging across the continent from both coasts into southern Canada and southward into Florida and northern Mexico (Fig. 1.1; Rosenfield and Bielefeldt 1993a and see Climate Change, Chapter 2). Within this range the bird nests in large forests of all species of trees, isolated woods in prairies,

Cooper's Hawks likely first evolved in forests and their relatively svelte body form and short, rounded wings allow for dexterous movement through thick vegetation, while the long tail acts as a rudder to facilitate apt maneuverability in such habitat. Photo by Thomas Muir.

shelterbelt stands, and more recently in cities and towns of all sizes. Although some populations are rather sedentary, most northerly birds are highly or partially migratory. The latter group consists of individuals that occupy breeding ranges year-round; migrating birds overwinter as far south as Mexico and Central America (Stout *et al.* 2008, Curtis *et al.* 2006).

The Cooper's Hawk is a close relative of two other widely distributed North American forest accipiter hawks, the smaller Sharp-shinned Hawk (*A. striatus*) and the larger Northern Goshawk (*A. gentilis*). All three accipiters have long tails and short, rounded wings, and similar feather color and plumage patterns by age. It's no surprise, therefore, that in the field they are difficult to distinguish from one another. Because of their closeness in size, Sharp-shinned and Cooper's Hawks are particularly difficult to separate. However, Cooper's Hawks tend to have a rather square-shaped, relatively larger head versus that of the smaller, rounded heads of Sharp-shins. The tail of the Cooper's Hawk is moderately rounded with a wider and more pronounced band of white at its end, versus the squared tail of the Sharp-shinned Hawk. Adult Goshawks have a noticeable

Figure 1.1   Distribution map of breeding Cooper's Hawks in North America.

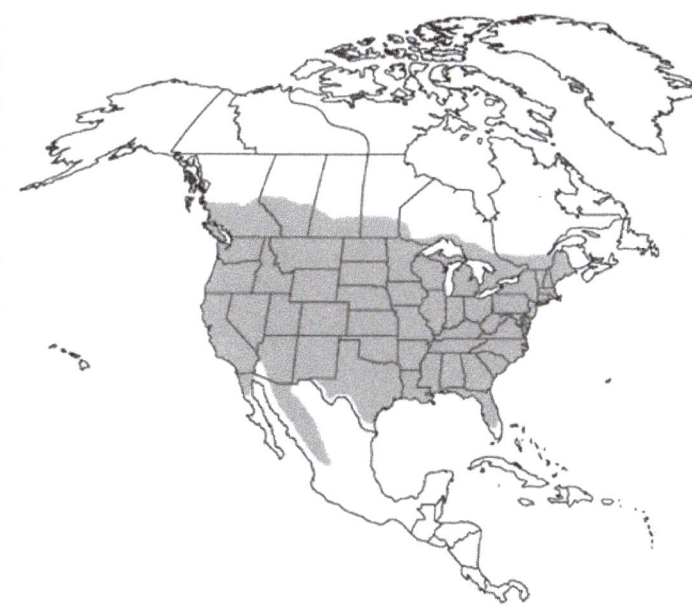

Chapter 1

The three species of North American accipiters in adult plumage. From left to right: male and female Sharp-shinned Hawk, male Cooper's Hawk, and female Northern Goshawk. Note proportionately larger, somewhat squared head of Cooper's Hawk vs. rounded head of Sharp-shinned and how dark blue-gray completely covers head and back of neck in Sharp-shin (dark blue gray only on 'cap' in Cooper's Hawk). Only Goshawk has white supercilium line above eye in adult plumage. Photo by Robert Rosenfield.

white supercilium line above the eye, which is absent in both adult Sharp-shinned and Cooper's Hawks.

These three accipiters also have relatively long legs and especially long toes to extend their reach. The toes are tipped with curved, relatively long, sharp talons to further enhance capture of agile bird prey and other animals. And, like almost all of the world's raptors, these hawks exhibit reversed sexual size dimorphism (RSD). However, the Cooper's Hawk exhibits one of the greatest degrees of RSD of all the world's raptors, with females weighing on average about 1.7 times more than males. Some males are only half the weight (or mass) of some females. Based on large samples of captured birds in Wisconsin, breeding males on average weigh 327 grams (12 ounces), and females 580 grams (21 ounces); thus males are a little under and females a bit over a pound, respectively, in Wisconsin.

However, one would expect that size of breeding birds would not be consistent throughout its continental distribution. That's because it is likely that North America's markedly different environmental conditions and landscapes would press for variations in the hawk's body size and body parts among populations, as has been shown to be the case for many vertebrates with large geographic ranges (Brown 1995, McNab 2012, Whaley and White 1994). Within a species, wing length also tends to differ between those populations that migrate and those that do not, as we'll discuss below. So, let's take a closer look at body size and other morphological, or body form, traits of breeding Cooper's Hawks across the continent.

Weight or mass is an honest index of overall body size in birds. Based on mass, we have demonstrated that similar-sized Cooper's Hawks breeding in western North Dakota and in British Columbia are on average about 28 grams (1 ounce) and 56 grams (2 ounces) smaller than Wisconsin males and females, respectively. These populations are not connected via direct movement of experienced breeders among these distant sites, which in part means that these populations effectively act as separate biological or evolutionary units (Gaston 2003, Meehan *et al.* 2001, 2003). We have suggested that body size in Cooper's Hawks is, as is true for many avian and mammalian carnivores, an anatomical response to the size and agility of the live prey they hunt (Rosenfield *et al.* 2010, Sonsthagen *et al.* 2012). In other words, the body size of the predator tracks the size of its prey. Accordingly, some western and northern breeding populations of smaller Cooper's Hawks in British Columbia and North Dakota typically hunt small to medium-sized songbirds, for example

Left: Mated pair of Cooper's Hawks. Note markedly smaller size of male (left) and gray tint to his cheek/side of face vs. brown on female's head. Eye color in breeding males, which is usually orange to red, is typically darker compared to that of its mate. It is unknown what function, if any, eye color plays in the natural history of this species. Our analyses of variation in eye color by age and sex in several breeding populations did not support the oft-pitched notion that female Cooper's Hawks choose male mates based on their eye color (see text). Photo by Robert Rosenfield. Right: A mated pair of Cooper's Hawks in temporary holding 'tubes.' Note the marked difference in overall foot size, toe length, and leg width between the male (right) and the female. Photo by Robert Rosenfield.

Chapter 1

Once caught, breeding adult Cooper's Hawks are temporarily held in 'tubes': cans hollowed out on one end and closed but with breathing holes in the other end. These tubes reduce movement and impart 'calming' darkness such that the captive hawk typically does not struggle. Direct and reliable hand-contact of the birds—especially by securing dangerous talon-laden feet—allow researchers to safely and expediently obtain measures of the wing, tail length, other body parts, and of course body mass or size. Such metrics have allowed much insight as to how Cooper's Hawk body form and size is influenced in part by diet and habitat (see Chapters 2 and 5). Photos by Madeline Hardin.

jays, thrushes, sparrows, specifically House Sparrows (*Passer domesticus*), and the American Robin (*Turdus migratorius*). Larger Wisconsin and other eastern nesting Cooper's Hawks do likewise, but also take heavier, less-agile prey, including the Eastern Chipmunk (*Tamais striatus*), and bigger species such as Rock Pigeons (*Columba livia*), Eastern Cottontail Rabbits (*Sylvilagus floridanus*), and less often, Gray Squirrels (*Sciurus carolinensis*) (Rosenfield and Bielefeldt 1993a, Bielefeldt *et al.* 1992). To illustrate this theme of predator-size tracking prey-size, consider this: larger breeding birds in Wisconsin are not genetically different from smaller western North Dakota birds, yet the North Dakota birds are genetically different from similar-sized British Columbia breeders (Sonsthagen *et al.* 2012). Clearly, nesting populations of Cooper's Hawks can, despite their genetic make-up, flex their body size (or to use the 'speak,' exhibit phenotypic plasticity). Note especially the genetically similar North Dakota and Wisconsin birds who vary significantly in size, in accord with the size of their prey.

We have also demonstrated that some body parts of Cooper's Hawks appear to respond adaptively to other non-genetic environmental influences. For example, migratory populations within species of birds usually have longer wings compared with their less migratory counterparts. This is because longer wings have been shown to provide more efficient flight; more flying power at a lower energy cost. In British Columbia adult nesting Cooper's Hawks are largely resident, but in western North Dakota they are highly migratory, and in eastern North Dakota and Wisconsin they are partially migratory. After statistically adjusting for differences in overall body size among these northern populations (which allowed us to assess whether birds of the same mass differed significantly by site in other body attributes), we found that wings of both sexes of the migratory or semi-migratory populations of western and eastern North Dakota, and Wisconsin, were significantly longer than those of sedentary hawks in British Columbia (Rosenfield *et al.* 2010, Sonsthagen *et al.* 2012).

We also found that tails in some breeding populations of Cooper's Hawks were longer, apparently in keeping with the need for enhanced maneuverability in relatively dense forested habitats (Wattel 1973). In fact, tails on average were significantly longer in breeding males in Wisconsin and British Columbia, where tracts of forest are larger and denser, than in western and eastern North Dakota, where birds nest in smaller woodlands surrounded by prairie grassland, cropland, and sparsely scattered trees (Rosenfield *et al.* 2010).

The Cooper's Hawk is rather well-known to both the birding public and to avian ecologists across North America. Famous enough, in fact, to prompt the Discovery Channel, Smithsonian Institute, *National Wildlife*, *National Geographic*, *Sports Afield*, and *Birder's World*, among others, to cover our Cooper's Hawk research in their television, website, and magazine pieces targeted for the general public. There may be three reasons for this celebrity. First, the Cooper's Hawk has a broad, continental distribution and a renowned ability to flex, or stretch, its niche, meaning it can survive and nest successfully in markedly diverse and fragmented habitats. These landscapes include small wooded tracts in grasslands of the Great Plains, tall conifer forests of the Pacific Northwest, deciduous forests of the eastern United States, and in cities of all sizes across North America. Such wide habitat breadth also places the Cooper's Hawk in relatively close proximity to humans throughout its range. Historically, the more farm-based population of the 1800s and early 1900s was aware of the Cooper's Hawk's nearby presence, but as a frequent unwanted "guest" seeking a meal at the hen-house. An early account noted that "This very common and impudent robber is the most destructive of the Raptores [sic] to the barnyard fowls." (Fisher 1893). Coupled with the general disdain of European settlers for predators, the Cooper's Hawk seemed to quickly earn an infamous reputation as one of the most villainous and "blood thirsty" hawks, the quintessential "Chicken Hawk" (Bent 1937). Unsurprisingly, persecution through shootings of this hawk, in part because of its depredations on poultry, probably contributed to early population declines of Cooper's Hawks around the early 1900s (Evans 1982).

A second reason for its celebrity is that the Cooper's Hawk was one of several high-profile raptors that suffered the ill-effects of DDT contamination, which resulted in aberrant adult courting behavior and thin-shelled eggs that broke under the weight of an incubating bird (Snyder et al. 1973). The disastrous ecological effects of the pesticide were highly profiled by many environmentalists, including Rachel Carson in her famous book Silent Spring (Carson 1962). Such ills underscored significant environmental concerns that in part prompted the birth of the wildlife conservation movement. Aggravating the ills of DDT were the high rates of habitat loss and illegal shootings, factors that together led to significant declines in the number of Cooper's Hawks that were noted in the mid-20th century along eastern U.S. migratory pathways popular with birders and researchers (Evans 1982, Bednarz et al. 1990). Some scientists predicted that Cooper's Hawk populations, especially in the eastern United States, were heading toward extinction in the 1960s and early '70s (Rosenfield and Bielefeldt 1993a). Consequently, many state agencies formally listed the Cooper's Hawk as endangered or threatened, along with other designations of conservation concern (LeFranc and Millsap 1984, Rosenfield et al. 2018). Fortunately, populations rebounded quickly after DDT was banned in 1972. This favorable outcome was probably aided by a reduction in shooting of Cooper's Hawks, thanks to law enforcement and educational actions (Rosenfield et al. 2018). Reports of Cooper's Hawks nesting in highly fragmented urban and suburban landscapes became relatively common after the 1970s (Stout et al. 2007). This de-

the species and its celebrity

Lower left: A fledgling Cooper's Hawk about 44 days of age 'proning' (laying down) on a car roof near the bird's urban nest. Young leave a nest about 25-30 days of age but will continue to use it or tree branches for resting. Urban fledglings also use various human structures for proning, including house roofs, lawns, and, as also shown, deck railings. Adults and fledglings use birdbaths and, rarely, we assume, even basketball hoops, which sites thereby underscore this species' flexibility in habitat use in human-dominated environments. Photos by Larry Sobolik (car, hoop, bird bath) and Brian Rusnica (railing).

spite the fact that, during this time, some researchers described the Cooper's Hawk as being an area-sensitive species (that is, it perhaps required large, unfragmented forests to survive) and that it might be adversely affected by forest fragmentation, human disturbance, and loss of nest site habitat (Robinson 1991, Bosakowski *et al.* 1993, Hannon *et al.* 2009). Cooper's Hawk populations in fact currently appear healthy across the continent in both rural and urban environments. The hawk no longer appears on any conservation listings (Rosenfield *et al.* 2018). The highest nesting densities, or numbers of breeding pairs per unit area, recorded for the species occur in cities, such as Tucson, Arizona, and Stevens Point and metropolitan Milwaukee, both in Wisconsin. An oft-stated reason for these high nesting densities is that urban environments have much greater numbers of songbird prey compared with rural habitats (Marzluff *et al.* 1998).

This urban nesting phenomenon underpins the third reason for the celebrity of the Cooper's Hawk: it's probably the most common nesting raptor in urban and suburban backyards across North America. In these settings, Cooper's Hawks are frequently seen using bird baths and hunting at bird feeders. One can readily view YouTube clips of these and other activities. Notably, bird feeding may be the most popular form around the globe of human-wildlife interaction. Providing food to wildlife has become incredibly popular (Martin and Baruta 2014), and 43% of U.S. households regularly feed birds (Robb *et al.* 2008). Bird feeding is likely to heighten public awareness of the pervasive phenomenon of urban breeding Cooper's Hawks, because more than two-thirds of the world's human population will live in cities by 2040 (Bradley and Altizer 2007, Rosenfield *et al.* 2018).

The fact remains, however, that most Cooper's Hawk populations are relatively new to breeding in cities, because the species initially evolved in and is adapted to forests. Science does not know well the fundamental ecology of urban raptors, especially on a long-term basis (Rutz 2008, Fidino and Magle 2017). Nor do scientists generally know how urban raptor ecology may or may not differ from birds living in exurban areas. ('Exurban' is a relatively popular term among ecologists and it generally refers to rural landscapes, but this term is sometimes used without definition and has been used to reference city-like, suburban landscapes [e.g., Millsap 2018]. I do not regard rural habitats and suburbs as ecological equivalents; see Chapter 4 and Chamberlain *et al.* 2009). I highlight that urbanization is perhaps the fastest habitat-altering force on the planet, and thus there is a need to document the behavioral adaptations and reproductive success of Cooper's Hawks and other wildlife in these ever-expanding fragmented landscapes (Miller 2005).

Contra to what's been written by Marzluff (2016) in his excellent review of urban ornithology, I believe that urbanization does not necessarily produce a uniform or homogenized urban environment for Cooper's Hawks, because cities differ markedly in size, habitat, prey populations, surrounding environments, and other ecological factors that potentially can affect the hawk's survival and reproductive success. Such high diversity among continent-wide urban environs should result in variation in the ecology of the Cooper's Hawk (Rosenfield *et al.* 2007c, 2018). Indeed, I'd suggest that a treasure trove of variety in the Cooper's Hawk's urban biology awaits discovery, and I eagerly look forward to new and exciting natural history findings about this bold backyard huntsman (Rosenfield *et al.* 2018).

Chapter Two

YOU ARE WHAT YOU EAT

*F*our fledglings, three females and one male, 20 days out of their nest, are flying about trees in a suburban backyard when the male swoops down and strikes at a Gray Squirrel on the ground. The squirrel runs into a nearby brush pile. Minutes later, all four hawks are on the ground next to the brush pile and seemingly are able to flush out the squirrel, which runs across the lawn toward some trees. The youngsters then block the squirrel's escape path, and eventually the squirrel jumps up, kicking, scratching, and teeth flailing, and thus drives off its attackers. Just then, the adult female flies in silently within a meter of the ground and just above her young, and the squirrel, eventually gaining a perch while giving an alarm call -cak-cak-cak- as she lands. She shows no sign of interest in the squirrel as prey. All the young seem to divert their attention toward her, and the squirrel then escapes to the brush pile. Two minutes later, the adult female flies to the brush pile, flushing an Eastern Chipmunk, which she captures. She then flies from view, with the three female fledglings following her. The juvenile male, which remained on the ground, then flies to the brush pile and pulls with its beak at sticks. This activity appears to flush another chipmunk, which is quickly captured by the male. Did the male mimic the actions of its parent to procure prey? And did the adult female's presence halt the attacks of her fledglings on the squirrel, whose counterattack might have seriously injured these juveniles?

Adult Cooper's Hawks occasionally take Gray Squirrels, but they generally appear to respond indifferently to Gray Squirrels or regard them as nest predators rather than perceive them as prey (and Cooper's Hawks do not give alarm calls and thus give up their potential advantage of a surprise attack while going after prey!). Interestingly, this was a very large female with a mass of 700 grams at the nestling stage, which is the second largest mass among 341 breeding female Cooper's Hawks caught in Wisconsin. In fact, her mass exceeded that of several adult male breeding Northern Goshawks *in Wisconsin, a larger accipiter that does prey on Gray Squirrels in Wisconsin (Nicewander and Rosenfield 2006, R.N. Rosenfield, unpubl. data). Yet, despite the large size of the female Cooper's Hawk, she did not attack the squirrel.*

Overview

To best understand the biology of a predator, it's important to know what it eats. So investigating its diet is a required exercise for a natural historian. Knowledge of a predator's diet and its foraging behavior provides, as discussed earlier, insights as to its body size and form. Diet may be linked directly to the suitability of a particular habitat for the predator and its role and influence in a community of other species. In fact, the ill effects of environmental contaminants like DDT on natural communities were revealed in part through diet studies that showed that raptors, including Cooper's Hawks, could bioaccumulate (or biomagnify) these pesticides by consuming 'infected' avian prey (Snyder *et al.* 1973, Rosenfield and Bielefeldt 1993a). It's also been suggested that top-apex predators like hawks may be particularly susceptible to the adverse effects of recent climate change. This is true particularly because of their longer generation turnover times, which may impede their ability to adapt quickly to shifts in timing of prey events (such as earlier migration of songbirds in spring), and an inability to match their reproductive timing with optimal brood-rearing conditions, such as when food is most available (Rosenfield *et al.* 2016b).

Wildlife managers have tried to assess the impact of raptors on prey populations, in their efforts to sustain a harvestable number of game animals. This research has included studies of predation by Cooper's Hawks on Northern Bobwhite (*Colinus virginianus*) in the southeastern U.S., where this game species' population has been declining since the late 1900s, and where some believe that predation by Cooper's Hawks may be a significant cause of these declines (Mueller 1989, Rollins and Carrol 2001, Millsap *et al.* 2013). Similarly, we encounter many urban residents expressing concern about the impact of Cooper's Hawk predation on the doves and songbirds

Photo by Brian Rusnica

that use bird feeders. Scientists are also curious to know whether—as some recent evidence suggests—urban breeding Cooper's Hawks are more susceptible to, and/or adversely affected by, diseases as a result of taking feeder birds or other urban prey. Such prey are potentially more likely to transmit diseases by virtue of their elevated abundance in urban areas, and especially at feeders (Boal and Mannan 1999, Wilcoxen *et al.* 2015, Wrobel *et al.* 2016).

Food habits study, diet, and foraging behavior

Before we delve into what scientists have specifically learned about the predatory habits of the Cooper's Hawk, and the possible effects of climate change on breeding birds, let's briefly explore how researchers objectively and accurately demonstrate their knowledge of a species' dietary habits. A focus on this process of scientific discovery is necessary because studies that assess raptor diets can be fraught with methodological challenges (Marti *et al.* 2007). Indeed, by demonstrating that several earlier investigations introduced significant biases in their methods of study, we were able to challenge the common claim that birds predominate in the diet of Cooper's Hawks (Bielefeldt *et al.* 1992). For example, pellet analysis is a technique that relies on the natural history fact that most raptors egest pellets that contain undigested remains of consumed prey, including bones, teeth, hair, and feathers. Pellets can be found at the nest or at perch sites near the nest. However, there are several shortcomings to studying pellets. Unlike owls, for example, diurnal raptors tend to completely digest the bones of their prey. Owls don't because their digestive fluids are not as acidic or as strong. Bones tend to be absent in Cooper's Hawk pellets, so there is less material to help researchers identify what they've been preying on. Another problem with using pellets is that you may not be able to find enough of them to accurately represent what was eaten. Methodological bias may also pop up in studies that mostly tally uneaten and/or plucked prey remains collected at nests or perch sites. These items are more likely to be larger items such as colorful feathers that are easily found (e.g., those of Blue Jay, *Cyanocitta cristata*) versus less conspicuous items like mammalian hair or drab-colored feathers from small birds. Reptiles and nestling birds, which are known Cooper's Hawk prey, unfortunately leave little in the way of remains.

Therefore, we used multiple methods to investigate some of these biases in our attempt to catalog accurately the diet of breeding Cooper's Hawks in Wisconsin. We collected prey remains at plucking posts (regularly used substrates such as fallen trees or elevated tree branches), and, along with the herculean help of field-savvy

Chapter 2

This researcher is standing close to an oak tree that was used as a plucking post, or food delivery site for Cooper's Hawks nesting in this Wisconsin pine plantation. Plucking post trees are usually noticeably larger than surrounding trees and as such they typically have large lower limbs which provide ample bases upon which breeding males transfer food to mates and sometimes cache food. These trees are also frequently used for perching by adult females during the pre-incubation period. Plucking posts are usually within 50 meters (164 feet) of the nest tree, and here the nest is visible in a pine tree toward the upper right portion of this image. Photo by Robert Rosenfield.

An adult male with starling prey at a plucking post, tree limb. Plucking posts serve as prey transfer sites—that is, males do not typically fly to their nests with food during the nestling stage. Rather, immediately upon arrival at the plucking post, a male will announce his presence to his mate with 'kik' calls. The female then flies to the limb to get food and then, while uttering 'whaa' calls, usually further deplumes ('processes') and eats the prey there if she is on eggs, or she will take it to the nest to feed her nestlings. Daily use of plucking posts by adults across several months results in much 'sign' at these sites, such as prey remains, streaks of adult 'whitewash' (feces), and molted feathers of adults on the ground. The same plucking posts are frequently reused across years (even by different individuals) should the territory remain occupied. In fact, the relatively easily spotted sign created by breeding birds near plucking posts helps to reveal occupied sites during nest searching. Photo by Brian Rusnica.

you are what you eat

Prey caught by adult breeding male Cooper's Hawks typically is delivered to their mates at routinely used plucking posts, which are usually large tree branches or logs near or on the ground within about 50 meters (164 feet) of a nest. Here at plucking posts near central Wisconsin nests is a whole and partially de-plumed fledgling House Finch (Haemorhous mexicanus) near a streak of hawk whitewash on a log and pluckings of a Belted Kingfisher (Megaceryle alcyon) nearby. In another image are many pluckings of various prey on the ground below a log. Note in the lower left center the small white chevron in the brownish tail feather and an orange-tipped breast feather both of an American Robin; the two, broadly white-tipped gray tail feathers in the upper right of a Mourning Dove (Zenaida macroura); the single and small, black-tipped, yellow tail feather of a Pine Siskin (Spinus pinus) in the center; the center located black-spotted and white tail feather of a Yellow-bellied Sapsucker (Sphyrapicus varius); and the furry tip of an Eastern Chipmunk's tail in extreme lower left. Tree canopy birds like the Siskin are uncommon-to-rare prey in Wisconsin as Cooper's Hawks mostly take ground- or shrub-foraging prey, like the finch, robin, dove, and chipmunk. Photos by Madeline Hardin.

Breeding male Cooper's Hawks will take nestling songbirds, such as this Common Grackle (Quiscalus quiscula) in Wisconsin, one at a time from a nest until it is apparently emptied, as evidenced by short intervals of only a few minutes between deliveries to their mates of nestling songbirds of the same species at the same stage of development. Photo by Madeline Hardin.

Accipiter toes are long, as are the talons, and for added help with catching and grasping prey in the air note the pads on the undersides of these Cooper's Hawk toes. Photo by Robert Rosenfield.

raptor researcher Joe Papp, directly observed prey deliveries by adults to nestlings via tree blinds manned by researchers during all daylight hours. Observed deliveries also included prey dropped in mist net traps at the time of adult capture. We did not use pellet analyses. We demonstrated that indirect collection of prey remains near nests overestimated the proportion of avian items (92%) in comparison to direct observations (51-68%).

This result was unsurprising and probably occurred because, as mentioned earlier, bird pluckings are larger and often more colorful, and hence more conspicuous than remains of mammals or other non-avian prey. The colorful Blue Jay, for example, accounted for 36% of the identifiable avian remains, but only 15% of the identifiable birds delivered to nests. Importantly, mammalian items were scarce in the samples of remains (8%) but averaged about 40% of items delivered to nests; this disparity again reflected the difficulty of finding hair in plucked remains (Bielefeldt *et al.* 1992). Most raptor researchers now implement study designs that minimize these and other well-documented biases. Indeed, many raptor biologists use multiple techniques in a single study, such as the recent intensive diet studies of Cooper's Hawks in Tucson, AZ (Estes and Mannan 2003), Victoria, BC (Cava *et al.* 2012), and in Florida (Millsap *et al.* 2013), all of which used remote video recorders placed near nests to track what was being delivered. Thus modern diet studies more accurately reflect raptor diets (Rosenfield *et al.* 1995b, Marti *et al.* 2007).

Most food habit data for the Cooper's Hawk stems from breeding-season studies because of the logistical ease of obtaining samples at or near a nest, where relatively frequent food deliveries by adults to young can be tallied. The list of prey items discovered in these studies numbers well over 80 species and includes birds up to the size of a Rock Pigeon and Red Junglefowl (or chicken, *Gallus gallus*), Cattle Egret (*Bubulcus ibis*); mammals from the size of mice to Eastern Cottontail Rabbits; reptiles, especially lizards; and even some insects (Rosenfield 1988, and see references in Table 2.1). However, birds and, secondarily, mammals appear to be most frequently delivered to nests throughout the Cooper's Hawk's breeding range.

Of 12 studies across North America that used unbiased methods, 10 (83%) reported bird prey to be dominant, ranging from 56% to 96% of the total items tallied in each of those 10 studies (Table 2.1). The most common from smaller to larger: House Sparrow (especially in cities like Victoria, BC, Milwaukee, WI, Grand Forks, ND, and Albuquerque, NM; Cava *et al.* 2012, R.N. Rosenfield pers. obs.); the Northern Cardinal (*Cardinalis cardinalis*) and Northern Mockingbird (*Mimus polyglottos*), (especially in rural Florida; Millsap *et al.* 2013); and the American Robin, European Starling (*Sturnus vulgaris*), Blue Jay, and the non-songbird Mourning

Table 2.1: Proportions of avian & mammalian prey in studies using direct observations of nest deliveries or crop contents or prey remains. Note that only the first two listed studies show a minority of birds as prey.

State/Province	No. Nests	No. Items	Percent Birds	Percent Mammals	Source
CA	1	38[1]	26	5	*Fitch et al. 1946*
MD	na[2]	57	30	70	*Janik and Mosher 1982*
AZ-NM	11	473	56	30	*Snyder et al. 1973*
NM	17	167[3]	60	37	*Kennedy 1991*
WI	5	329	61	39	*Bielefeldt et al. 1992*
ND	2	74	70	30	*Peterson and Murphy 1992*
WI	3	24	71	29	*Errington 1933*
MI	4	262	84	16	*Hamerstrom and Hamerstrom 1951*
WA	6	240	90	10	*Kennedy 1980*
FL	95[4]	1,100	88	4	*Millsap et al. 2013*
BC	133[5]	4,451	96	3	*Cava et al. 2012*
AZ[6]	36	228	90	2	*Estes and Mannan 2003*

[1] 69% reptilian.
[2] Not available.
[3] 3% reptilian.
[4] 10 nests with direct observation, 85 with prey remains; 4% mammal, rest reptilian and unknown.
[5] 87 nests with direct observation, (2 with videos), 44 nests with prey remains.
[6] 8% reptilian; only direct observations.

Dove, in both urban and rural habitats throughout North America (Bielefeldt *et al.* 1992, Cava *et al.* 2012, Millsap *et al.* 2013).

Therefore, excluding the Mourning Dove, which as an adult weighs about 100 grams, it appears breeding Cooper's Hawks mostly capture small to medium-sized songbirds weighing between 30 and 70 grams. This range converts roughly to about 1-2 ounces of weight per avian item, or about 5-10% and 9-18% of the average weight of a breeding female and male Cooper's Hawk in Wisconsin, respectively. Similar in weight, one adult Eastern Chipmunk or Mourning Dove comprises about 18% and 30% of the adult mass of a breeding female and male Wisconsin Cooper's Hawk, respectively.

Because birds dominate the prey deliveries to nests, most diet studies accordingly demonstrate that biomass, or weight of prey delivered to nests, is predominately avian. However, mammalian prey, especially the Eastern Chipmunk, which on average weighs 107 grams, more weight than the typical 30-70 gram avian prey item, was shown to predominate in terms of total biomass at some nests in Wisconsin even though it was delivered less frequently than birds (Bielefeldt *et al.* 1992). In fact, the Eastern Chipmunk appears to be an important prey item in frequency and/or biomass in several areas of eastern North America (Meng 1959, Janik and Mosher 1982, Rosenfield and Bielefeldt 1993a). Similarly, chipmunks (*Eutamias* sp.) and ground squirrels (*Spermophilus* sp.) were important prey in some western North American studies of breeding Cooper's Hawk diets (e.g., Fischer 1986, Rosenfield *et al.* 2010).

There tends to be a shift in ages of prey taken during the breeding season in many Cooper's Hawk populations. That is, adult birds and mammals tend to predominate in the hawk's diet early in the breeding season, while nestling and fledgling birds and young chipmunks, which aren't as available early in the season, dominate as prey when they become more available during the nestling stage. Males capture prey items one at a time and, for example, will return to a songbird nest repeatedly to take a single individual until the nest is emptied; they also have been observed capturing various songbirds at avian nest boxes (Stewart 2003, Millsap *et al.* 2013, R.N. Rosenfield, pers. obs.). As seen in direct observations of nest deliveries, the young of the year also provide the majority of prey items taken by various other raptor species, including Sharp-shinned Hawks, Broad-winged Hawks (*Buteo platypterus*) and the Peregrine Falcon (*Falco peregrinus*; Bielefeldt *et al.* 1992, Rosenfield *et al.* 1984, 1995b). It seems that Cooper's Hawks and these other raptors probably take the prey easiest to catch during the breeding season.

Sub-adult and ground-foraging animals may be particularly vulnerable to the hunting tactics of Cooper's Hawks. They typically employ a series of brief perch-and-scan episodes to locate potential prey and probably take most prey by surprise attack—sometimes from behind an obstruction such as a building—rather than active aerial pursuit (Fischer 1986, Kennedy 1991, Roth and Lima 2003, Millsap *et al.* 2013). Such tactics should be most effective and economical against nestling birds, non-agile fledglings, and other inexperienced juvenile animals, as well as ground-foraging individuals (especially mammals) whose avenues of predator detection and escape are more limited than those of arboreal, or tree-dwelling, species (Reynolds and Meslow 1984). Studies throughout North America suggest that nearly all mammalian prey and large majorities of avian prey can be classed as ground- or shrub-foraging species (Rosenfield and Bielefeldt 1993a). An exception is in Florida, where researchers frequently observed male Cooper's Hawks searching tree canopies for bird nests (Millsap *et al.* 2013). These scientists also noted that their study populations produced relatively fewer offspring, which the researchers attributed to food being limited in their study areas. They highlighted the absence of ground-dwelling squirrel and chipmunk prey as the key factor limiting the reproduction of Florida Cooper's Hawks. That said, some urban Cooper's Hawk populations maintain high productivity and breeding densities without using mammalian prey (e.g., Tucson, AZ, and Victoria, BC), but this perhaps is possible because of the greater abundance of suitable avian prey in urban environments (Boal and Mannan 1999, Rosenfield *et al.* 2010, Cava *et al.* 2012). Curiously, introduced species, such as House Sparrows and European Starlings, both of which can cause damage to native ecosystems by out-competing native species for food or nest sites, strongly dominated (more than 85%), along with the native American Robin, the collective prey for breeding Cooper's Hawks in Victoria, BC (Cava *et al.* 2012). The dominance of a few prey species has been observed in most Cooper's Hawk diet studies.

Prey species used during the breeding season strongly reflect the hunting abilities of adult male Cooper's Hawks, because the male is the primary food provider for himself, his mate, and the young, from courtship through the nestling stage. Males appear to 'graze' throughout the day on their captures, as many of the items they deliver through the nestling stage arrive partially eaten, in fact often decapitated. Grazing on prey by males during the nestling stage may suggest that they deliver every prey item they capture to their mates and/or their young. However, we do not really know if breeding males target vulnerable prey or if researchers tally captures that are the result of higher attack success rates. We note that researchers in Florida reported that the Northern Bobwhite comprised 34% of Cooper's Hawk prey during the breeding season (57% during the non-breeding season), and they suggested that this ground-dwelling quail species may be preferred prey there (Millsap *et al.* 2013). Similarly, Fischer (1986) speculated that

Chapter 2

Hunting Cooper's Hawks will readily pursue prey into thick cover. This adult male 'plunged' into this hedgerow shrub and left with a House Sparrow moments later. Photo by John Seibel.

ground-dwelling chipmunks (*Eutamius* sp.) and ground squirrels (*Spermophilus* sp.) may be the preferred prey of breeding Cooper's Hawks in central Utah because they were "on the average larger and easier to catch than birds." And Millsap *et al.* (2013) suggested that non-breeding female Cooper's Hawks prefer Cattle Egrets as prey in rural Florida. 'Preferred' prey is that which is taken out of proportion to its availability (or abundance levels). But despite some of the above suggestions, to our knowledge no such investigations demonstrating preferred prey *per se* exist for breeding Cooper's Hawks.

Findings from intensive telemetry studies and all-day trapping of breeding adults near nests with young generally suggest that males are persistently active and likely hunting (perhaps at their maximum capacity) throughout the day. We note that males tend not to linger near nests after prey deliveries during the nestling stage, which may suggest that they quickly resume hunting (Snyder and Snyder 1973, Murphy *et al.* 1988, Millsap *et al.* 2013, R.N. Rosenfield, pers. obs.). That said, we reported an adult male who, while tending four nestlings at his urban nest in Oshkosh, WI, was building on his nest from the immediate previous year. This unusual timing of alternative nest-building seemed anomalous to us, as we assumed him to be maximally tasked with hunting for his mate and four young (all of which fledged). On the other hand, perhaps the urban landscape, which typically is regarded as rich with prey, provided a surplus of energy reserves that could be used by him for building a nest for a future attempt. In fact, the male resumed building the next spring at the alternative nest and fledged young there (Rosenfield and Sobolik 2017).

Some researchers have reported daily lulls in the foraging activities of Cooper's Hawks during the nestling stage in the western United States. The lulls perhaps were associated with inactive periods for prey, such as during early mornings in Utah, when the possible preferred prey, chipmunks and squirrels, were inactive (Fischer 1986). Similarly, breeding hawks in California were mostly active in late morning and late afternoons, when common lizard prey, especially the whiptail, (*Cnemidophorus tesselatus*) were active (Fitch *et al.* 1946).

A notable novel feature of the timing of hunting behavior of Cooper's Hawks was the discovery that overwintering, telemetered birds in Indiana hunted roosting prey at night, using the illumination of urban lighting and the moon, and more so in urban settings than hawks hunting in rural areas (Roth *et al.* 2005).

Males delivered prey to incubating females in Wisconsin on average about three times a day, with deliveries spaced two to three hours apart (Rosenfield and Bielefeldt 1993a, R.N. Rosenfield, unpubl. data). Delivery rates by adult males to nestlings averaged 0.3–0.9 per hour in most studies, or an average of about six to 12 items per day. To our knowledge, the maximum number of deliveries in one day was 17 (all songbirds) at a nest with five nestlings in Victoria, BC (A.C. Stewart, unpubl. data). Rate of prey deliveries for nestlings, however, may vary with size of prey, and comparatively lower prey-delivery rates would be offset if the biomass of prey captured was relatively large. Infrequently, time between male food deliveries is so short that female Cooper's Hawks will cache uneaten prey away from the nest, because the young are satiated and unable or unwilling to eat more. Females periodically retrieve food from caches to feed the young (Bielefeldt *et al.* 1992, Estes and Mannan 2003, R.N. Rosenfield, pers. obs). These cache sites in Wisconsin are

Cooper's Hawks mostly hunt ground- and shrub-foraging birds and chipmunks via a series of brief perch-and-scan episodes in trees to locate prey, which are then pursued with a sudden and speedy burst of flight. But sometimes they will chase their prey by running. This yearling male is in hot pursuit of House Sparrows hiding in a backyard garden. Photo by John Seibel.

plucking posts, or transfer sites, and other substrates elevated above the ground, such as tree branches and squirrel nests, where perhaps their food bounty is safe from being pirated by other animals (R.N. Rosenfield, pers. obs.). We note that both sexes will cache unconsumed food throughout the nesting season (Rosenfield 1990, Bielefeldt et al. 1992)

The timing and landscape locations of foraging behavior of breeding Cooper's Hawks have not been widely studied. In the first ever study of the foraging behavior of a suburban-nesting male Cooper's Hawk, we found the seasonal home range (defined by scientists as the area in which an animal moves on a periodic basis) throughout the nestling and post-fledging stages, or about three months, was 784 hectares (about 3.0 square miles). However, this telemetered individual exhibited much smaller daily ranges of 231 hectares (about 1.0 square mile). He spent most of his time during the season within a half kilometer (0.3 miles) of his Wisconsin nest, and 99% of all foraging was within 2 kilometers (1.3 miles) of the nest (Murphy et al. 1988). Indeed, he seemed to have one favorite hunting spot, which was a small wood about 0.7 kilometers (0.4 miles) from the nest, where he caught about 60% of the prey we observed being delivered to the nest. Similarly, telemetered breeding male Cooper's Hawks in Florida captured most prey within 2 kilometers (1.3 miles) of their nests (Millsap et al. 2013). Mannan and Boal (2000) suggest that nest location is what influences where male Cooper's Hawks hunt. If true, the size of breeding-season home ranges should therefore be in proportion to foraging distances of males from their nests. Seasonal home ranges of nesting male Cooper's Hawks vary in size from 0.66 square kilometers (0.25 square miles) in urban areas of Tucson, Arizona (Mannan and Boal 2000), 4.81 square kilometers (1.6 square miles) and 6.09 square kilometers (2.4 square miles) in urban and rural habitats, respectively, in California (Chiang et al. 2012), to 7.84 square kilometers (3.0 square miles) in suburban Wisconsin (Murphy et al. 1988), and 12.06 square kilometers (4.7 square miles) in rural New Mexico (Kennedy 1989). The increasing size of the home range, which varied 18-fold from urban to rural environments, suggests that food is more abundant in urban areas, so city males do not have to range far from their nests to capture prey (see Chapter 4). Similarly, breeding Cooper's Hawks delivered two times more prey biomass per hour at urban nests in Tucson, Arizona, versus nearby rural sites (Estes and Mannan 2003).

Notably, breeding-season ranges of male Cooper's Hawks were much larger (14.6 square kilometers, or 5.5 square miles) in rural Florida, perhaps because about 35% of prey were captured beyond 2 kilometers (1.3 miles) of the nest. Researchers there speculated that home range and foraging distances of nesting males were comparatively larger there due to the limitations imposed by lower food levels, so males had to forage farther to find suitable prey (Millsap *et al.* 2013). That said, Florida researchers also reported regular spacing of Cooper's Hawk nests, which would not seem to be in accord with limited food conditions. Regular or generally uniform spacing of nests is typical in areas where food apparently is more readily available (Rosenfield *et al.* 1995a, Mannan and Boal 2000). In a landscape where prey is particularly limited, there would likely be scattered and irregular spacing of food (Krebs 1994), which should cause an irregular spacing of breeding territories and nests. But, I reiterate, the temporal and spatial dynamics of the foraging behavior of nesting Cooper's Hawks have not been widely studied. This lack of natural history knowledge is aggravated by poor documentation, so far, of the behaviors of territorial and floater Cooper's Hawks, who are potentially interacting (see Chapter 2; Moreno 2016, Rosenfield *et al.* 2016c). It is possible that dynamics of Cooper's Hawk sociality that have yet to be documented, including complex extra-pair paternity behaviors that involve courtship feeding by males (including floaters), may influence the spacing of nests and therefore where foraging occurs, the locations of extra-pair trysts, and locations where breeding males may be defending their territory (Moreno 2016, Rosenfield *et al.* 2016c).

Breeding females generally do not travel much beyond about 100 meters of the nest over the incubation and the nestling stage, and they rarely hunt during the nesting season until their young are about 3 weeks old, about a week before they fledge (R.N.Rosenfield, pers. obs., Millsap *et al.* 2013). Even then, females may only be hunting opportunistically. In one intensive study of telemetered adult breeding Cooper's Hawks, males were responsible for 85% of all prey captures, and only four of 10 nesting females were observed to begin foraging again during the entire breeding season while they were closely monitored (Millsap *et al.* 2013). That said, females in Wisconsin hunted prey opportunistically in the pre-incubation stages (see Chapter 3). Interestingly, at all nests in a Florida study where breeding males died, all of the females deserted these sites, and thus all the abandoned nestlings died. By contrast, in Wisconsin we have documented some adult, widowed females hunting and delivering prey to their nestlings, and even fledging young on their own (R.N. Rosenfield, pers.obs).

BIRD FEEDER USE AND DISEASE

One readily observable aspect of the predatory behavior of urban Cooper's Hawks that has drawn much attention is their use of bird feeders. As was said earlier, feeding wildlife has become incredibly popular (Martin and Baruta 2014), and

Chapter 2

about 43% of U.S. households regularly feed birds (Robb *et al.* 2008). Some 53 million Americans over the age of 16 collectively spend more than $5 billion a year on bird feeding, bird baths, bird houses and other accessories (U.S. Fish and Wildlife Service 2012)! One aspect of the spatial ecology of wintering urban Cooper's Hawks is their use of bird feeders as a favored site for predation. Among 25 species of predators, Cooper's Hawks, along with the Sharp-shinned Hawk and domestic cat, were responsible for 80% of recorded incidents in which a known predator was observed lurking at a bird feeder in Project Feederwatch, a North American-wide survey of winter birds at feeders (Dunn and Tessaglia 1994). It was suggested that the increase in feeders in the northeastern United States might have been responsible, in part, for the observed decrease in migration counts of these two hawk species at banding stations farther south, because the hawks apparently stayed north to hunt feeder birds (Viverette *et al.* 1996). Notably, feeder birds represent the size class of birds that Cooper's Hawks generally prey upon: small to medium-sized songbirds and doves. We reiterate that males, not females, are primarily responsible for procuring prey for nestlings and their larger mates during the nesting season and thus males would more likely be seen at feeders taking these size classes of birds at this time. We note some data, but not all, suggest that males take smaller prey than females during the breeding season (Snyder and Wiley 1976, Kennedy and Johnson 1986, Rosenfield and Bielefeldt 1993a), and that females typically take larger prey than males during the non-breeding season (e.g., Millsap *et al.* 2013). Among individually color-marked birds, males were about six times more likely than females to be seen hunting at feeders during the non-breeding season in Victoria, British

Cooper's Hawks throughout North America are commonly detected at backyard bird feeders, as was this adult in Victoria, British Columbia. This might be because most feeder birds are the size of birds typically preyed upon by Cooper's Hawks. Unfortunately, the specific ecological roles that bird feeders play regarding the biology of breeding Cooper's Hawks is unknown because few feeder studies exist. For example, do feeders influence the breeding density or the reproductive success of nesting hawks, and do these areas of bird 'congestion' generate a greater risk of disease transmission to this predator?
Photo by Rick Page.

Columbia where adults of both sexes overwinter; females also took larger prey than males at this time (Stewart *et al.* 2009, A.C. Stewart, unpubl. data).

It is also possible that the apparent importance of feeders to Cooper's Hawks may simply reflect the fact that humans are most likely to see hawks at bird feeders. That's a perspective supported by Roth *et al.* (2008), who observed no systematic use of bird feeders by telemetered Cooper's Hawks wintering in Terra Haute, Indiana. Although a few individual hawks visited feeders more often than expected, just as many avoided them. Roth speculated that the lack of a strong tendency to hunt around feeders may be "prey management" by Cooper's Hawks, whereby hawks avoid repeated attacks at areas (feeders) frequently visited by prey that would respond by avoiding the feeder in future, thus ensuring for themselves a usable source of prey over the long term. However, there was an apparent sex bias in his study as seven of the eight urban Cooper's Hawks in this study were females. Regardless, we typically encounter residents in Wisconsin who claim that breeding Cooper's Hawks dramatically reduce use of bird feeders by various species of birds (R.N. Rosenfield, pers. obs.). However, most residents seem pleased to have hawks nesting nearby, especially given that in Wisconsin, Cooper's Hawks regularly take Eastern Chipmunks, a rodent much disliked by many homeowners for their ground-digging and chewing near or on human structures. Similarly, Mannan *et al.* (2004) found that the majority (82%) of residents whose property was occupied by, or near breeding Cooper's Hawks versus those of random residents (67%) in Tucson, AZ, responded positively about the diet of the Cooper's Hawk. These findings are particularly curious given that 80% of households in their study area put out food or water for attracting birds, not hawks *per se.*

Robb *et al.* (2008) indicated that bird feeding affects all aspects of avian biology. One theme of particular import to humans is the risk of disease. Bird feeders have been implicated in outbreaks of salmonellosis, aspergillosis, various large die-offs of songbirds, and trichomoniasis (Martin and Baruta 2014). A long-established ecological principle is that disease transmission occurs at greater rates in populations and communities that are more densely populated than those that are more sparsely populated (McCallum *et al.* 2001, Wrobel *et al.* 2016). Bird feeders, especially those in urban environments, create a common food source for large and concentrated numbers of birds of the same and different species, thereby increasing the possibility of disease transmission. One recent study reported a higher disease prevalence in birds at feeder sites compared with non-feeder sites in Illinois (Wilcoxen *et al.* 2015). That said, feeder birds in that study were overall healthier than non-feeder birds, but few studies have attempted to link disease transmission between feeder birds and Cooper's Hawks. However, another recent study demonstrated that antibodies against disease agents like viruses and bacteria that in feeder birds cause avian pox and conjunctivitis, respectively, were common in several raptor species, but comparatively twice as high in Cooper's Hawks and Eastern Screech-Owls (*Megascops asio*) among raptors admitted to a rehabilitation center in Illinois. Researchers noted that Cooper's Hawks and Screech-Owls regularly inhabit urban and suburban areas where bird feeders are abundant, and that these raptors prey on species that use backyard feeders (Wrobel *et al.* 2016). This study also indicated that all raptors showed infrequent sign of disease, and that the frequent antibody presence suggested that exposure to pathogens is not a rare occurrence and that these birds of prey, including Cooper's Hawks, are capable of mounting an effective adaptive immune response that generally prevents development of pathology. Similarly, we reported that migrating and breeding adult and nestling Cooper's Hawks in Minnesota and Wisconsin commonly harbored blood parasites (*Haemoproteus* sp. and *Leucocytozoon toddi*). These infections result from insect vectors, but the parasites showed no detectable ill-effects on these birds (Taft *et al.* 1994, 1996).

The type and availability of prey can (or has the potential to) negatively affect reproductive success or heighten the risk of mortality for urban Cooper's Hawks. For instance, Boal *et al.* (1998) recorded high levels of trichomoniasis, an upper digestive tract disease that can result in plaque-like growths, which can, in severe cases, block the food and air canals such that birds starve and/or die from asphyxiation. This disease caused a 40% mortality rate among nestling Cooper's Hawks in Tucson, AZ It was likely contracted through high consumption of abundant columbid, that is, pigeon or dove prey (especially Mourning, White-winged [*Z. asiatica*], and Inca Doves [*Columbina inca*]) that harbor the disease agent, a parasitic protozoan worm

An adult male Cooper's Hawk stooping on pigeons from a perch atop a nine-story hospital in Massachusetts. Use of cities—and their urban structures—is now rather common among many different raptor species worldwide.
Photo by Brian Rusnica.

(*Trichomonas gallinae*). Similarly, trichomoniasis was reported as a "somewhat frequent" cause of mortality for Cooper's Hawks in and around Albuquerque, NM (Cartron *et al.* 2010). Lower reproductive rates were found at urban than rural Cooper's Hawk nests in Arizona, due largely to nestling mortality from trichomoniasis. The urban death rates led these researchers to suggest that Tucson may be an 'ecological trap' for Cooper's Hawks (Boal and Mannan 1999, Rosenfield *et al.* 2018).

An ecological trap is a habitat that attracts a species with seemingly favorable environmental conditions (e.g., abundant food, quality nesting cover), but in reality, the habitat results in mortality rates higher than reproduction can counter. Anthropogenic activities may cause most traps, so it seems plausible that animals in urbanized environments may be especially susceptible to ecological traps (Robertson and Hutto 2006). We must discuss the concept of an ecological trap before we continue, because this theme has become very popular with ecologists and wildlife managers. Unfortunately, the term is often used in an untenable and confusing manner (Bielefeldt and Rosenfield 2000, Robertson and Hutto 2006). I emphasize that to establish that a trap exists, the researcher must show behaviorally that the attractive but actually poor habitat (as revealed perhaps through reduced reproduction and/or a low number of adult survivors) acts like a magnet, drawing breeders that would have otherwise nested and/or survived more successfully elsewhere. Thus, if a city acts as a trap, there must be evidence of a net movement, or emigration of adults (breeding dispersal), or recruits (natal dispersal of sexually matured young) from exurban to urban areas. While we have demonstrated natal and breeding dispersal of individuals of both sexes between rural and urban habitats in Wisconsin (Rosenfield *et al.* 2016c, R.N. Rosenfield, unpubl. data), I know of no raptor study that has credibly established this behavior for any habitat cast as an ecological trap. Research that reports habitat-specific reduced production or survival by Cooper's Hawks or other birds may rather have identified a 'population sink,' where the habitat may be of poor or marginal quality. Perhaps it is worth pointing out explicitly that, while all traps are sinks, not all sinks disproportionately attract birds and thus function as traps. Incidentally, the ecological opposite of sinks is 'source populations,' bird populations living in habitats so favorable that productivity is high enough to offset adult mortality and generate emigration elsewhere (Pulliam 1988). The specific type of emigration, or dispersal movement, is poorly documented in many animal metapopulations (i.e., a group of partially isolated populations of the same species), but such movement would seemingly include natal dispersal (see Chapter 4). Regardless, we have suggested, based in part on molecular data and high productivity indices in both urban and rural nests, that Wisconsin has acted as a source site in metapopulations of Cooper's Hawks in north-central

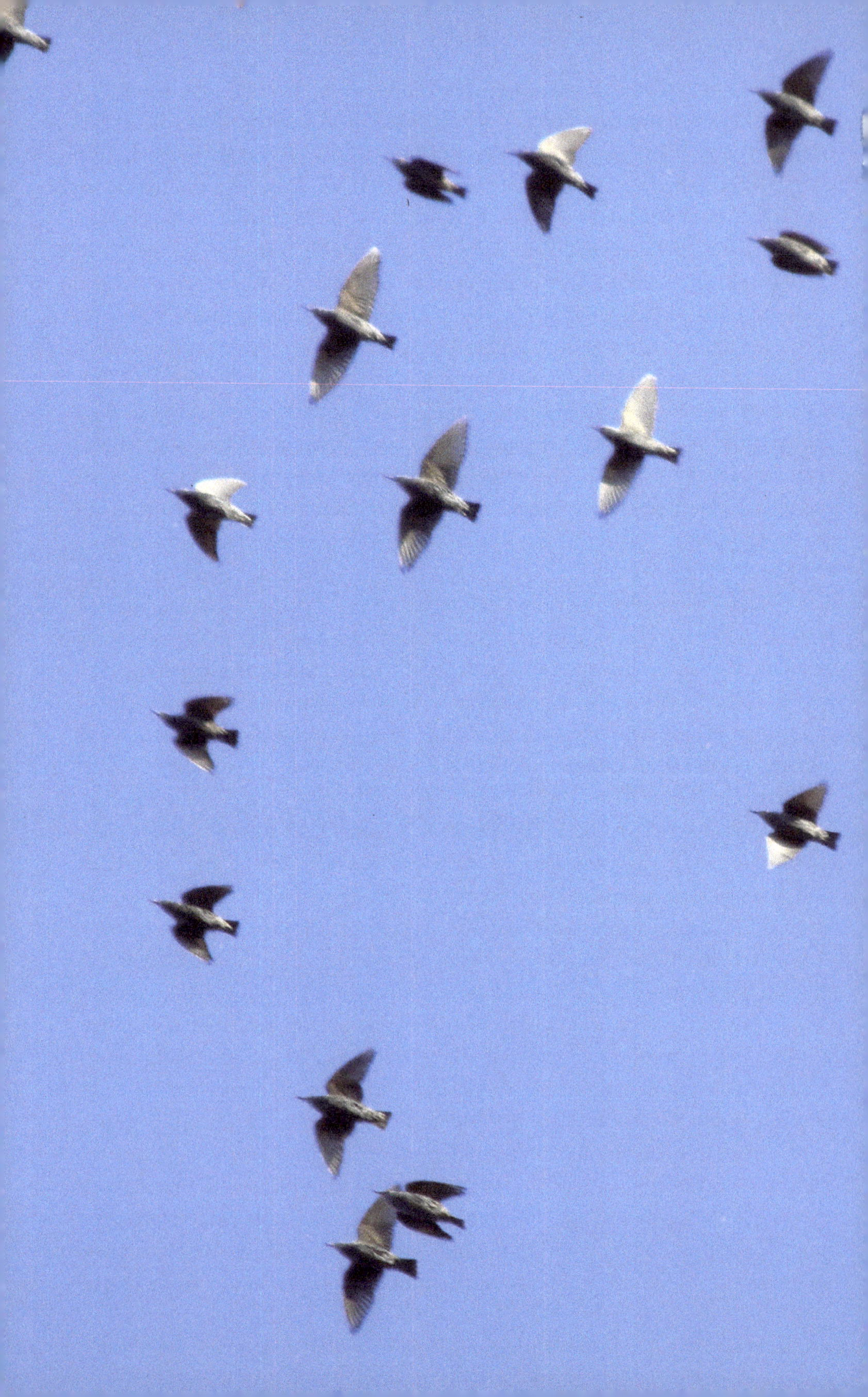

Much research suggests that abundant avian prey, such as urban starlings shown here being passively chased by a Cooper's Hawk, renders cities very favorable habitat for breeding raptors. Photo by Brian Rusnica.

North America. This probably took place in the late 20th century and the early part of the 2000s, with dispersal from Wisconsin west into North Dakota, where the prairie and grassland habitat is suitable for breeding Cooper's Hawks but productivity in some populations is lower than in Wisconsin (Sonsthagen *et al.* 2012; see Chapter 4). North Dakota also seems to have served as a relatively more historical and regional source of dispersers (Sonsthagen *et al.* 2012). It's obviously important for management reasons to establish whether a habitat is of high or low quality, but researchers (e.g. Kettel *et al.* 2017) should not confuse a sink with an ecological trap.

Indeed, returning to the Tucson study, additional research did not support the suggestion that the urban Arizona population of Cooper's Hawks was an ecological trap. Further analyses demonstrated the disease issue was time-specific, and that the urban area had a rapidly growing population with high production of young and high rates of adult and offspring survival, particularly of hawks in their first year of life, if they survived trichomoniasis (Mannan *et al.* 2008, Rosenfield *et al.* 2018). Researchers studying Cooper's Hawks elsewhere in North America, including British Columbia, North Dakota, Wisconsin, and Minnesota, reported that urban and exurban nestlings, breeding adults, and migrating birds had had low rates of infection (less than 3% of 257 birds) with the disease organism that causes trichomoniasis, and no nestling deaths attributable to trichomoniasis (Rosenfield *et al.* 2002b, 2009b). We earlier suggested that a much lower proportion of doves (5-8%) in the diet of Cooper's Hawks in some of these other venues, versus the large proportion (83%) of columbids in the diets of urban Cooper's Hawks in Tucson, may help explain the higher prevalence of infection and consequent mortality at urban nests in Arizona (Rosenfield *et al.* 2002b). That said, the relative roles of infection rates in prey, the proportion of infected prey in diets, and the severity of trichomoniasis infection in nestling hawks causing mortality remain unknown.

In the United States, urban birds, including feeder birds, may be the most competent species for West Nile Virus (WNV; Kilpatrick 2011, Kilpatrick *et al.* 2006), and these birds may be preferred for feeding by the mosquitos (*Culex* sp.) that carry the virus. A study of urban raptors in metropolitan Milwaukee, WI (Stout *et al.* 2005), found WNV antibodies in 88% of breeding adults and 2.1% of nestling Cooper's Hawks. They suggested, however, that this population didn't show any detectable adverse effects from WNV infection. It's important to highlight that we understand very little at this time about urban avian host-parasite ecology, except for a few parasites with implications for human health (Martin and Boruta 2014). Indeed, a recent discovery that a Cooper's Hawk harbored songbird-feeding ticks that tested positive for *Borrelia burgdorferi*, the bacterium that causes Lyme disease, prompted researchers to suggest that raptors may amplify this infectious agent in nature, and thus increase the likelihood of people contracting Lyme disease, especially in coastal areas (Scott *et al.* 2013).

We reiterate that few bird feeder studies exist, especially involving the breeding season, so it's unclear how feeders affect the risk of avian infections in cities (Martin and Baruta 2014, Rosenfield *et al.* 2018). The paucity of disease-related investigations is a concern, given that changes in disease and vector prevalence found elsewhere in avian communities may be related to the effects of climate change. Rising temperatures can influence disease distribution by providing favorable conditions for the movement of disease-carrying insects (Grimm *et al.* 2008, Paxton *et al.* 2016).

However, behavioral and population responses to the effects of urbanization on food-dynamics are understudied in raptors, including the Cooper's Hawk. The ability of breeding birds to respond to habitat change, such as cities taking over native or natural habitat and other ecological factors including climate change, is particularly hampered in raptors, partly by their relatively low reproductive capacities and their longer generation turnover times.

Some researchers claim that because cities are concentrated centers of production, consumption, and other factors that drive change in land use, they represent microcosms of global environmental change (e.g., Paxton *et al.* 2016). Thus, perhaps the continent-wide dynamic of bird-feeder use by urban Cooper's Hawks presents an opportunity to contribute to global-change science studies.

Climate Change

A recent study indicated concern about the viability of the Cooper's Hawk and other raptor populations in the Great Lakes region due to earlier dates of spring migration, attributed to recent climate change, or warming, between 1979 and 2012 (Sullivan *et al.* 2016). Earlier migration could lead to an earlier timing of breeding, which could result in mismatches between reproductive timing and food availability. Decoupling of breeding and food supply is expected to become more severe among higher trophic level (top-of-food-chain) species, such as raptors (Rosenfield *et al.* 2011, Sullivan *et al.* 2016). Conversely, it is possible that adaptively favorable outcomes could occur thanks to advanced timing of migratory songbird prey for Cooper's Hawks. Some scientists have claimed that spring arrival of songbird prey may trigger egg-laying in Cooper's Hawks (Snyder and Wiley 1976, Millsap *et al.* 2013). In fact, in Wisconsin, the American Robin—one of the most frequently detected prey items at both urban and exurban Cooper's Hawk nest sites during the pre-incubation stage—did, along with other migratory songbirds, advance its spring migration in the late 1990s, consistent with recent climate warming (Bradley *et al.* 1999, Rosenfield *et al.* 2016b). Notably, we found that six consecutive generations of Wisconsin Cooper's Hawks in the Great Lakes region started laying eggs 4 to 5 days earlier in urban and exurban habitats between 1980 and 2015, a pace similar to the advanced arrival of spring in Wisconsin– 6 to 7 days earlier on average– during the years of our study. Further, a gradual shift of 0.13 days per year in spring to earlier egg-laying in Cooper's Hawks was similar to the gradual 0.21 days per year, on average, of earlier timing of spring phenologies (or calendric schedules) of 55 species of Wisconsin plants and mostly migratory songbirds during our study years. It seems reasonable and likely to conclude that recent climate change is influencing the natural history of many biological communities in Wisconsin, including the Cooper's Hawk.

However, we found no adverse effects on the reproductive output of Cooper's Hawks because of this earlier nesting in this study's healthy nesting population (Rosenfield *et al.* 2016b). More specifically, we found no trend in average clutch and brood counts (overall, nests averaged 4.3 eggs and 3.7 young) across this 36-year period, in both urban and exurban environments. These long-term, stable indices of reproduction are the highest ever reported for the species and perhaps represent the physio-ecological maximum for Wisconsin Cooper's Hawks (see Chapter 4). To our knowledge, ours is the only raptor study in which variation in clutch size was investigated as a potential population response to climate change. This is surprising, because clutch size might well be the most immediate reproductive response to the earlier arrival of prey in spring (Rosenfield *et al.* 2016b). Also, species with larger clutch sizes, such as the Cooper's Hawk, have a more effective buffer against population crashes and should be able to recover from them more quickly (Krüger and Radford 2008).

The shift to earlier egg-laying could be related to a change or evolution to a larger body size in Cooper's Hawks. That's because bigger birds in any given year within a population breed earlier and have more young (see Chapters 1 and 5). It's important to note that body size and breeding phenology are traits that can be inherited. However, the body size of breeders and their diet hadn't changed over our study years (Rosenfield *et al.* 2016c). So we concluded that recent climate change was a plausible cause of the shift in egg-laying we documented for Cooper's Hawks in Wisconsin, and that our population appeared resilient to and was not adversely influenced by the rate of climate change during our study years. These conclusions about breeding accord with the recent low level of conservation concern for Cooper's Hawks across the continent (Langham *et al.* 2015). But the rate of climate change is expected to increase across its range in years to come, so further monitoring is needed to reveal the potential influence of climate change on breeding birds.

It should be noted that an advanced nesting schedule could benefit Cooper's Hawks in ways other than the productivity metrics we measured. For example, it is possible that Cooper's Hawks advanced their timing of nesting in part for social reasons regarding territoriality. An advanced nesting schedule may enhance the ability of an individual to secure and defend a territory as early as environmental conditions (e.g., food availability) permit. That behavior, in turn, may enhance that individual's ability to prevent another bird from taking over his territory before the conditions are in place for breeding. Initiating nesting earlier also provides more opportunity to try again if the first clutch fails. Similarly, and although I'm not aware of any published reports on this, it is conceivable that Cooper's Hawks in food-rich cities are more likely than exurban birds to re-nest if a first clutch fails. Earlier nesting also might enhance the survival of juveniles and give them longer to develop foraging and flight skills before the fall migration begins. The duration of the nesting period did not increase for Cooper's Hawks, and the whole process advanced in timing across all of the study years, which would consequently lengthen the time between fledging and migration in Wisconsin, where the onset of fall has been delayed. Unfortunately, we were unable to address these hypotheses or alternative explanations with our study design. We have urged others with long-term data sets to focus on the possible effects of recent climate change on these natural history dynamics (Rosenfield *et al.* 2016b).

Lastly, ecologists have suggested that opportunities to hybridize may increase as species distributions shift and populations colonize new habitats in response to recent climate change. Cooper's Hawks have demonstrated recent breeding range shifts farther northward into Canada (Rosenfield et al. 2010, A.C. Stewart, pers. comm.), and southward into urban, central Mexico (González-Oreja et al. 2019). We recently genetically confirmed that a juvenile accipiter caught during fall migration at Cape May, New Jersey, and who showed features of both a Northern Goshawk and a Cooper's Hawk (e.g., a white-line above the eyes as in goshawk and intermediate in size between these two raptors), was in fact a female hybrid between these two species. This is the first documentation of a natural hybrid for these species (Haughey *et al.* 2019) and we note that molecular analyses indicated that the male parent was a Cooper's Hawk and the female parent a Northern Goshawk! Thus, it's conceivable that range shifts associated with climate change, whereby Cooper's Hawks may now be more preponderant in the traditional northern continental breeding distribution of the Northern Goshawk, may have contributed to this hybrid event.

Chapter Three

COURTSHIP AND NESTING BIOLOGY

So I am camouflaged and lying flat and still on my back on the ground under and alongside the plucking post log that, with much effort, I have lowered close to the ground. My plan is that when the adult male from the nearby nest lands on the log to transfer food to his mate I can jump up and scare him into my mist net, set just to the other side of the log. Gosh, I hope this works. He's wearing a red leg band with a unique alpha-numeric code on his left leg, indicating I banded him as an adult. But I have been unable to recapture him this year because he's 'trap shy' from having been caught in previous years with use of the same decoy owl, and I'm guessing he recognizes it unfavorably. Either way, he won't attack my trapping owl, and I really need to get this hawk so that I can draw blood for our new paternity study in Stevens Point, which may allow me to identify which offspring he sired and maybe even which female(s) he has courted in our urban study population. I sense a whir of air, and in an instant he's inches above me, having just landed with a lifeless robin— I reflexively lunge and yell at the same time to 'scare' him, and he flushes right into my net! Then a speck of his blood is obtained for his DNA...YES!!! I'm guessing it'll be harder to trick him into a capture in the future, and so I grip him for a few extra seconds, admiring his regal look before releasing him, as I figure it'll be (and it was) the last time I hold this long-lived 'stud,' as he's replaced the next year with the new kid in town.

OVERVIEW AND NEST BUILDING

Undeniably, the best-studied aspect of raptor ecology is nesting biology. This is likely because, as with most birds, socially monogamous Cooper's Hawks become predictably present daily at or near a nest during the same months each year. During this time, the vocalizations and persistent presence of the pair in nest building, food deliveries by adults to young, and defense of the nest site from predators or territorial rivals render the birds more detectable. In fact, and as we shall see, seemingly collaborative efforts by a nesting male and female reflect individual strategies that sometimes are in conflict. Thus, they must strike compromises to marshal the main task of their existence: to produce young who in turn will join future breeding generations. In fact, and as naturalist Charles Darwin pitched, the ultimate goal for an individual is to produce, or in effect contribute more young into a population versus others of the same species. Competition among counterparts is a main driving force for the behaviors exhibited by social partners. The basis for these behavioral or evolved adaptations is that they are, in part, expressions of copies of genes that they obtained from their parents. So, offspring typically exhibit many behaviors inherited from their parents, enhancing their own viability and competitive success when they begin breeding.

Let's first overview some facts about Cooper's Hawk nests, nesting events and the duration of such events, to provide some context for the more specific details to follow about courtship, vocalizations, and paternity issues. Cooper's Hawks generally produce a single brood each year, and several of their breeding events come in 'fours.' Adults take about 3-4 weeks to build the nest in spring (though some nest-building occurs in the non-breeding season), about 34 days to incubate eggs, and about 4 more weeks to feed and care for pre-flight young. It's mostly the females who incubate and tend to the young at the nest. Both adults will deliver food to young for several weeks after they leave the nest, or fledge, but females eventually leave dependent fledglings after they are out of the nest for 2-3 weeks, and adult females become less associated with the immediate nest site and the breeding territory. Males, on the other hand, provide the bulk of food to fledglings while they are gaining independence, but over time they provide less and less food to the offspring. So the young must eventually hunt on their own. Fledged young will often follow and imitate each other's behaviors, and hence they hunt together (and rarely share food). Often they're grouped within several meters of each other during this post-fledging period, which lasts about 4-6 weeks. Infrequently, and unlike many non-raptors, the Cooper's Hawk and other birds of prey continue to use the nest for loafing, sleeping, and feeding during the post-fledging period (Boal 1997, Meng and Rosenfield 1988, Nicewander and Rosenfield 2006). Altogether, the breeding period lasts about 4-5 months, typically beginning in mid- to-late March and lasting through July in Wisconsin (this period can be extended by a few pairs in a population who re-nest after a failure during the egg stage such that active nests occur in August). Interestingly, this schedule is generally similar to other populations of Cooper's Hawks throughout North America (Rosenfield and Bielefeldt 1993a, Millsap *et al.* 2013).

Adult female Cooper's Hawk with 14-day-old young. Young are essentially all white with down feathers up until this age when tips of growing darker feathers begin to show. Note feces or 'whitewash' of young whose squirts of their waste land on nest rim, tree branches, leaves, and the ground. Thus the nest's interior is kept relatively clean and it thus may, for example, be less likely to attract parasitic insects.
Photo by Robert Rosenfield.

Left & Bottom Left: Adult female arriving with starling prey for less than 1-week-old young. It is the female that primarily tends the nest, feeding and brooding the young. Photos by Thomas Muir.

Above: Weak and hungry 3-day-old young apparently reacting to my movements at the nest by opening their mouths for food. Notice white egg-tooth on top end of bills. An egg-tooth facilitates breaking an egg-shell at hatching and usually disappears when young reach 10 days of age. There too is a leg of a woodpecker prey item on nest rim. Photo by Robert Rosenfield.

Incubating adult female Cooper's Hawk on typical Wisconsin nest that abuts main stem of conifer; nest is about 50 centimeters (20 inches) wide and 25 centimeters (10 inches) deep. This female bred for seven consecutive years on the same territory and would not leave the nest when a researcher climbed to count eggs (one partially visible on her left) and later to band young. Thus we could hand-grab her for marking, etc. Here she, as with many incubating hens, is hunkered down low in a possible attempt to conceal her presence to me.
Photo by Robert Rosenfield.

Completed clutch of 5, typically pale bluish eggs at a nest in a white pine tree in Wisconsin. Note abundant red pine bark flakes that line inside of nest and downy white feathers on nest rim from adult female's underside as her brood patch forms to expose skin to enhance transmission of heat to eggs. Bark flakes from trees are typically added during egg-laying and occasionally throughout the 34-day incubation period. The female typically begins incubation after the first 3 eggs are laid. Thus with same duration of incubation time to hatching for each egg, the first 3 eggs hatch on same day, 4th and 5th eggs about 1 and even up to 3 days later, respectively. Such asynchronous hatching results in later-hatched young being noticeably smaller than their older siblings. Photo by Robert Rosenfield.

An adult female (right) has just arrived at her nest to resume her duties as primary nest attendant. Males typically incubate eggs or broods of very small young only for short time periods of about 10-15 minutes when their female mates are away from a nest to feed on delivered prey, defecate, and/or bathe. Note that this male has a brown cheek rather than the gray face of most males.
Photo by Thomas Muir.

Returning to the start of the nesting season in spring, we have estimated that male Cooper's Hawks do about 70% of the twig collection for nests. Twigs are delivered one at a time to a nest during building. Females occasionally land on nests under construction without any building material and thus may be simply 'inspecting' its progress (Meng and Rosenfield 1988, Rosenfield et al. 1991a). It is rare for both birds to be on the nest at the same time during its construction.

Nests typically abut the main tree stem, are usually within the cover of the lower reaches of tree canopy, and average about 14 meters (45 feet) above ground in Wisconsin (Trexel et al. 1999). Nest height typically is at about 60% of total tree height, a proportion that appears to apply to many other Cooper's Hawk breeding populations throughout North America, irrespective of the tree species used for nesting (see below, Bosakowski et al. 1992, and Rosenfield et al. 2002a). The nest is a relatively large structure about 50 centimeters (20 inches) in diameter and 25 centimeters (10 inches) deep. Cooper's Hawks typically build a new nest—in fact they build several—each year on a territory (see Chapter 4). Nests are often not started from scratch in Wisconsin. In fact, about 40% to 60% of nests each year are built on pre-existing structures such as squirrel or old Cooper's Hawk nests (R.N. Rosenfield, unpubl. data). Millsap *et al.* (2013) reported 21% reuse of the previous year's nest in Florida.

In one fortuitous instance, a courting pair stopped building on a nest about 50 meters (150 feet) from my ground blind, and the female, with the male flying close

Right: Adult Cooper's Hawks have to molt, that is drop and replace worn out old feathers each year. Breeding activities, including different nest duties by the sexes, likely influence the molt process. These images representing captured gray birds at least 2 years old, or after-second-year (ASY) breeders, depict in a generalized pattern the molting process in flight feathers of the wing and tail of Cooper's Hawks in Wisconsin (white, old feathers; gray, new flight feathers; N is sample size). Neither sex begins molt during the pre-incubation period. Although unknown, perhaps at this time both sexes avoid molting in part because they need all their plumage to signal to possible mates their individual integrity in courtship display and flight efficiency (in fact both males and females in Wisconsin choose their mates; see Chapter 5). Notably, molt gaps in the wing reduces aerodynamic flight performance in birds (Hedenström and Sunada 1999). Breeding males and females begin molt during the mid-incubation period (about mid-May). By contrast, in some other raptors, including the ecologically similar Eurasian Sparrowhawk (A. nisus), males begin molt later during egg-hatching and the early nestling period (Newton 1986, Steenhof and McKinley 2006). However, as in other raptors, molt in female Cooper's Hawks occurs to a greater extent, in fact, involving about twice as many total flight feathers as the male Cooper's Hawk in each of the incubation and nestling stages. Further, the male restricts its molt to the 'primaries', which feather group is the outermost 10 feathers of the wing. The difference in extent in molt between the sexes probably occurs because females do not have to route as much energy to flying as they principally tend eggs and young at a relatively small area around the nest. Thus unlike males, who are energetically and aerodynamically tasked with hunting and carrying prey throughout a territory due to their primary role as food provider, females can direct more of their energy toward molting during the incubation and nestling stages.

courtship & nesting biology

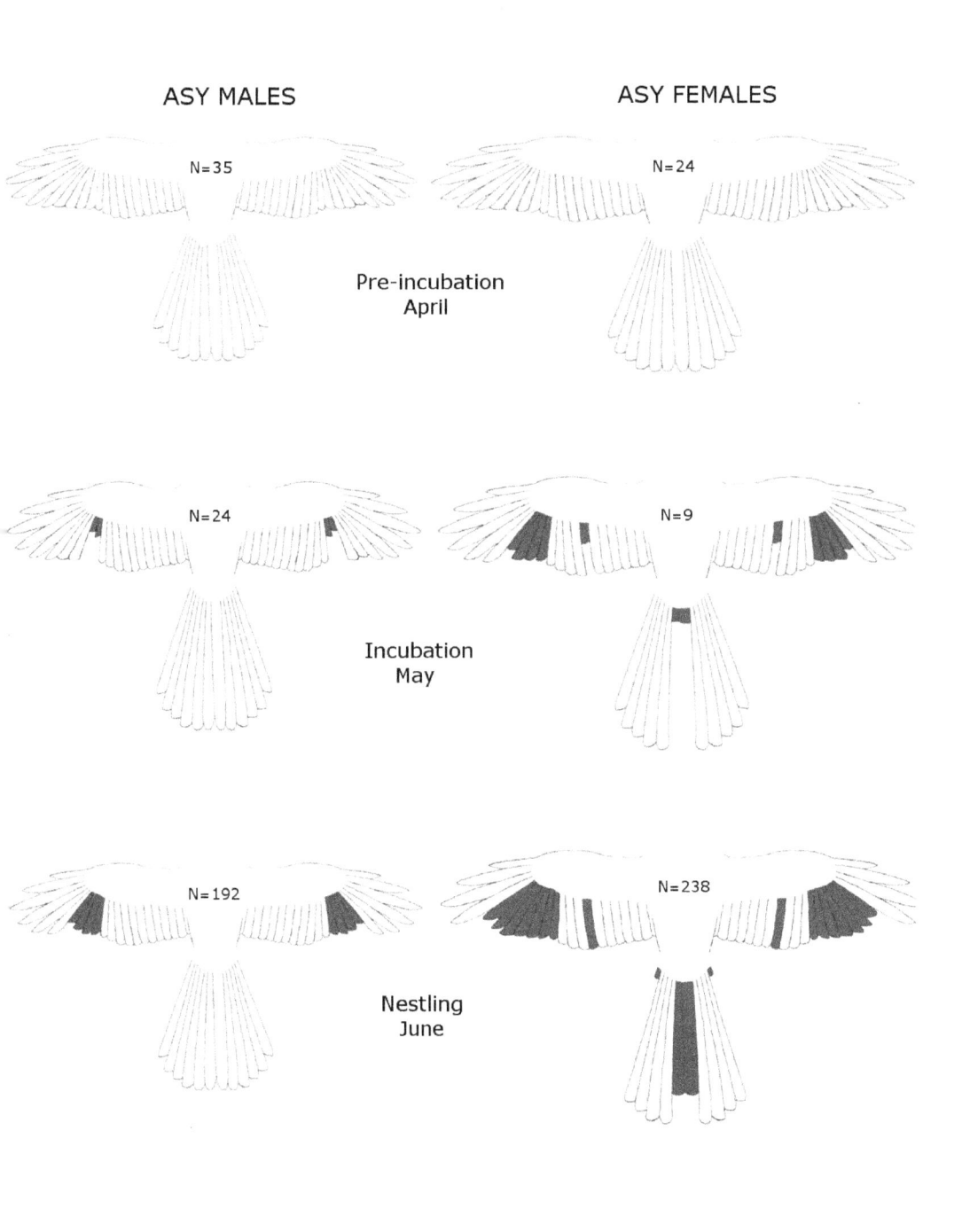

ASY MALES / ASY FEMALES

N=35 / N=24
Pre-incubation
April

N=24 / N=9
Incubation
May

N=192 / N=238
Nestling
June

On average perhaps the highest Cooper's Hawk nests occur in tall conifers of the Pacific Northwest. Here the author is ascending to a nest just over 31 meters (102 feet) in a Douglas-fir tree in Victoria, British Columbia. Canadian researchers Andy and Irene Stewart often cannot readily find study nests in this city because they are so difficult to see from the ground so they resort to early morning observations of nest-building hawks whose activities reveal nest locations.
Photos courtesy of Eric Wagner.

behind her, flew over and onto a squirrel nest in a tree just above my hide. The male did not land at the nest and perched in another tree. The female then started to 'shuffle' about the structure while lying on her chest (I note that she was not holding any twigs when she arrived at the nest). Her actions on the nest over about 30 seconds were so forceful that she knocked several leaves from the structure, which landed on me. She then flew off and perched nearby. Then her mate flew to neighboring trees, where he broke sticks one at a time (at least 13 in total), which were used for nest-building on the squirrel's nest. The female eventually flew off, and the male almost immediately followed her out of my view. These events were probably the beginning of nest building on that structure, because later that day, when the pair was off-site, I climbed to and counted only 13 fresh sticks on that squirrel nest. My impression at the time was that her movements on the nest were simply to assess its structural integrity, but she also could have been checking whether the nest was occupied by squirrels (a possible egg predator). It was not. It also seemed to me that her actions influenced or prompted the male to build there. Nevertheless, I did not see the pair use this nest further that year. Without providing evidence, Meng (1951) indicated that the male Cooper's Hawk selects the nest tree in New York, while Moore and Henny (1984) assumed that the female does this task in Oregon. I have no evidence to indicate, generally, which sex chooses the nest tree.

Cooper's Hawks nest in a very wide array of tree species across the continent in both rural and urban settings. For example, they use white pine (*Pinus strobus*) in Massachusetts and Wisconsin; American beech (*Fagus grandifolia*) in New York and Florida; various oaks (*Quercus* spp.) in California, Florida, Maryland, Iowa, and Wisconsin; Douglas-fir (*Pseudotsuga menziesii*) in Oregon, Washington and British Columbia; and green ash (*Fraxinus pennsylvanica*), trembling aspen (*Populus tremuloides*) and even Rocky Mountain juniper (*Juniperus scopulorum*) in North Dakota (Rosenfield and Bielefeldt 1993a, Rosenfield *et al.* 2002a, Millsap *et al.* 2013). There is evidence that Cooper's Hawks prefer nesting in white pine in Wisconsin and that pine plantations are important habitat for breeding Cooper's Hawks throughout the Midwestern U.S. (Rosenfield *et al.* 1991b, 2000, see Chapter 4). Unlike other raptors that will use man-made structures for nests (e.g., buildings and billboards by Red-tailed Hawks [*Buteo jamaicensis*], smokestacks and bridges by Peregrine Falcons; Bird *et al.* 1996) urban nesting Cooper's Hawks apparently are averse to using anything other than trees (Stout and Rosenfield 2010).

Several of the breeding activities and pre-incubation events already mentioned are common in many other raptors, but one recent, surprising discovery shows the Cooper's Hawk to be markedly unlike all other birds of prey studied to date. Most raptors are socially and genetically monogamous, with only occasional trysts that result in nests with young sired by at least two different males. This latter phenomenon is known as extra-pair paternity, or EPP. Cooper's Hawks, however, are highly unfaithful to their social partners. In fact, their mating system seems more like that of songbirds, a group of mostly sparrow-sized birds renowned for their sexual promiscuity despite their social monogamy. EPP seems particularly detrimental to the fitness (meaning, ability to produce young that would in turn become breeders) of the resident male who, in Wisconsin, invests all of the reproductive periods of his life into one territory where, theoretically, he should be raising his own young. This site investment is accentuated by the fact that males, not females, establish breeding territories; invest more than females do in reproductive efforts via nest building and anti-predator behavior before the eggs are fertilized; and are principally responsible for procuring prey for themselves, their mates, and their young right through to independence after fledgling (Rosenfield and Bielefeldt 1991a,b, 1993a). There clearly is a marked difference between the sexes in reproductive investments in a nesting effort. And although males in Wisconsin make lifetime or career decisions as to which site (a nest-centered area/territory 800 meters in diameter, about half mile) they will breed in, some females switch sites and, over the years, divorce mates

(Rosenfield and Bielefeldt 1996). The factors that dictate mating dynamics of the sexes can be difficult to identify, but some insights will be discussed in Chapter 5. Nevertheless, successful nesting at any nest site requires cooperation between the sexes. This begins with courtship.

Courting

Courtship includes interactions between the sexes that involve pairing and other behaviors that should lead to production of eggs and young. Unfortunately, there is little (especially quantitative) information on the specific behaviors that lead to pairing. Aerial displays, either in tandem or singly, are a common and seemingly important behavior that may facilitate pairing in raptors (Olsen 1995). In spring, and less frequently in fall, male Cooper's Hawks (and females less so), exhibit a pronounced or exaggerated deep wingbeat during a slow, somewhat undulating and rocking flight above treetops (sometimes as high as 100 meters [300 feet] above the ground). That makes the birds appear, at least to my eye, very light or buoyant in flight. Their under-tail, brilliant white covert feathers tend to be flared in such flights, and we have heard males occasionally give *kik* calls during these displays. This apparent and early courtship display, which may initiate or facilitate pairing, is similar to the buoyant wing flapping of Common Nighthawks (*Chordeiles minor*).

Thus this behavior in Cooper's Hawks is called 'night-hawk flapping.' We have seen male and female Cooper's Hawks in simultaneous night-hawk flapping. It seems practical that a forest raptor would advertise his (her?) availability, territory vacancy and/or occupancy to potential mates or rivals more obviously in the open sky than in a more enclosed, darkened forest. I have twice seen a night-hawk flapping male being 'chased' by another male using direct and fast flapping, which to me suggested an impending attack (R.N. Rosenfield, pers. obs.). Unfortunately, I did not see the outcome of these chases. Male Cooper's Hawks will readily attack each other in contesting ownership of breeding territories, and there is evidence that these territorial interactions can have lethal outcomes (Millsap *et al.* 2013; see Chapter 4).

Indeed, I found two dead males, about a meter (3 feet) apart at the base of a nest tree with an incubating female present. Both males had several small puncture wounds about the upper chest. I speculate that they had fought a few days earlier (based on the equal 'freshness' of the carcasses) and inflicted lethal wounds to each other. Several days after finding these bodies, I climbed to the nest at this site and found cold eggs and no sign of the female, who had probably been obliged to desert the nest to hunt and feed herself, with no mate present to feed her. One of these dead

Spring courtship includes flight displays in which white under-tail covert feathers are noticeably splayed as shown here in upper photo.
Photo by John Seibel.

Dr. Steve Taft saw these two adult male Cooper's Hawks collide in mid-air and while gripping each other, fall to an ice-covered lake on the outskirts of Stevens Point, Wisconsin, in March, when courting seasonally commences. They remained 'talon-locked' for several minutes before releasing their grip on one another and flying off. Cooper's Hawks will physically attack and sometimes kill each other in territorial disputes (see Chapter 3).
Photo by Steve Taft.

birds included what was then my oldest breeding male (9 years old) and a 1-year-old, brown bird. This probable battle for the nesting site between a 'senior' and a 'teenager' occurred after a complete clutch of five eggs had been laid, so it seems territorial contests aren't restricted to the courtship period. (Similarly, Cooper's Hawks in Albuquerque, New Mexico, will build nests outside the spring courtship period, in the fall; B.A. Millsap, unpubl. data). In addition, a colleague of mine, zoologist Dr. Steve Taft, witnessed two adult Cooper's Hawks collide in mid-air, and, while locked in each other's grip, fall onto the snow on a frozen central Wisconsin lake in late March. For several minutes, the birds' talons appeared locked into each other's bodies, before they each let go and flew away. It was not apparent who 'won,' nor what extent of wounding was inflicted on either bird.

This hostile engagement during the courtship period probably reflected a conflict over territory. We have no observations of adults preying upon each other for food. But we did observe a subadult, 1-year-old female Cooper's Hawk take a very young (less than 1 week old) nestling from a nest in an apparently rare case of infanticide in Cooper's Hawks (Rosenfield and Papp 1988). This intruder took the young while the female was away from the nest and out of sight of the observer watching from a blind near the nest.

Courting generally appears to last several weeks each year in Cooper's Hawks and is an ecological dynamic that has been very poorly studied in wild birds of prey.

A bowing display that may signal a readiness to nest-build in Cooper's Hawks. We documented quick bursts of bowing mostly at dawn just before nest building for the day began. Bowing resembled movements of birds when they place sticks into a nest. The display never lasted more than a minute, and males, the sex that does the majority of building, gave this display more than females. This posture also may facilitate pairing, as we observed it mostly in new mates several weeks before eggs were laid. Drawing by Bryce Robinson.

This gap in our knowledge about raptor courtship is partly the result of logistical problems. For example, being relatively large birds, raptors range farther from the nest site than smaller birds do and are therefore difficult to track. Raptors also are generally less vocal than non-raptors, and many are quite wary of being approached by human observers. Nonetheless, we have learned much about Cooper's Hawk courtship, mostly through direct observation of marked birds. Viewing has been made easier by the recent and ubiquitous presence of large numbers of nesting Cooper's Hawks in sparsely vegetated settings of cities throughout North America. More recently, we have used molecular techniques to reveal the identity of birds, gene flow (i.e., the movement of genes via individual mobility) across populations, and to document the maternity and paternity of nestlings. These latter findings have revealed rather remarkable, if not puzzling, unseen parental behaviors between the sexes prior to egg-laying.

Most of what has been published in quantified form about courtship behaviors stems from my doctoral research on the pre-incubation behavior of dozens of pairs of individually marked Cooper's Hawks in Wisconsin (Rosenfield 1990). This work with my friend and colleague, the late John Bielefeldt, was aided by our awareness that in spring, Wisconsin Cooper's Hawks are predictably present on their nest sites about 30 minutes before sunrise each day, even during extended periods of light rain- and snow-fall. And, because they do not roost near partially constructed nests, we made it a point to arrive at nest sites in early morning darkness, presumably undetected by the Cooper's Hawks. There we sat, quietly and still, for hours while documenting their early morning arrival and other behaviors. Sometimes we would trap hawks with dove or starling prey in these early morning visits. We were fortunate, in that the birds virtually always called when they arrived, so we knew of their presence even in low light conditions. If they were not calling, we often could detect their presence by the audible and distinct cracking sound of twigs being broken by hawks as they built their nests in the still morning air.

A relatively stereotypical schedule of events in the morning was that both male and females immediately called as they arrived. Males almost always called from perches, initially 30 to 100 meters (99 - 330 feet) away from the nest. Females' initial calling positions were difficult to determine, because they called while in flight to the nest or to the male's position. Females were typically about 80 to 200 meters (260 - 660 feet) from their nests when they began calling. Male-to-female distances at initial calls averaged 65 meters (215 feet).

During several of our dawn visits we observed an undocumented bowing display in this species. This display was seen 10 times among nine birds; eight marked males and one female (Rosenfield and Bielefeldt 1991c). Displaying birds assumed

Cooper's Hawks build their stick nests in a main crotch of a tree or on branches against its main trunk. Building in spring occurs daily and usually begins about 30 minutes before the sun rises. Most building occurs in the morning but it can occur in all daylight hours. Typically, one bird builds at a time and the male does most of the construction. Twigs are gathered in trees by tugging at them with the beak, although sticks infrequently are collected on the ground. The nest on the left is being built atop that of a squirrel's, which latter structure can be recognized by the aggregate of leaves below the exclusive and rather 'porous' layer of sticks brought by hawks. Cooper's Hawks do not incorporate leaves in the base of their nests, but for reasons unknown, they will add sprigs (i.e., twigs with green leaves/pine needles) atop a completely built nest. A completed nest lacks the porous or 'airy' look shown here.

Top photo of nest by Thomas Muir; bottom photo by Brian Rusnica.

a horizontal standing position on a tree branch, from which bursts of quick bowing movements (three to 10) occurred. Each bow was interrupted by very short (less than 1-second) pauses, with the forebody at the horizontal plane. Wings and tails were not spread. In one male, the white under-tail covert feathers were spread; these covert feathers are used in other displays by males but apparently less so by females. Most males gave *kik* calls (see below) during this behavior, and the same call is given upon their arrival at dawn and when males arrive at a nesting area with prey. Bowing never exceeded 60 seconds, typically occurred before nest-building began for the day, and the pair never exhibited the behavior simultaneously. The single female seen bowing gave one single *kik* call at the beginning of bowing. This posture may, as in some other birds, function as demonstrative nest-building, signaling a bird's readiness to engage in actual nest-building (Rosenfield 1990).

Cooper's Hawks build nests by shoving twigs into the structure, repeatedly grabbing the sticks at different points along their length and pushing them into the base. Such repeated grabbing results in head and body movements similar to those in bowing. Bowing was seen mostly in males, the sex that does the majority of the building in most pairs (Rosenfield *et al.* 1991a). Bowing displays have been reported in many different birds, including other raptors, and may have evolved for different reasons in different species (Rosenfield and Bielefeldt 1991c). Male raptors may also bow to convey their 'submissiveness' to their larger mates. Alternatively, Andy Stewart (pers. comm.) suggests that bowing is ritualized prey plucking by male Cooper's Hawks as the motion resembles the dynamics of their plucking of prey presented to females. Thus, bowing may signal food provisioning competence in males. These explanations, of course, are not mutually exclusive.

Bowing may be more common at the time that pairs are forming or in new pairs, as displays tend to become superfluous in birds, raptor or not, with previous breeding experience (Rosenfield and Bielefeldt 1991c). Indeed, of the 10 times we observed bowing, seven were about 3-4 weeks before first eggs were laid in these observed pairs, and at least five of the 10 pairs in which bowing was seen included a new mate.

Following the hawks' arrival near a nest at dawn, only one bird builds at a time. Sticks typically are collected, that is, broken off tree branches, by tugging with the beak, while the bird is perched in a tree typically within about 80 meters of the nest. Birds will infrequently collect twigs from the ground. The non-building mate typically remains nearby, occasionally changing perches within about 40 meters of the nest and its mate. Building continues for a variable portion of the morning. Daily courtship activities then peak over several weeks. Copulations occur during nest building and in fact are strongly associated with construction of nests, with most copulations immediately following delivery of sticks to nests by males. (Copulations are also strongly associated with food deliveries by males to females; see extra-pair paternity below). Males fly toward females to copulate during nest building; I have never seen a female fly toward a male immediately before a copulation during nest building. Copulations occur throughout the almost 4-week-period before incubation, typically in the morning, but also throughout the day. Generally they happen on a tree branch, rarely on the ground (Rosenfield *et al.* 1991a).

Females tend to remain near the nest throughout much of the day, but males are absent several times each day while procuring food for themselves and their mates. However, direct observations of leg-marked birds and findings from some recent excellent telemetry studies have shown that during the pre-incubation stage, females (some seemingly paired) infrequently visit other Cooper's Hawk territories, which

Chapter 3

Copulations in Cooper's Hawks, which last about 5 seconds, typically occur as shown here in trees, and rarely on the ground. In spring copulations happen throughout a 4-week period prior to egg-laying, and typically occur just after a male has either delivered food (note the prey item in the female's mouth) or after he has delivered a twig to a nest. Our estimate of 372 copulations per clutch of eggs for Cooper's Hawks is among the highest such measure for all the world's birds.
Photos by Brian Rusnica.

can be adjacent sites or territories miles away (Driscoll and Rosenfield 2015, Millsap *et al.* 2013, Deal *et al.* 2017). It is likely that females are generally not hunting at this time, though females do opportunistically take prey during the pre-incubation stage (we have lured and captured females with live prey near nests at this stage of breeding [Rosenfield and Bielefeldt 1993b]). These extra-territorial movements may represent strategies for procuring food resources elsewhere, and may involve copulations from extra-pair males and/or evaluation and competition for prospective mates.

VOCALIZATIONS

As is true for many bird species, adult vocalizations are a pervasive and thus presumably important natural history phenomenon during courtship and throughout the remainder of the nesting season (Kroodsma 1996, Rosenfield and Bielefeldt 1991a). Among songbirds, males generally call more often and have a larger repertoire of vocalizations than females. The reverse is true for Cooper's Hawks and perhaps other raptor species (Sanchez 2007). Breeding female Cooper's Hawks have a larger repertoire of calls than breeding males and call more frequently when in the presence of their mates. Females also call during a wider array of activities

(Rosenfield and Bielefeldt 1991a). In marked contrast, except for occasional calls uttered during night-hawk flapping mostly in early spring, courting males generally do not call while in flight, while collecting twigs for nests, or when females are at nests. Females routinely called during these activities and when they were at the nest while it was under construction. In fact, except for vocalizations in spring during their arrival at dawn, during copulations, and during the first few nest visits of the day, courting males are relatively silent in the presence of their mates.

The contrast between songbirds and raptors when it comes to vocalization is most interesting, because the role of the male in establishing and defending breeding territories is generally the same in both types of birds. Perhaps this sex-difference in vocalizations is related to the synergy between reversed sexual size dimorphism (males smaller than females), dangerous weaponry, and the strong motivation for killing in raptors. Maybe larger female raptors feel a need to be disarming by sending vocal messages of non-aggression to their male partners, to reassure them that it is not dangerous to be near them. Many times we have witnessed females displace male Cooper's Hawks from perches. It appeared to us that males were frightened or intimidated by their much larger mates. Notably, size in animals is generally correlated with strength and the ability to inflict injury in actual or potential conflicts or fights (Arnott and Elwood 2009). It also could be that the marked difference in vocalizations between the sexes in raptors stems from the female's need to convey more information; it's possible that females may control male-female interactions (Mueller 1986).

This idea is widely referenced and there is some supportive evidence. But more behavioral data are needed to support this theme in Cooper's Hawks and in other raptor species. For example, given that females depend on food deliveries from males, it is conceivable that a male has (or could exercise) much control over his potential or actual social mate via his willingness to courtship-feed a female during the pre-incubation period. Our studies show that both males and females exercise choice of social partners, but unfortunately, I do not know the behavioral dynamics of this phenomenon (Rosenfield and Bielefeldt 1999, Rosenfield *et al.* 2016b; see Chapter 5).

We stress that vocalization by raptors, breeding or not, is a very understudied, if not neglected, area of their natural history and urge that more attention be devoted to this social behavior. The need for more attention to this is underscored by recent research showing that the behavior of many species of birds, including Cooper's Hawks, reflects adjustments to new environmental factors in cities. For example, breeding adult Cooper's Hawks vocalized less during feeding activities in urban than rural environments in and around Tucson, AZ. Females in the food-rich city were less likely to give *whaa* calls (also spelled *whaaa*) at urban nests, apparently because of lower food stress compared with rural sites that have smaller food reserves (Estes and Mannan 2003, Rosenfield *et al.* 2018).

In his excellent doctoral dissertation based largely on comprehensive studies of nesting Cooper's Hawks in New York, Meng (1951) reported 64 distinct adult calls, but we categorized only 4 types, rendering less distinction between variations within call-type groups. These 4 call types (i.e., *cak-cak-cak, kik, whaa*, and abbreviated *whaa* calls) are the ones typically used by breeding birds. We highlight these, along with some calls of the young, because they are the vocalizations most often heard by human observers near Cooper's Hawks nests throughout North America (Rosenfield and Bielefeldt 1991a, 1993a). Adult male calls are typically higher pitched than female calls, but this is difficult to discern when a single individual of a pair is calling.

The loud *cak-cak-cak*, or "alarm call," is probably best known because it is heard most often. It is typically given when a nest is disturbed or threatened. It lasts about 2-5 seconds, but when alarmed, an adult male or female will loudly utter it many times in sequence, either on the wing or perched in the vicinity of the nest (or at the nest, by females when they are nest building). During courtship it is often prefixed or interspersed with 1 or more *kik* notes by females, especially at dawn, when both sexes begin daily mating activities. We believe that *cak-cak-cak* calls signal aggressive intent, because we heard adult males use them only during nest defense. Females, too, use them during nest defense, but females also use them in brief (1-7 minute) exchanges of calls at dawn, perhaps to indicate presence and/or to reassert their dominance on a daily basis. 'Excitement or alarm' does not seem to adequately describe the context of *cak-cak-cak* calls, because a male is likely to be excited or intensely motivated at times other than nest defense, and the female need not be alarmed at dawn. Young may give weak *cak-cak-cak* or *ki-ki-ki* adult-like alarm calls once they are at least 3 weeks of age. We believe that, as with adults, they function in aggressive intent, as we heard them only when a predator was nearby.

The *kik* is an adult male's most frequent call and likely is used to announce his presence, identity, and location to a mate near the nest (within about 100 meters [330 feet]), either when returning with food for his mate and/or young, or on a daily basis at dawn during courtship. At both times, females are unlikely to be able to see the male's arrival, especially in more vegetated rural areas where sightlines are diminished. We note that when males are delivering food they do not give *kik* calls until (and I stress immediately when) they have landed at "plucking posts." These are fallen trees of at least 18 centimeters (about 7 inches) diameter on the ground or on horizontal tree limbs at least 8 centimeters (about 3 inches) in diameter, typically about 5-7 meters (about 20 feet) above ground. We note that males in Victoria, British Columbia rarely use logs or other substrates on the ground (A.C. Stewart, pers. comm.). Males also give *kik* calls at the nest during nest-building and during a postural bowing display, which may convey readiness to nest-build and simultaneously to signal reduced aggression, or to convey submissiveness (Rosenfield and Bielefeldt 1991c). Females also give single *kik* calls, but less often than males. During pre-incubation, females give *kik* notes mostly at dawn when in flight toward the nest, while collecting twigs for nests, and while perched near males when the latter are nest-building. I have observed some of our individually marked, adult males utter *kik* calls during September and early October from about 70 meters (230 feet) to 1 kilometer (3,300 ft) from their previously used nests, which may suggest that these calls are used to signal territorial rights outside of the typical spring courting time. And hence, that some contests for territory among males (and/or signaling to prospective mates?) occurs well outside the breeding season. But I have never detected another Cooper's Hawk in the vicinity of a calling bird in autumn.

Whaa calls are primarily given by adult females when flying toward males for food, during food exchanges between mates, when plucking prey delivered by males, and when flying back to nestlings with food, but not while feeding young at the nest. Before incubation, *whaa* calls are given in clusters of 1-4, almost exclusively by females, when perched near males when the latter are nest-building, when in flight to or from the nest, from perches preparatory to collecting twigs, but less so when loafing near the nest while males are away apparently hunting (see below regarding extra-pair copulation behavior). So, if one hears this call in spring, it's likely coming from a female within about 50 meters (164 feet) of a nest. *Whaa* calls may be a non-aggressive or submissive signal of female's willingness to suspend the potential for aggression and join in breeding, thus reassuring her much smaller mate that it is not dangerous to be near her. It is also conceivable that females are calling while their social partners are away from the nest to announce their presence and/or receptivity to non-resident, extra-pair males or potential social mates who might offer food in trade for copulations. We highlight that females certainly do not know when, or if, resident males will return with food or return at all. Thus it would seem advantageous for females to exhibit behaviors that maximize food deliveries, regardless of the identity of the male provider. Indeed, food deliveries are essential for a female's survival and egg production over about a month. Breeding Wisconsin females are at their heaviest during the pre-incubation stage – on average about 9% heavier than at the nesting stage – and they gradually and significantly drop weight until they hit their lowest body mass at the nestling stage (Rosenfield and Bielefeldt 1999, Sonsthagen *et al.* 2012). Vocalizations by a pre-laying female might help ensure her access to food via any male willing to respond and accommodate her food needs. So, it is conceivable that vocalizations by courting birds may not, contrary to earlier suggestions by us (Rosenfield and Bielefeldt 1991a), involve only communications between the resident pair.

Mated pairs aside, Cooper's Hawks are not known to move about, hunt, or otherwise function in groups as adults, typically do not share food as nestlings or, so far as previously known, as fledglings. Yet in Wisconsin, and for about 6 weeks post-fledging, we observed juveniles, as shown here, closely follow each other regularly, hunt in groups, and infrequently share food. Indeed, siblings at this stage seem 'inseparable' for weeks, as described by one observer (Nicewander and Rosenfield 2006). Photo by Larry Sobolik.

Multi-noted, abbreviated (2 to 6 second) *whaa* calls were given by both sexes during the 5 second average length of copulations; always by females, but not always by males. It is unknown what function, if any, these calls perform.

Cheep or *chirrp* is the first call of young and is given when eggs are pipped. The chip call is given by young when they are at least a week old, but not beyond the age of 3 weeks; it is given when birds are irritated, as by direct sunlight. Cheep and chip calls are typically low volume and difficult for an observer to hear from the ground. Much louder and easily heard *eeeeeeee*, *eeeeeeee-oo*, or *speeeeeeeeo* calls are given by fledged young and apparently function as food-begging calls (Rosenfield and Bielefeldt 1993a).

Extra-pair Paternity

Female birds can be certain of their genetic relationship or maternity with their own eggs and nestlings. Males, however, have no assurance of their paternity because of the possibility of extra-pair copulations (Birkhead and Møller 1992). In monogamous species in which both partners rear offspring, a need for confidence in paternity therefore arises, because cuckolded males (i.e., those raising young sired by another, or extra-pair male who provides no parental care) would waste reproductive investment and lose individual fitness in raising unrelated offspring (Trivers 1972). It has been suggested that mixed-male reproductive strategies (i.e., being unfaithful to a social mate) are to be expected in monogamous species in which males provide parental care. There is a strong physiological basis for this theory: males have far more sex cells (gametes or sperm) than do females (eggs).

In fact, female birds are apparently born (hatch) with all the eggs they will have their entire lives and are thus, compared to males, limited in their reproduction, because they can only produce one to several eggs in each breeding episode. However, male birds, like human males, essentially have the ability to produce seemingly unlimited numbers of sperm throughout their entire lives. Consequentially, while being socially mated to one female, a male should not waste his excess sperm and should attempt to inseminate other females and thereby use his vastly superior number of gametes to increase his reproductive potential, and hence his fitness. This mixed reproductive strategy is generally common in animals. Many higher animal species exhibit social bonds called polygyny; that is, one male is socially bonded to several females. Males could also simply be promiscuous and copulate with many females in one breeding season. In fact, social monogamy is rather rare in animals (Alcock 2009). Yet it is oft-estimated that 90% of all bird species are socially monogamous, probably because a male and a female need to collaborate to successfully raise a brood of young (Lack 1968, Bennett and Owens 2002). Polygyny occurs in only about 10% of all bird species (Bennett and Owens 2002).

That said, we genetically confirmed the paternity of a male Cooper's Hawk in successful social polygyny with two females. This trio produced three fledglings in each of two simultaneous urban nests about 300 meters (1000 feet) apart, as investigated and discovered by our collaborator Dr. Timothy G. Driscoll in Grand Forks, N.D. (Rosenfield *et al.* 2007b). Polygyny is rare in birds of prey but more common in raptors that take mammalian prey (e.g., some harrier hawks [e.g., Northern Harrier, *Circus cyaneus*] and the Boreal Owl [*Aegolius funereus*]). To our knowledge, ours was the first documented case of polygyny in Cooper's Hawks and the first successful instance of polygyny in any of the world's accipiters. Interestingly, this polygynous male's reproductive output may have been enhanced in this urban setting, whereas that of the female's may have been compromised, as each female's output of three young was below the average number of young fledged (3.6) in successful nests in that urban population. The male's collective production of six young from both polygynous nests exceeded by one the maximum brood size of all but one monogamous pair of Cooper's Hawks in Grand Forks. Production of six young at one nest is the maximum documented for this species and is rare among Cooper's Hawk populations (for example, we detected production of six young in only 0.9% of 740 nests across 36 years in Wisconsin; Rosenfield *et al.* 2016b). Notably, this polygynous male exhibited three different breeding strategies—monogamy, polygyny, and extra-pair copulation—while he nested successfully in each of 7 years (in 6 of which he was monogamous), producing a grand total of 30 young, which was the most by any male on that study site (Driscoll and Rosenfield 2015). In fact, one male fledgling at each nest of the two polygynous nests eventually became a breeder in Grand Forks. The polygynous male's own collective production, along with that of his two sons, disproportionately produced young across this 11-year study in that urban population (Driscoll and Rosenfield 2015).

Polygyny has been behaviorally observed (with no genetic confirmation) in another trio of Cooper's Hawks by our colleague Brian Millsap in the city of Albuquerque, NM (Driscoll and Rosenfield 2015). It is tempting to speculate that the elevated abundance of avian prey in cities fosters this alternative breeding strategy, just as mammal-eating raptors who exhibit polygyny are probably responding to the periodic and markedly high population increases of their prey and therefore have enough food to accommodate at least two families (Korpimäki 1988). But it is also possible that it is easier to detect polygyny in cities thanks to the relative ease of watching nests and mates in less-vegetated urban habitat. Nevertheless, polygyny apparently is rare in Cooper's Hawks. Other than these two reported accounts, and despite our intensive work on pre-incubation behavior, we have no observations of marked adults that would indicate polygyny during our repeated visits to more than 1,000 nests in our multi-decadal research on this species (Rosenfield *et al.* 2007b). We suggested that polygyny is not likely to evolve to a considerable extent in urban settings in Cooper's Hawks, because we view polygyny and extra-pair copulations as competing strategies in this species. Extra-pair copulations would involve fewer costs and risks than polygyny, which requires a male to be the principal food provider and to defend more than one family over several months. An extra-pair copulation by a male certainly requires much less investment. This prediction is supported by long-term observations documenting no polygyny but relatively common extra-pair copulations and/or fertilizations across breeding generations in high-density populations of Cooper's Hawks in the cities of Victoria, BC, and Milwaukee and Stevens Point, WI (Driscoll and Rosenfield 2015, Rosenfield *et al.* 2015a, S.A. Sonsthagen, A.C. Stewart, and R.N. Rosenfield, unpubl. data).

Much recent research supports the view that males and females do indeed go outside their social bonds and engage in extra-pair copulations, especially in songbirds, or passerines, where more than 86% of all species studied engage in extra-pair copulations. And about 45% of non-passerines exhibit such behavior (Westneat and Sherman 1997). In general, the risk of cuckoldry is high in birds. In an attempt to assure their paternity, territorial male raptors exhibit two behavioral strategies: mate guarding (close following of the female while she is fertile) and frequent copulation. The latter occurs in two broad categories of birds that do not perform mate guarding: colonial birds, in which one member of the pair remains at the breeding site while the other forages (think seabirds like albatrosses; Birkhead *et al.* 1987), and birds of prey, in which the male generally feeds the female from the time of pair formation through the incubation stage. Thus a male while hunting will be absent from the nest site for extended periods (generally about 2 hours but up to 5 hours daily in Cooper's Hawks). Male Cooper's Hawks are at high risk of being cuckolded because they provide most of their mates' food during the pre-incubation period and must leave females unguarded while they hunt away from them and the immediate nest site. Aggravating the challenge of mate guarding for male Cooper's Hawks is the recent discovery that female Cooper's Hawks make extra-territorial movements during the pre-laying period and engage in extra-pair copulations during such movements (Rosenfield *et al.* 2015a, Millsap *et al.* 2013, Deal *et al.* 2017). To devalue, or possibly displace, the sperm of competitors, called sperm competition, male Cooper's Hawks, like other male raptors, are believed to copulate more times than necessary to fertilize the several eggs their social mates produce in one breeding season. In fact, evidence suggests that the ejaculate from a single copulation is sufficient to fertilize all the eggs in a bird's clutch (Birkhead and Møller 1992). Most birds copulate fewer than 20 times per clutch (Birkhead and Møller 1992). Raptors, however, exhibit the highest number of copulations per clutch in all birds. For example, the Osprey (*Pandion haliaetus*) copulates about 59 times per clutch (Birkhead and Lessells 1988), the Northern Goshawk about 518 times per clutch (Squires and Reynolds 1997), although Kenward (2006) suggested 100 - 300 copulations was more typical for most goshawks. The Cooper's Hawk, with 372 copulations per clutch, is one of the highest such measures for any bird.

One recent review paper concluded that mate guarding and high rates of within-pair copulations are effective paternity guards in raptors (Mougeot 2004). In fact, studies of raptors had revealed either no evidence of extra-pair paternity, as in owls overall, and the Merlin, a small falcon (*F. columbarius*, Warkentin *et al.* 1994), or very low levels of about 3% to 11% of extra-pair young collectively, among all nestlings. A maximum of about 9.5% of nests with extra-pair offspring were found in the America Kestrel (*Falco sparverius*, Villarroel *et al.* 1998). Earlier, in my dissertation on the pre-incubation behavior of Cooper's Hawks, I suggested that high copulatory rates were the consequence of the high risk of cuckoldry, due to the fact that a males' ability to mate-guard was compromised by his primary role as food-gatherer, which compelled him to be away from his mate several times daily. During such times, the unattended female could be inseminated by another male. I had recorded a few intrusions by extra-pair males while resident males were away from the nest but never an extra-pair copulation, even though some females seemed receptive to the intruders' presence (Rosenfield 1990).

I had anticipated that a study of extra-pair paternity in our population would reveal low rates of EPP, as had been found in other studies of birds of prey, including the ecologically similar and closely related Northern Goshawk. Indeed, in one study only one of 77 Goshawk nestlings was sired by a different male (Mougeot 2004, Gavin *et al.* 1998). Logically, we thought that high rates of copulations within pairs of socially bonded

Cooper's Hawks would, as in the Goshawk and other raptors, serve as effective paternity guards. Nonetheless, our piqued curiosity prompted us to investigate EPP in collaboration with Dr. Bill Stout in his long-term studies of nesting Cooper's Hawks in metropolitan Milwaukee (Stout et al. 2007). Our thinking was that our chances of detecting EPP might be greater there, because even if low levels of promiscuous behavior existed, the probability of detecting it was greater thanks to Milwaukee's large number and high density of breeding birds, where possible extra-pair partners are often within 800 meters (about a half-mile) of territorial birds. We also thought this an ecologically intriguing study site because Milwaukee has, like many urban environments, a relatively large proportion of brown, or younger, 1-year-old or SY breeding females (in their second year of life). These young birds typically take seasonally longer than older females (gray birds at least 2 year old, or after-second year [ASY]) to acquire the resources for egg-laying. We reasoned that SY birds may be more likely than older females to accept prey from extra-pair males in possible trades for copulations, which would result in extra-pair young in nests of SY females. Cities, as previously noted, tend to have a greater abundance of avian songbird prey than rural environments (Rosenfield et al. 2018). Unlike other raptors, there is a strong association between courtship feeding and copulations in the Cooper's Hawk; most copulations almost immediately follow food deliveries by males, and copulations often occur while the female is feeding. Further, SY females are smaller than older females, and smaller birds in general take longer to acquire resources needed for egg production. They also produce fewer young. So we predicted that EPP, if found, was more likely to occur at nests with younger, SY females. We also guessed that because body size is positively related to clutch and brood sizes (larger birds have greater productivity than smaller birds; Rosenfield and Bielefeldt 1999), larger males may be better providers of the resources needed for egg-laying, meaning that females mated to larger males would not seek food as trade for extra-pair copulations. So we speculated that extra-pair paternity, if found, would be related to differences in age, body size and perhaps brood size; EPP rates would be higher in younger and smaller birds, and higher in broods with smaller numbers of nestlings.

However beautiful the hypotheses, so the saying goes, the facts can be ugly. But only in part. I vividly recall the phone call from Dr. Sarah Sonsthagen, a former undergraduate research assistant in my lab and now a population geneticist at the U.S. Geological Survey's Alaska Science Center, in which she relayed the results of the paternity analyses from the blood samples that Bill Stout and I collected from adult and nestling Cooper's Hawks in Milwaukee. She had in fact found evidence of EPP; I asked how much, and she said that 34% (15) of the total 44 study nests had at least one extra-pair young, and that 19% (27) of all 140 nestlings were sired by extra-pair males! I was both ecstatic and puzzled, and exclaimed, "Are you sure? No one will believe those numbers! Those values are too high for a raptor!" True to form, she calmly indicated that she had already re-run her analyses for quality control and that the findings were solid. I was incredulous and instantly contacted Bill Stout to tell him the surprising news. My gosh, I wondered, what specifically about the natural history of the Cooper's Hawk, which has several similarities to the breeding behavior of many other raptor species (including other accipiters!) that exhibit low rates of EPP, would conversely produce such high rates of EPP in Cooper's Hawks? Indeed, about four times higher per nest than the previous highest EPP value for raptors overall (about 9% per nest); and almost twice the previous high of 11% of all young among all nests reported in any other study of birds of prey. Accentuating the baffling but exciting findings about the promiscuous behavior of Wisconsin Cooper's Hawks, I suggest that the 34% mark probably represents the minimum level of a larger (but unknown) proportion of females involved in extra-pair copulations. Given what little we know about the copulatory behavior and reproductive physiology of wild birds, I believe it is highly unlikely that all extra-pair copulations in Milwaukee females resulted in successful fertilizations (Birkhead and Møller 1992). (We'll never know the full number, as copulations *per se* cannot be detected with molecular techniques). Further, we detected fertilizations only in successful nests, and we speculate that some nests with extra-pair fertilizations failed before we could obtain blood from their young.

Other findings from our paternity analyses deserve highlighting. No maternal-offspring mismatches were found and thus no other females laid eggs in (or "parasitized") the nests of other female Cooper's Hawks. Intra-specific (that is, within a species) brood parasitism occurs in several groups of birds, for example in ducks and woodpeckers. However, to my knowledge, the only raptor species in which this has been reported is the colonial-breeding Lesser Kestrel (*Falco naumanni*) of Eurasia. In that study, researchers documented two nestlings in two nests (of 26 total) that resulted from intra-specific parasitism (Negro *et al.* 1996). Notably, I have observed female Cooper's Hawks near or in nests (seemingly incubating) early in the breeding season in Wisconsin outside Milwaukee who were not the females we caught defending these nests later during the nestling stage. Did these 'early' hens desert the territory, or die, or were they potentially parasitic females we saw in the act of laying eggs? I do not know.

Regarding potential sires, of the 27 extra-pair nestlings in our study on Cooper's Hawks, we were able to identify only two extra-pair sires, one male at each of two (13%) of the 15 total nests with extra-pair sires (Rosenfield *et al.* 2015a). These sires were associated, though not all in the same year of the tissue sampling, with nests or territories ranging from about 2.6 kilometers (1.5 miles) to 12.8 kilometers (8 miles) away from nests with extra-pair young. Further, the number of extra-pair sires was at least two at two nests (thus, three total sires at these sites), and the territorial male at each of two other nests did not sire any of the young they were raising! Losers.

And now for some other ugly and baffling results: it turned out that the age of the female and the mass of adults, with larger and older (ASY) birds typically producing more young than smaller and younger (SY) hawks in our Wisconsin populations, were, and counter to our predictions, factors unrelated to EPP in broods. Only brood size (one-to-six young for our population) was a positive predictor of the presence of extra-pair young in nests. That is, nests with larger broods were more likely to have at least one extra-pair young.

We do not know why Cooper's Hawks exhibit such comparatively high rates of EPP among the raptors studied to date. However, we hypothesize that female Cooper's Hawks may use a strategy of maximizing energy intake, via an element of their natural history that is different from that of other raptors: the fact that copulations are strongly linked to courtship feeding by males. This may allow females to maximize energy intake, both for their survival and for production of eggs over several weeks, while they rely on males for food. Thus, females can accumulate ample body reserves to optimize their reproductive output (Lien *et al.* 2015, Rosenfield *et al.* 2015a). Such a strategy would presumably be enhanced in a high nesting density area such as Milwaukee, where the greater potential for frequent courtship feeding by (neighboring territorial males) might prompt a higher frequency of extra-pair copulations in a prey-rich urban setting. (But note that, despite the similar ecological conditions of a city, Caballero *et al.* [2016] recently reported a very low frequency of EPP— about 3% of nests— in urban Peregrine Falcons). We would thus expect comparatively lower rates of EPP in rural areas, where the nesting density is lower.

And yet more ugly: preliminary analyses of continuing work on EPP may not support our energy maximization hypothesis regarding urban females, as we did detect EPP at somewhat similar rates in Cooper's Hawk nests in rural environments near the city of Stevens Point (S.A. Sonsthagen, R.N. Rosenfield, unpubl. data). The influence of urbanization— and its highly fragmented environments—on avian mating systems is only beginning to be explored (Smith *et al.* 2016). And, although it's not intellectually comforting, we currently are in good company with our peers in our inability to accurately identify biological forces driving the EPP of socially monogamous female birds, including this phenomenon in Cooper's Hawks (Westneat and Stewart 2003, Neudorff 2004, Sardell *et al.* 2012). Any attempt to generalize about what drives EPP in avian mating systems is prohibited by a lack of knowledge about the natural histories of mating in birds. Indeed, the vast majority are poorly documented and/or completely unknown (West and Sheldon 2002, Stutchbury and Morton 2008, Smith *et al.* 2016). Aggravating these limitations a bit, at least in raptor biology, is that one recent review paper by Mougeot (2004) misrepresented several of the breeding and courtship natural histories of the world's raptors, including our own findings on Cooper's Hawks (see Table S1 in Rosenfield *et al.* 2015a). We thus hope that our colleagues use some parts of this important review with caution.

courtship & nesting biology

The number of young within a brood of extra-pair origin is inherently difficult to explain because it involves so many unknown factors. For example, molecular analysis of blood used in paternity analyses do not allow us to identify where or when extra-pair copulations of Cooper's Hawks took place. For want of observational data, we do not know the behaviors associated with these trysts. We also do not know what role potential sperm storage plays (female birds can store sperm in sperm storage tubules that occur at the junction of the uterus and the vagina in the hen's reproductive tract [Birkhead and Møller 1992]). In addition, it's likely that some extra-pair copulations do not result in fertilization, and we do not have locational or behavioral data on such encounters. Given the high proportion of nests (89%) at which we trapped and obtained tissue samples from male Cooper's Hawks in Milwaukee, we hoped we would have identified a higher number of the extra-pair sires. Perhaps some sires of extra-pair young were floaters, sexually mature males who did not have breeding territories and were therefore difficult to detect and thus sample. These floater males, free from territorial tasks such as its defense, seemingly 'want their money for nothing and their chicks for free!'

Healthy and high-density populations of birds, such as the Milwaukee population of Cooper's Hawks, probably have a substantial number of floaters (Rosenfield *et al.* 2015a, Hunt 1998, Moreno 2016). Some evidence suggests that the number of territorial breeders may comprise less than half of all adults in healthy raptor populations (Hunt 1998, Kenward *et al.* 2000). Indeed, for each paired bird with eggs there were three floaters in a European population of Common Buzzards (*Buteo buteo*; Kenward *et al.* [2000]), a raptor similar in size and ecology to North America's Red-tailed Hawk). Unfortunately, we know virtually nothing about the abundance levels or behaviors of floaters in our Wisconsin populations of Cooper's Hawks. That said, most extra-pair males observed near urban and rural nests in our study population have been SY males who likely were floaters (Rosenfield *et al.* 2015a, R.N. Rosenfield, unpubl. data). Interestingly, in a recent review paper it was reported that female floaters are less abundant in avian populations than male floaters (Moreno 2016). Similarly, Millsap (2018) reported that essentially all urban, yearling female Cooper's Hawks he tracked in Albuquerque, NM, settled on nesting territories rather than spending the first year as nonbreeding floaters. Thus, he suggested that there were few if any floater females originating from nests in his city population, whereas males, who typically did not breed as yearlings (as is true of most Cooper's Hawk populations; see Chapter 4), were present at unreported levels as floaters in his urban study area.

Notably, there are accounts of three adult Cooper's Hawks tending each of two nests, one in Milwaukee (Stout *et al.* 2007) and the other in Tucson (Boal and Spaulding 2000). In both circumstances, the additional bird was a yearling or SY male, also known as a 'helper'. The other males and both females were more than 2 years old, or ASY birds.

Both helpers aggressively defended the nests, and one helper delivered food to the female. Theoretically, by helping, a bird may acquire copulations with the tending female, and/or enhance its genetic fitness if the helper is related to either of the other adults. Unfortunately, no copulations involving any of the males were observed at either nest. And no tissue samples were taken from birds at the Arizona nest, so the possible genetic relationships among the three adults and the young were unknown. (The authors suggested that the helper was unrelated to the adult female, as she failed in her nesting attempt the previous year.) However, blood samples at the Wisconsin nest indicated a second-order genetic relationship (e.g., half-siblings or grandparent/grandchild) between the female and the ASY offspring sire, whereas the yearling male, who did not sire any of the offspring, was unrelated to the female. Helpers do occur in several other raptor species, but this phenomenon is uncommon and poorly understood in birds of prey.

We suggest that EPP and other mating dynamics in Cooper's Hawks are the outcome of a mostly undocumented complex social system (Rosenfield *et al.* 2016c). Unfortunately, most research on mating in birds is skewed toward data from breeders. The role of (potentially more numerous) non-breeders in mating dynamics is virtually unknown (Rosenfield 2017). Accordingly, we will gain much additional insight into the natural history and understanding of mating in Cooper's Hawks by documenting the pre-incubation behaviors of all sexual partners—socially bonded or not—including their individual characteristics such as body size, age, health, fighting abilities, along with what factors influence the birds' movements and their timing. These facets must be investigated to discover which, if any, are related to reproductive output, because adaptive behaviors and other individual characteristics that are favored should be correlated with reproductive output (see Chapter 5). These are daunting but necessary tasks to enhance our understanding of the behavioral strategies, within and between the sexes, that promote successful reproduction. Filling these gaps in our knowledge may also shed light on why the Cooper's Hawk deviates so markedly from other raptors in the natural history of its copulatory and other mating behaviors. Incidentally, I am glad that I did not assume that Cooper's Hawks were like other raptors, that is, they were mostly faithful to each other as mates. Think how wrong I would have been about their natural history of mating if we had not studied their paternity!

Chapter Four

The Breeding Population and Habitat Suitability

❝ *Finding my first Cooper's Hawk nests was incredibly exhilarating, but it was strikingly clear that many birds were very secretive, as many did not stay or even call near their nests. In fact, I banded young at a couple of nests where, rather eerily, I never saw or heard an adult while I was present. I thus wondered if, when nest searching, I could manipulate the behavior of nesting birds by perhaps luring them toward me and/or eliciting their vocalizations via broadcasts of recorded calls of Cooper's Hawks. If I could make breeding birds more detectable, I could possibly enhance my chances of finding their nests to help attain an accurate estimate of the size of the Wisconsin breeding population. I knew that broadcasts of owl calls worked with finding their nests but use of such a technique for finding hawk nests at the time was essentially unknown. In my first year of field work, renowned raptor researcher Fran Hamerstrom told me that she had been seeing 'Coops' near her rural home and that perhaps a nest was nearby. So, equipped with a small, hand-held tape cassette recorder, I showed up at her property to search a large stand of thick white pines for a possible nest. At one point I stood in place and played the taped 'cak-cak-cak' calls, and within seconds of the first broadcasts an adult female Cooper's Hawk flew silently right at me— veering off within a foot or two of my head (!) before flying from view. I was elated and quickly moved several meters, rebroadcast the calls, and got the same response, presumably by the same female. I then walked in the direction she had flown away from me, which was the same in both interactions, and walked directly to a Cooper's Hawk nest about 40 meters (132 feet) from the first spot I had lured the hawk. Awesome! That first manipulation of a breeding bird with call broadcasts led to us experimentally demonstrating the strong value of this technique for finding Cooper's Hawk nests (Rosenfield et al. 1988). I am now NEVER without my recorder when nest searching and I often elicit responses from breeding birds by playing my recorder from my open car window while parked in suburban streets. And man, the odd looks I get from some folks...."*

Overview

Populations exhibit several attributes, or demographics, that interest the public, natural historians, and ecologists alike. These demographics include the size of the population in an area like a city or a state, the sex ratios of offspring and adults, and the ages of breeding individuals. Population biologists quantify overviews of these attributes as well as their changing structure, or dynamics, across time to understand the viability or health of a population. For a population of nesting birds the dynamics of the following four demographic attributes conventionally are measured, especially for raptors:

1) numbers of breeding pairs per unit area, or density (which is often reported as one nest per number of hectares [one hectare is about 2.5 acres]),
2) reproductive output, or productivity (often reported as the number of advanced-aged young per nest with young [i.e., a successful nest]),
3) nest success (or the proportion of nests with incubating females that produced at least one older nestling), and,
4) annual survival rates of breeding adults (proportion of marked birds alive per year; the converse, or annual mortality rates, is often commonly invoked in survival rate discussions).

These population attributes are minimally essential for accurate assessment of the viability or sustainability of a population through time by comparing, for example, demographic outputs of one population of the species to the same outputs for another population of that species. In fact, comparing the recent productivity of a species' population to an older baseline known (or assumed) to represent a healthy or viable population has helped raptor researchers determine whether current productivity is sufficient enough for a population to sustain itself (Grier 1982, Cade *et al.* 1988, Rosenfield *et al.* 2007c). Further, evaluation of a population's health rests with an accounting of the suitability of habitat, as many studies show that this may be a key factor influencing the long-term viability of breeding populations.

Linking demographic data such as breeding density, productivity, and annual rates of survival of breeding adults to types of habitat—urban versus rural for example—can potentially index the quality of habitat. We will explore such links throughout this chapter. But we also will explicitly and separately discuss habitat suitability in this chapter's last section by addressing some findings from the midwestern U.S. that suggest a preference for pine plantations by nesting birds. We will close with a discussion of dispersal behavior by experienced adults and matured young, as such behavior may provide insights into the suitability of habitat, given the increasing fragmentation of habitat and its possible influence on habitat suitability and the viability of Cooper's Hawk populations.

Population abundance and finding nests

Total population size, particularly of breeding birds, would seem to be a valuable and possibly preferred demographic on which to base any assessment of the health of a population and its habitat. However, population size is hard to obtain logistically for most species with large populations over large areas, because one simply cannot find all breeding pairs in big landscapes. It's also unnecessary to conduct a complete census throughout a large area of known size, such as a national forest or a state, if one has enough random samples of densities of breeding pairs in smaller parts (or, to use technical speak, strata) of the representative habitats of the larger area. Such samples, if taken randomly, are unbiased and will be indicative of (i.e., index) the density of the whole population in a circumscribed area (Krebs 1994). Highlighting the significance of having density estimates, it is worth emphasizing here the words of the late, world-renowned population ecologist Graeme Caughley, who said that density provides "the biologically real measure of abundance" (Caughley 1977). This implies that density is the biologically meaningful measure of population abundance, meaningful I suggest, to a large degree because the density of a breeding, territorial species reveals, at a minimum, the outcome of social dynamics that dictated the dispersion of nests or breeding pairs in a particular area. Conversely, a simple number such as the total population size of Cooper's Hawks in Wisconsin, reveals nothing about where the birds may be, nor the spacing that this population exhibits in probable relation to resources necessary for a breeding pair to be successful. Accordingly, accurate and biologically meaningful abundance estimates of the total number of nesting pairs of Cooper's Hawks in an administrative unit such as the state of Wisconsin must include densities from the (wide) array of known nesting habitats within the unit for example, both pine plantations and cities (e.g., Rosenfield et al. 1995a, 2016a).

I must again stress the difficulty (and high expense and effort) of locating raptor nests, because breeding pairs occur at low densities and raptors tend to be more secretive than other territorial bird species. That said, raptor researchers often index abundance levels (and changes in such) across large areas through counts of breeding pairs on randomly located, smaller areas (Andersen et al. 2004, Rosenfield et al. 1995a, 2016a). Earlier we reported a conservative estimate of 7,500 breeding pairs (or 15,000 individual) Cooper's Hawks throughout Wisconsin based on extrapolations of nest densities from several smaller plots throughout Wisconsin (Bielefeldt et al. 1998). I note that these estimates of nesting population size in a single average-size state are about the same as the continental estimate of 20,000 adults (apparently breeding or otherwise) proposed in the late 20th century by Johnsgard (1990). This disparity in estimates leads us to suggest that population sizes of Cooper's Hawks in North America may once have been misperceived and possibly underestimated in other states as well as Wisconsin, at least in the late 1990s (Bielefeldt et al. 1998). That said, Partners in Flight recently estimated there was a breeding population in the United States and Canada of 700,000 adults and a United States population of 600,000. Interestingly, our previous estimate of 15,000 birds in the average-sized U.S. state of Wisconsin, times 48 states, equals 720,000 individuals, a number close to the nation-wide estimate (Partners in Flight 2017).

The formal technique used to determine nesting density is quadrat sampling. This method involves a biologist walking (or driving a car if in an urban area, or flying in a small, fixed-wing plane over inaccessible, remote wilderness environments) throughout a pre-determined plot, or quadrat, of some size. For objectivity, the boundaries of this plot should be set before searching begins. The shape of the plot is mostly irrelevant, but searching should reveal a nearest neighboring pair in any direction from a previously found nest. The biologist tallies within the study plot all occupied and active nests. Occupied sites are those where a pair is associated with a nest (that may or may not end up with eggs/young), and active nests are those attended by a pair of adults that have eggs (preferably) or young. Quadrat sampling in exurban areas for nesting forest raptors is particularly difficult, because a researcher is typically on foot and must see/search all trees, because any one tree could serve as a nest-site. Conifer or evergreen trees are particularly time-consuming to survey, because you have to approach the tree more closely (ergo more walking) than you do a deciduous tree, as a nest is harder to see within the ever-present, thick needle-like conifer leaves. In contrast, a researcher has a distinct advantage in detecting nests early in the spring on a plot dominated by deciduous trees, because there are few

breeding population & habitat suitability

Backyard Cooper's Hawk nests like this one in a deciduous tree in the city of Oshkosh, Wisconsin (human population of about 60,000) are relatively easy to see before leaf-out and make for efficient nest-spotting even by car when, of course, driving below the speed limit.
Photo by Madeline Hardin.

leaves to obstruct one's view at that time. For that reason, most searching should be completed in spring (see below).

I have spent thousands of hours conducting quadrat sampling for forest-nesting raptors in Wisconsin, including Broad-winged Hawks (Rosenfield *et al.* 1984), Northern Goshawks (Rosenfield *et al.* 1998), and of course the Cooper's Hawk (Rosenfield *et al.* 1995a, 2016a). For all species, I selected plots for which I had no advance knowledge of the presence or absence of nesting hawks, nor any advance information on the suitability of the habitat for breeding hawks via the technical literature or professional opinion. In this way, my work was free from biased estimates of density that would accrue by simply searching habitat where I pre-supposed that I was more likely to find nesting birds. All plots for all species were about 3,116 hectares (12 square miles) in size, and it took roughly 3-4 weeks of daily searches for, 8-10 hours a day to search an entire quadrat. Search duration was heavily influenced by type and amount of tree cover, elevation, and of course the weather (searching occurred on rainless days, as I did not want to frighten a bird during egg-laying in adverse weather). One of my biggest concerns, besides searching carefully for breeding birds, nests, or signs of bird presence, was completing my search of a quadrat before incubation began or, at the latest, in the first week of the 4-week incubation period. In this way, I would probably not underestimate breeding density by missing nests that failed prior to discovery. Indeed, if one searched mostly during the nestling stage in June, for example, it would be easier to find Cooper's Hawk nests because of the presence of whitewash under a nest tree; young squirt their white feces over the nest rim and it can be readily seen on the ground around the base of the tree. Also, it is more likely that you'll detect nests with young versus nests with incubating females, because adults tend to be quiet and often crouch low over their eggs unless you tap on or linger near the nesting tree, which can cause a bird to flush. I note that female Cooper's Hawks flushed off eggs in Wisconsin typically fly silently from view and return to incubate in about 10 minutes, as long as the researcher has left the immediate area of the nest tree. Conversely, adult females that are brooding young are more mobile and more likely to fly near their nests while scolding '*cak-cak-cak*' at an intruder even when the researcher is beyond 50 meters (164 feet) from the nest tree. Most importantly, quadrat sampling conducted exclusively at or mostly during the nestling stage skews the count of nesting pairs toward successful nests, which will probably make estimates of nesting density inaccurate. When attempting to get reliable abundance estimates of breeding birds, it clearly is important to have a firm grasp of the natural history of the species, especially the breeding phenology, that is, the calendar timing of nesting events, and the type of behavior including vocalizations (see Chapter 3) exhibited by breeding birds.

Detecting and correctly interpreting Cooper's Hawk sign is also an exceedingly important aid to finding nests. I generally find most nests each year during the pre-incubation period by detecting prey remains and hawk whitewash (feces), both of which–if on the ground–are typically obvious within about 70 meters (230 feet) of a nest. A very important natural history fact that enhances the ability to locate breeding pairs, and hence a nest, is that Cooper's Hawks routinely use plucking posts (or 'butcher blocks'), which typically are fallen trees on the ground or horizontal tree limbs, usually a minimum of 10 centimeters (4 inches) thick, typically about 5-7 meters (about 20 feet) above ground. These sites serve as spots where prey are transferred to females, and where prey are 'processed'—feathers or fur removed, for example. The repeated use of these sites, even across years by the same or different hawks, results in the presence of 'slices' or streaks of whitewash; prey remains, including entrails; and, starting in mid-incubation (early-to-mid-May in Wisconsin), molted flight feathers from adults. Sometimes we encounter whole bodies of prey that may represent surplus food or an item that a frightened hawk left upon our arrival. There tends to be at least two plucking posts per nest, which enhances the chance of finding signs of their presence and hence nests. In urban areas, I also look under tree limbs for whitewash on sidewalks and streets; such feces can be readily seen on concrete, from a slow-moving car or on foot.

We also encourage the use of broadcasts of recorded alarm calls (*cak-cak-cak*) of breeding Cooper's Hawks to complement surveys for breeding pairs, having been the first to demonstrate that this increases the chance of detecting breeding Cooper's Hawks. We have lured birds (calling in flight and also approaching silently) to our broadcast position from as far as 200 meters (660 feet) using only a small hand-held tape-recorder. Broadcasts of calls appear to work best during the several weeks before eggs are laid, and again when there are nestlings or fledglings (incubating females are generally reluctant to leave their eggs). However, we stress that broadcasts

Locating active breeding territories is greatly enhanced by finding and 'reading' sign, such as this fresh bird carcass (Mourning Dove) (right), these feather pluckings (American Robin) (bottom right), and molted feather and whitewash of a Cooper's Hawk (bottom left), all of which typically occur within about 70 meters (230 feet) of nests. Photos by Robert Rosenfield.

of calls are not a substitute for thorough ground searches for nests, because not all breeding birds respond to call broadcasts (Rosenfield *et al.* 1988).

Finding breeding pairs and their nests can also be done via early morning visits in the pre-incubation period to find potential breeding sites, because Cooper's Hawks predictably arrive near their partially constructed nests virtually every morning about 30 minutes before sunrise, and their vocalizations and frequent nest-building flights during this time make birds more easily detectable. My colleagues and friends Andy and Irene Stewart routinely conducted early morning, pre-incubation visits (most days, several months per year, across 17 years!) throughout the city of Victoria, BC, to detect behaviors (especially vocalizations) of breeding pairs, because of the difficulty of locating nests built in the upper reaches of tall conifers (Stewart *et al.* 1996). Also, and as previously mentioned, plucking posts in Victoria are typically well above ground, in fact, near or at the height of nests. In addition, whitewash and prey remains are often more dispersed or intercepted by

Chapter 4

Active Cooper's Hawk nests, that is those with eggs and an incubating bird, can often be confirmed from the ground early in spring by noting the obvious (long) tail feathers of an incubating adult sticking out from the nest's edge. Longer tails of accipiter hawks function as rudders that facilitate maneuvering through thick wooded vegetation in which the bird likely first evolved.
Photo by Madeline Hardin.

vegetation, thereby underscoring the importance of early morning observations to detect breeding birds in that city.

Knowledge of other natural histories of the Cooper's Hawk can enhance one's ability to find their nests. At least in Wisconsin, Cooper's Hawks regularly build their own nests on top of squirrel nests, which appear as ball-like aggregates of dried brown or (if freshly built) green leaves. From the ground, it can be difficult to see the hawks' stick nest atop that of the squirrel's, and sometimes even more difficult when there is only a small layer of sticks laid atop a nest. I often back far enough away from a tree with a squirrel nest to get a better angle of sight so as to see the top of the nest. Sticks collected by Cooper's Hawks for nests typically are dead branches that are broken by the beak; such 'fresh' twigs typically have a noticeable color difference—a very light brown—at their ends, compared with the dark brown tips of older sticks, a difference that can be readily seen through binoculars. Lighter-colored tips indicate 'freshly' broken sticks likely gathered by a hawk. A particularly frustrating aspect of their nesting behavior is that it is common for Cooper's Hawks to build more than one alternative nest (sometimes four!) before eggs are laid in one nest. (Incidentally, I have speculated that nest building in spring, which is mostly done by males, might serve as a pre-copulatory display, because copulations are commonly preceded by stick deliveries to a nest by a male.) Alternative nests may serve as other display sites at which nest-building induces females to copulate (Rosenfield *et al.* 1991a). Thus, when I return to a nest to confirm incubation I sometimes cannot find fresh sign and instead find an empty nest with no adults nearby. The search then resumes for the active nest, which I typically can find if it exists within 200 meters (660 feet) of the initial nest. The greatest distance between an initial nest and the eventual active nest on one nesting site in Wisconsin was 335 meters (1,100 feet), while the average distance was about 170 meters (560 feet; Rosenfield and Bielefeldt 1993a).

Nesting Densities

Cooper's Hawk nesting densities vary markedly across North America: ranges of densities of 1 nest/671-2,321 hectares (2.6-9.0 square miles) were reported in the western states and 1 nest/272-5,000 hectares (1-19 square miles) in midwestern and eastern states (Stout and Rosenfield 2010, Rosenfield *et al.* 1995a, 2018). These nest densities vary 18-fold between the highest and lowest measures. The lowest density metrics, with fewer breeding pairs per unit area, all stem from rural settings (for example, 1 nest/1,494 hectares in Florida, 1 nest/1,554 hectares in Michigan, 1 nest/2,321 hectares in Oregon, 1 nest/5,000 hectares in North Dakota; Reynolds and Wight 1978, Rosenfield *et al.* 1991b, Millsap *et al.* 2013). Such large variation perhaps is unsurprising, given the markedly different types of possible habitats in which this species can nest, concomitant with the premise that habitats probably vary in quality for breeding. The highest nesting densities have been found in cities (e.g., 1 nest/272 hectares and 1 nest/295 hectares in 1993 and 2017, respectively, in Stevens Point, WI, with a human population of about 38,000 [Fig. 4.1]; 1 nest/330 hectares in Milwaukee, WI, with about 1,000,000 people; and 1 nest/437 hectares in Tucson, AZ, with about 900,000 people). However, some rural density metrics were comparable to these urban measures (e.g., 1/nest 294 hectares in rural Florida and 1 nest/331 hectares in rural Wisconsin; Millsap et al. 2013; Rosenfield *et al.* 1995a). Of particular note are the high nesting densities of 1 nest/292 hectares and 1 nest/395 hectares in the isolated woodlands of the Northern Great Plains of north-central North Dakota (Nenneman *et al.* 2002).

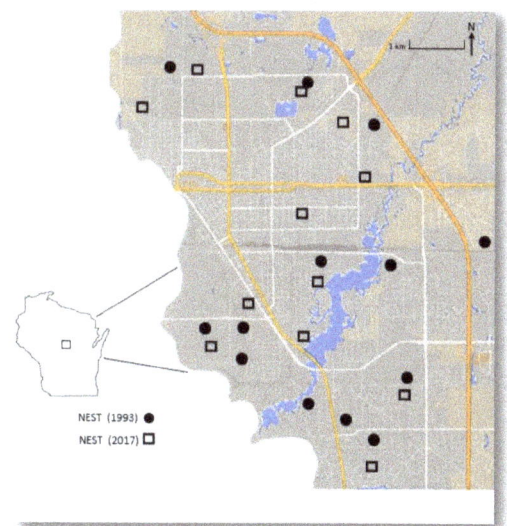

Figure 4.1. Distribution of Cooper's Hawk nests on the urban 3540-hectare (~12 square-mile) study plot in Stevens Point, WI, in 1993, and 24 years, or four breeding generations, later in 2017. Indicative of a territorial species, note the regular nest spacing, suggesting habitat saturation in both years, and especially the close spacing of about 0.8 kilometer (about a half-mile) between nests in the southernmost part of the study site in 1993. Comparable high nesting densities were found in Tucson, AZ., Milwaukee, WI., Victoria, BC, and in the grasslands of the Northern Great Plains of North Dakota during the 1990s and the early 2000s (see text). Modified from Rosenfield et al. (2018).

Dr. Robert Murphy (left) and author with mated pair of Cooper's Hawks at nest woods in north-central North Dakota. Surprising to many birders and biologists, Cooper's Hawks exhibit high nesting densities in the sparsely scattered, deciduous woodlands of coulees (ravines) in prairie and grassland landscapes of North America. In fact, the Cooper's Hawk may be the most abundant breeding raptor in the woodlands of the northern Great Plains (Nenneman et al. 2003). Photo by Robert Rosenfield.

It may be easier to visualize density in terms of distance between active nests. Closest nesting pairs may be on average only about 800 meters (a half-mile) apart at the highest densities for this territorial species. Such distances suggest about one nesting pair in every square mile. In Albuquerque and in Victoria, some pairs nest successfully within 160 meters (524 feet) and 270 meters (885 feet) of each other, respectively (B.A. Millsap and A.C. Stewart, unpubl. data). In contrast, nearest nesting pairs in exurban areas are generally an average of about 2.6 kilometers (about 1.6 mile) apart, which suggests a density of one nesting pair in about 5.2 square kilometers, or every 2 square miles (Rosenfield *et al.* 2018). Thus, Cooper's Hawks may attain higher densities in urban areas than exurban ones. Although several hypotheses have been offered to explain this disparity, including reduced predation and availability of water in cities (especially in the dry landscapes of Arizona and New Mexico), it may be that greater food availability in urban environments is the cause (Rosenfield *et al.* 2018, Millsap 2018). That said, we note that Cooper's Hawks can attain high nesting densities in some local areas that lack permanent sources of water, such as in Wisconsin (Rosenfield and Anderson 2016, Trexel *et al.* 1999) and North Dakota (Nenneman *et al.* 2003).

The number of individuals and overall biomass of avian prey for this bird-eating hawk are typically much higher in urban environments than exurban environments.

Indeed, telemetry studies generally reveal that urban breeding and wintering Cooper's Hawks do not have to range as far as their rural counterparts to obtain food. Curiously, introduced species in cities, such as prevalent large populations of House Sparrows and European Starlings (both of which can cause damage to native ecosystems by out-competing native birds for food and/or nest-sites) provide a dominant food source for native breeding Cooper's Hawks in Victoria (Cava *et al.* 2012). In fact, House Sparrows appear to be common prey of Cooper's Hawks in numerous other cities throughout North America (Cava *et al.* 2012). Regardless of the specific reasons for the seemingly higher suitability of urban habitat, cities represent relatively new habitats for Cooper's Hawks, so future research should focus on identifying what specific factors support such high urban densities. I suggest that these factors will vary among cities because of the marked variation in size among them, and the different habitats within and surrounding cities. That said, it appears there is less variation in nesting densities among cities compared with the variation of nest densities in exurban environments.

I emphasize that comparing densities of different populations of nesting birds with the goal of using these measures to indicate habitat quality might be perilous if the researcher does not take into account that breeding density may, as with some density data presented herein for Cooper's Hawks, differ by time periods (e.g., Stout and Rosenfield 2010, and see Reynolds *et al.* 2017 for similar caveats regarding breeding densities for Northern Goshawks). Indeed, nesting densities may in fact reflect a time-specific environmental circumstance (e.g., a poor food year due to drought, cold, and wet spring) and/or reflect a stage of population trajectory at the time of sampling (Murphy 1993). These time-specific circumstances would especially be aggravating in studies of short duration, which could compromise accurate interpretation (sensu Rosenfield 2016a). Researchers should qualify their estimates of abundance levels according to environmental or research design circumstances. For example, it is likely that Cooper's Hawk nesting densities during the DDT era (from about the mid-1940s to the early 1970s) were lower than in ensuing years, after this chemical had been banned and there was a period of population recovery. Similarly, in response to increasing woodland habitat across 50 years (1938-1991), breeding densities of Cooper's Hawk (including pioneering grassland) populations were increasing in north-central North Dakota during the 1980s (Murphy 1993). I speculate, with some supporting evidence (e.g., Rosenfield *et al.* 2002a), that the low density of 1 nest/5,000 hectares noted above for North Dakota (reported for a 2-year period in western North Dakota in the late 1970s) reflected a time-specific measure for a recovering and/or pioneering population. Relatively lower density estimates during a recovery or a pioneering population dynamic do not necessarily represent poor habitat quality, as we could reasonably assume that density would increase in suitable or good habitat until almost all potential breeding territories become occupied, and remain relatively so, in a stable and healthy population (see Rosenfield *et al.* 1995a). We note that nesting populations of Cooper's Hawks can grow relatively quickly; the urban pioneering populations of Cooper's Hawks doubled in 9 years and tripled in just 12 years in Albuquerque, NM, and Milwaukee, WI, respectively (Millsap 2018, Stout and Rosenfield 2010). For context, 9 years is just a bit longer than one breeding generation, which is about 6 years for females in urban New Mexico, and the same time as one generation of breeders of both sexes in Wisconsin.

Similarly, we note that the demographic properties of growing breeding populations of Cooper's Hawks may differ from those of stable populations (Rosenfield *et al.* 2015b, Smith *et al.* 2015). For example, although productivity did not differ significantly across a 12-year period, the proportion of 1-year-old female breeders declined significantly during this time, as this pioneer, colonizing population of Cooper's Hawks in Milwaukee grew at a fast rate (Stout and Rosenfield 2010, Stout *et al.* 2007). As with the age structure of breeding adults in other raptor species, younger individuals generally tend to be more common in small and growing populations until numbers of competitively superior adults build up and replace the younger birds in the decreasing number of territories that remain available (Stout *et al.* 2007, Stout and Rosenfield 2010). Interestingly, although reproductive output can decrease as population density increases for some bird species, including raptors (perhaps because of the poorer physiological condition of individuals resulting from heightened competition among counterparts for resources), average productivity for Cooper's Hawks in Milwaukee *increased* with increasing breeding density. This dynamic may be a characteristic of a population in a relatively rapid growth phase (Stout and Rosenfield 2010).

The sex ratio of offspring is another demographic attribute that may be affected by population trajectory. But, before continuing, I need to indicate that in birds, unlike mammals, females determine the sex of the young and do so at the time of conception and/or egg-laying. Although hormones appear to play a role, the specific physiological process by which sex is determined is unknown in female birds (Pike and Petrie 2003, Alonso-Alvarez 2006). I also note that population-level estimates of offspring sex ratios in birds are generally 1:1, one male to one female (Donald 2007). However, raptor offspring sex ratios are often skewed toward males (Rosenfield *et al.* 2015b, Reynolds *et al.* 2017; but see Millsap 2018, who reported an approximately 1:1 offspring sex ratio across 3-years, but 58% female young in another year in his Albuquerque population of Cooper's Hawks). Such skewing toward males may occur for various reasons, but most likely because males are smaller than females

breeding population & habitat suitability

Marked difference in overall foot size, toe-length, and leg-width between 16-day-old male (right) and female nestling (left) Cooper's Hawks. These disparities between the sexes can usually be discerned when young have reached 12 days of age. Photo by Robert Rosenfield.

(especially in Cooper's Hawks, where extreme reversed size dimorphism occurs) and males are therefore cheaper to produce, assuming equal parental investment in providing food and care to offspring (Howe 1977).

We predicted, and demonstrated across 11 years (2001-2011), almost two breeding generations, that a stable and saturated population (i.e., few if any new breeding sites available) produced a consistent preponderance of male offspring at the time of egg-laying in Wisconsin, excluding Milwaukee. The breakdown was about 60% males, 40% females. We expected more males based on our earlier, 21-year efforts in the state, where offspring sex ratios were generally skewed toward males, but we did not precisely predict the 60:40 ratio for this saturated population (Rosenfield *et al.* 1996a, 2015b). We note that hatching sex ratios in Cooper's Hawks accurately represent their fledgling sex ratios, as we have no evidence across 38 years of research in Wisconsin of differences in mortality of nestlings by sex. Nor are we aware of such differences in any other Cooper's Hawk population (Rosenfield *et al.* 2015b, Millsap 2018, R.N. Rosenfield, unpubl. data).

Now, if a growing population of breeding Cooper's Hawks also produced a preponderance of male offspring (60%), and that preponderance is expressed in the number of breeders, there might be a shortage of females for males to breed with at the yet available nest-sites. We therefore predicted, and were able to confirm, in the fast-growing, colonizing Milwaukee population, that breeding females consistently adjusted the sex ratio at conception to produce comparatively more female offspring (overall about 51% males, 49% females) than the stable outside-Milwaukee breeding population during the same study years. Note that outside Milwaukee, 40% were female, versus 49% in the growing Milwaukee population. We had not precisely predicted the Milwaukee offspring sex ratio, either. Thus a Milwaukee breeding female was, we hypothesized, likely to get more of her young (especially females) into the breeding population where there were more available nest-sites than one who was part of the saturated population outside Milwaukee (Rosenfield *et al.* 2015b). These findings suggest that Cooper's Hawks can adjust their offspring sex ratios to adapt to changing population levels. This adjustment in sex ratios is poorly documented and controversial in birds, in part because studies are too short (one to five years) in duration to investigate the potential role of population flux on nestling sex ratios. Notably, Reynolds *et al.* (2017) suggested that Northern Goshawks, an accipiter closely related to Cooper's Hawks, adaptively adjusted their brood sex ratios to produce more of the rarer (male) sex in response to lower survivorship of adult males. This was found as part of 20-year, cross-generation studies in Arizona, where the number of breeders changed markedly due to variations in precipitation. In Milwaukee, we predict there will be a different offspring sex ratio, with fewer female Cooper's Hawks, once the population becomes saturated and stable over time. We eagerly await what our continuing work in Milwaukee will show in this regard.

Another demographic that may vary with changing population trajectory is the age-structure of breeding adults. Our long-term mark-recapture data on nesting adults revealed long-term age-structure changes in breeding males that no other Cooper's Hawk study has demonstrated, specifically the changing proportion of brown birds in their second year of life (SY birds, or yearlings) versus males at least 2-years old in gray plumage (ASY males). This shifting age-structure allowed us to say with some confidence that we had tracked a recovering population growing into a stable one in Wisconsin.

Male raptors, unlike females, generally do not begin breeding at the age of 1 year, probably because it takes a young male more time to acquire the skills needed to obtain a territory and become the principal provider of food for himself, his mate, and his young. Hence males should exhibit, to use the speak, delayed reproduction, or else pay some deleterious 'price' for breeding early. Most studies of Cooper's Hawks across North America have never or rarely detected SY breeding males. In a 32-year (1980-2011) analysis, we found a very low frequency of breeding SY males: among 732 captures in Wisconsin, only 13 (2%) were SY, versus 719 (98%) ASY males. SY males made up almost 13% of all breeding birds in any year when at least one SY male was detected (mean = 6%). The frequency of occurrence of SY birds differed markedly and statistically during the study, as 12 (92%) and one (8%) of the total 13 SY males were detected in the first and second 16 years of our study, respectively. Further, breeding by SY males was relatively consistent annually early in the study, as we did not detect it in only 3 of the first 12 years of the study (Fig. 4.2).

Generally, investigators have reported a disproportionately greater number of yearling individuals breeding for the first time in colonizing and/or recolonizing (and growing) populations. When populations increased, the proportion of inexperienced breeders declined as more experienced birds became more prevalent. It is believed that inexperienced birds cannot successfully compete for territories with

Rare occurrence of brown-feathered, yearling breeding male (right front) with starling prey at his Wisconsin nest. Some new, dark blue feathers are visible on his left folded wing and in his tail. The 24-day-old female nestling in left front is noticeably larger than her dad. These young are at the branching stage and soon to fledge. They can readily climb onto nearby tree branches to perch. Photo by Robert Rosenfield.

older, more experienced birds when they become more prevalent. SY males may, however, become relaxed from this constraint when they're in an area that lacks breeders– as in a growing population– because they face fewer territorial contests with older and competitively experienced breeders (Rosenfield *et al.* 2013). The higher prevalence of SY males in the earlier years of the study than in later years may reflect temporarily reduced costs for breeding by 1-year-old males, which could more likely find unoccupied nesting places in what was then a smaller breeding population with lower density (Fig. 4.2). In fact, increasing migration counts of Cooper's Hawks in Wisconsin and our own nesting density data support the premise that greater numbers of SY males were nesting while the breeding population was growing. And what was the ill price SY males paid for breeding so early in life? Maximum longevity. The oldest age attained by an SY breeding male was six years, whereas males that exercised restraint and waited until two years old to breed attained ages up to 11. Consequently, SY males who started breeding young compromised fitness because lifetime reproductive output strongly correlated with longevity (Rosenfield *et al.* 2009a, 2013).

Interestingly, 92%, or 12 of the 13 SY breeding males in our Wisconsin study, were paired with ASY females, whereas in Tucson, AZ., Boal (2001) reported that 78%, or seven of nine, SY breeding males were paired with SY females. Boal suggested that experienced females favored more experienced ASY males. We do not know what may explain this marked contrast in proportion of ages of females paired with SY nesting males between these two studies. We note that average brood size in

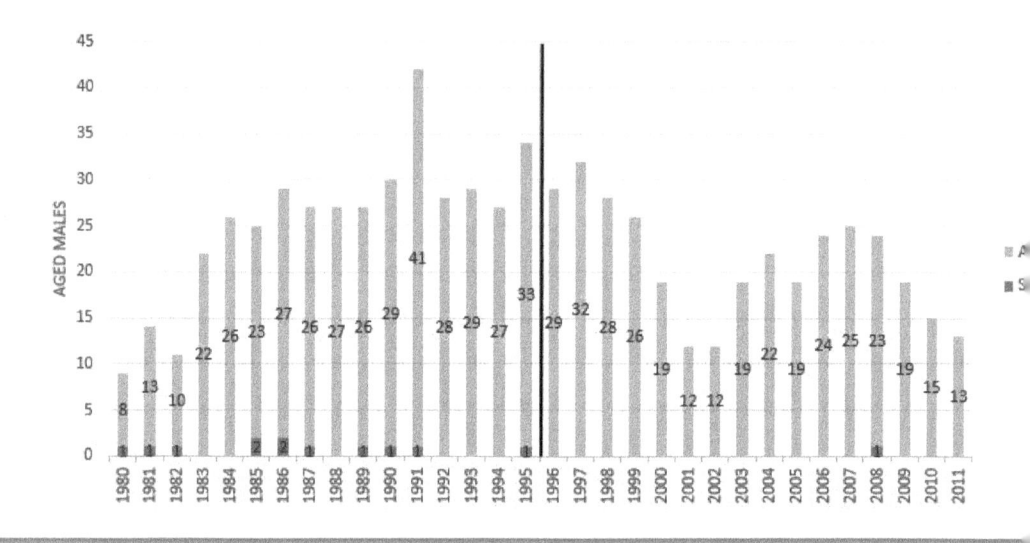

Figure 4.2. Variation over time in age-structure of breeding male Cooper's Hawks in Wisconsin. In this 32-year analysis, note especially the incidence and number of 1-year-old, or SY, males (in their second year of life) within blackened portions of a bar. Thirteen males representing only 2% of a total 732 breeding male captures, were SY birds, or brown, yearlings. ASY birds are gray birds at least 2 years of age. Mid-bar number is the total number of aged males detected each year, and the bold vertical black line separates the first 16 years of the study from the second 16 years. We suggested that SY males could more likely obtain nesting places in the earlier years in a smaller and growing (in fact recovering) breeding population because they didn't have to compete with the older, competitively experienced ASY breeders that became more prevalent later in a larger and more stable population (see text and Rosenfield et al. 2013). Despite the rarity of documenting breeding SY male Cooper's Hawks in North America, timing of detections of only 13 such birds across several breeding generations demonstrated temporal variation in the age-structure of nesting males. These data strongly underscore the value of long-term data sets to reveal ecological patterns in population biology. Modified from Rosenfield et al. (2013).

Wisconsin SY males was greater than that of SY male pairings reported in Arizona (Rosenfield *et al.* 2013).

Reproductive output

Figures on reproduction, or productivity, of nesting Cooper's Hawks are typically obtained via brood counts. These tallies conventionally are obtained by climbing to nests to count young when they are at least two weeks old, but more typically about three weeks, or about 70% of fledging age. Fledging occurs when young are about 25 to 30 days old. Males, who develop faster perhaps due to their smaller size, generally leave the nest two or three days before their female siblings. Researchers routinely mark young with U.S. Geological Survey aluminum leg-bands at the time of counting. I note that when Cooper's Hawk young are at least two weeks old, one can, with minimal training, reliably determine their sex by noting the proportionate size of legs and feet of same-age young; again, males are markedly smaller than females of the same age in this raptor. A researcher typically determines when young are old enough for banding through infrequent visits to track the amount of whitewash that offspring routinely squirt from their nests. When possible, researchers can also view the young from the ground, taking note of their stage of feather development to estimate their age.

To ensure a reliable count, it is imperative not to climb to nests too early and disturb adults with 'fragile' young who may not yet be able to thermoregulate (and thus could die from exposure) or that are too small to band. More important, well-timed counts of advanced-aged young do a better job of accurately estimating the number of offspring that will survive and probably fledge. I stress that climbs to nests with young at and especially older than three weeks are more likely to cause them to prematurely fledge (frightened young will jump out of the nest before they can fly), and thus a researcher may compromise the young's ability to survive, not to mention get inaccurate brood counts (Rosenfield *et al.* 2007a). Again, natural history knowledge of nest activities is paramount to obtaining sound data and minimizing disturbance to nesting birds.

I have, in all 38 years of research on Wisconsin Cooper's Hawks, climbed to most nests each year during the mid-incubation period (about mid-May in Wisconsin) to obtain complete clutch counts. These relatively quick climbs occur on rainless and warm days of at least 18°C (65°F). Typically, I can be in and out of a tree in under eight minutes if the nest is less than about 20 meters (66 feet) up a tree. This duration usually minimizes potential adverse chilling of eggs. I tend to avoid climbing nest trees at the incubation stage if I deem a tree 'unsafe,' meaning it has poor structural integrity or the nest is too high to allow for a quick climb. Clutch counts across North America range from one to eight eggs, with most nests containing three to five (Rosenfield and Bielefeldt 1993a, Stout 2009). Eggs are not always counted by other Cooper's Hawk researchers (e.g., Millsap 2018, Stout *et al.* 2007, Chiang *et al.* 2012, Millsap *et al.* 2013). However, clutch counts have allowed me to gain numerous insights into the reproductive biology of Cooper's Hawks that I would not have been able to do otherwise, as discussed below (and see Climate Change in Chapter 3). Similarly, we have 'retroactively' determined offspring sex ratios at hatching (which are presumably the same as at fertilization) in nests where complete clutch sizes were known, all eggs hatched, and all young survived to an age of sex determination (Rosenfield *et al.* 1996a). As I wrote in Chapter 3, species with large clutch sizes, such as the Cooper's Hawk, are more effectively buffered from population

Chapter 4

Here a brown, yearling female Cooper's Hawk is reacting to my climb to count her eggs. Some females are reluctant to leave their clutch and will spread their wing and tail feathers while shuffling back and forth over the nest seemingly to protect the eggs during my ascent. Most birds, however, fly silently from view for the several minutes I am in the tree. Photos by Madeline Hardin.

crashes, as they can reproductively recover more quickly from population declines (Krüger and Radford 2008).

Cooper's Hawk brood counts range from one to six nestlings, and most nests contain two to four young, but more commonly 3 or 4 nestlings per nest, across North America. Estimates of average brood sizes at successful nests (i.e., those with young) among different populations range from 2.7 to 4.0. Some of the highest reproductive rates, with averages ranging from 3.6 to 4.0 young at successful nests, are from cities, while there are lower estimates ranging from 2.8 to 3.0 from some exurban studies (Nenneman *et al.* 2002, Millsap *et al.* 2013, Rosenfield *et al.* 2016a, 2018). We caution, however, that lower reproductive indices do not necessarily indicate lower population viability and/or lower habitat quality. Indeed, lower average brood sizes in a western North Dakota prairie population were apparently not related to increased hatchling mortality rates, or limited food or reduced nest-site availability. In fact, breeding habitat was probably increasing in the North Dakota study site, as woodland cover more than doubled there over the years 1938-1991 (Nenneman *et al.* 2003). We reiterate that it is generally believed that food and nest-site availability are the primary factors limiting breeding populations of raptors (Newton 1979, Stout and Rosenfield 2010). The highly migratory population in North Dakota consistently nested about two to three weeks later across a seven-year study than the breeding populations of Cooper's Hawks that exhibited reduced migratory behavior in concurrent study years, at comparable northerly latitudes in British Columbia and

Wisconsin. My colleagues and I speculated that the energetic demands of migration and the phenological (i.e., seasonal schedule) constraints of a shorter breeding season may have limited the ability of North Dakota hawks to accumulate energy reserves for egg production immediately after a long spring migration. Indeed, this North Dakota population had comparatively smaller average clutch counts (3.5 eggs/clutch versus 4.4 in British Columbia and 4.3 in Wisconsin), and hence smaller average brood counts (3.0) compared to 3.6 in British Columbia and 3.7 in Wisconsin. However, this prairie population was apparently viable, as it was increasing. Resource managers could possibly draw incorrect conclusions about the suitability of breeding habitat in western North Dakota if it was assumed that the comparatively lower brood counts indicated productivity deficiencies (Rosenfield *et al.* 2007c). In fact, lower production of nestlings was likely a consequence of lower clutch counts (rather than, say, reduced brood counts stemming from high hatchling mortality from nests with high clutch counts; Rosenfield *et al.* 2007c). We concluded that clutch size data in that study were crucial for assessing reproduction and relating productivity to habitat suitability. For these reasons, we encouraged raptor researchers to obtain clutch counts in their studies when feasible. We note that clutch size is perhaps the most central index to avian reproduction, as it strongly correlates with age at maturity, and with offspring and adult survival in birds (Jetz *et al.* 2008, Rosenfield *et al.* 2016b). We are fortunate that Cooper's Hawks are tolerant of our climbs to nests to obtain valuable clutch counts during the incubation stage. Indeed, some raptors are intolerant of this type of disturbance (Rosenfield *et al.* 2007a).

The range of productivity estimates among continental populations may suggest that local ecological and natural history factors vary widely among populations of Cooper's Hawks, irrespective of whether breeding populations are stable or growing. Unfortunately, we do not know precisely the mechanisms by which these various factors influence the variations in productivity estimates reported for nesting populations of Cooper's Hawks. This is mostly because few studies were designed *per se* to identify the factors governing reproductive rates among populations. There are, however, a few studies that provide other insights about environmental factors influencing variations in production in Cooper's Hawk populations.

For example, researchers in a rural Florida study speculated that home range and foraging distances of telemetered nesting males were comparatively larger than those measures in other studies due to the limitations of lower food levels (including types of suitable prey, especially chipmunks). Males tended to forage farther to procure prey (Millsap *et al.* 2013). The Florida researchers hypothesized that the lower reproductive rates (averaging about 2.8 young/nest) were due to a paucity of food. Also, high mortality (about 40%) of nestlings due to the respiratory disease trichomoniasis (contracted via an urban diet of doves that differed from the exurban diet) resulted in lower productivity at urban Tucson sites than in nests outside the city (Boal and Mannan 1999). However, those results regarding disease appeared to be restricted to specific years rather than occurring on a long-term basis (Urban and Mannan 2014, Mannan *et al.* 2008; see Chapter 2).

An ecological theme that has received much recent attention is whether productivity at Cooper's Hawk nests in cities may be higher than that at exurban nests (Rosenfield *et al.* 2018). If true, such a disparity may be due to a greater abundance of avian prey available in cities than in exurban habitats (Marzluff *et al.* 1998, Rosenfield *et al.* 2018). However, there have been few comparative paired studies of the reproductive rates of urban versus exurban Cooper's Hawk populations. That said, two studies reported higher average brood sizes in urban than exurban nests: 3.1 versus 2.8 (though these values were not statistically different) in Arizona (Boal and Mannan 1999) and 3.7 versus 1.5 in California (Chiang *et al.* 2012); this latter study was limited by very small sample sizes. In contrast, there were no significant differences in average clutch counts (about 4.3 eggs) and average brood counts (approximately 3.6 young) in relatively large annual samples between Cooper's Hawk nests in urban versus exurban habitats across 36 years in Wisconsin (Rosenfield *et al.* 1995a, 2015b, 2016b). Further, nesting phenology did not differ between urban and exurban nests in Wisconsin (Rosenfield *et al.* 2016b), in contrast to the aforementioned Tucson study, in which urban birds nested 16 days earlier than exurban ones (Boal and Mannan 1999). Apparently, food-rich Tucson birds had enough prey to seasonally nest earlier than their rural Arizona counterparts. I reiterate that urban landscapes vary greatly in size, habitat diversity, habitat gradients, prey populations, and other ecological factors that potentially affect the reproductive success of raptors. Such high variability of urban environs may help explain the variation in some aspects of the reproductive ecology of the Cooper's Hawk across North America. However, more studies are needed to address definitively the underlying causes of the demographic and natural history differences between urban and non-urban nesting populations of Cooper's Hawks. Such studies would be likely to provide greater insights (and perhaps novel discoveries, like the adjustment of offspring sex ratios by Cooper's Hawks described in this chapter) into habitat suitability if they were conducted on a long-term basis. Most studies of reproductive output in Cooper's Hawks to date are less than six years in duration, that is, most likely less than one breeding generation. Their findings are somewhat tenuous to compare with results from long-term studies (see above; Reynolds *et al.* 2017). Moreover, long-term studies can overcome the possible effects of, for example, short-term weather influences on breeders, small sample sizes, and an inability to obtain precision, or

For safer handling during sampling of tissues (such as drawing blood, which can be challenging up in a tree nest), we sometimes lower young from the nest in a backpack. Photo by Madeline Hardin.

These 14-day-old young were thus leg-banded and otherwise 'processed' on the ground at an urban nest site. Such activity also allows us to demonstrate our research activities to the curious public, along with allowing residents to get close up views—and especially to take pictures —of 'their' neighborhood birds.
Photos by Madeline Hardin.

Six Cooper's Hawk nestlings with oldest at 18 days of age in a backyard nest in Stevens Point, Wisconsin, where the highest nesting density of Cooper's Hawks has been reported, about 1 pair per 272 ha (or about one pair per square mile). This is the maximum brood size reported for the species, and has been found in only 1% of our study nests across 38 years. Interestingly, the adult female at this nest was banded by me as a nestling in another brood of six young elsewhere in Stevens Point. And her father was the oldest breeding bird in our study– reaching at least 11 years of age!
Photo by Robert Rosenfield.

inter-year annual repeatability, with respect to reproductive outcomes as they relate to habitat suitability.

Nest Success

Another important measure of avian reproduction is nest success, which is the proportion of nests with incubating adults that produce nestlings to an advanced age, or at least two weeks old for Cooper's Hawks. Nest success rates across North America range from 47% to 91% for Cooper's Hawks, with most studies reporting about a 70% success rate (Rosenfield and Bielefeldt 1993a, Nenneman *et al.* 2002, Brogan *et al.* 2017, Rosenfield *et al.* 2002a, 2018). It is difficult to generalize about why nests fail for Cooper's Hawks, because most nests fail for unknown reasons, as is true in other raptor and non-raptor species. However, numerous ecologists have demonstrated that predation is the major cause of nest failure in birds (e.g., Flaspohler *et al.* 2001, Faaborg *et al.* 2010). Meng (1951) suggested that up to half of the Cooper's Hawk nests in his New York study lost young to Great Horned Owls. Indeed, predation at Cooper's Hawk nests by Red-tailed Hawks, Great Horned Owls, and raccoons (*Procyon lotor*) seems important and widespread (Rosenfield *et al.* 2018).

Cooper's Hawk nests placed closer to the ground may have greater predation risk (likely from mammals) than nests placed higher up. Nest success rates differed among three study sites, with British Columbia (91%) significantly higher than Wisconsin (82%), and North Dakota (68%) significantly lower than the other two sites. That corresponds to the quantitative difference in average nest heights at 18, 13, and 9 meters, in British Columbia, Wisconsin, and North Dakota, respectively (Rosenfield *et al.* 2002a, A.C. Stewart, unpubl. data). In fact, nest success rates were lower in western and north-central North Dakota than the other two

Juvenile Cooper's Hawk in its first autumn on a sidewalk in Milwaukee, Wisconsin. Apparently large volumes of non-migratory, urban avian prey such as House Sparrows and European Starlings forestalls migration in many Cooper's Hawks and thus even inexperienced juveniles are commonly observed overwintering in northern cities in North America. Photo courtesy of author.

Being able to see a captured mated pair of Cooper's Hawks close up, and note the striking size difference between the sexes (male on top) and eye colors of these birds, are just some body features that readily attract a curious public to our research activities in urban settings. Photo by Madeline Hardin.

Chapter 4

It is difficult to determine the cause of nest failures as such events mostly occur unseen. We guess that this 19-day-old nestling was killed in a fall about 6 meters (20 feet) from its nest. Perhaps it tried to escape from a predator or storm winds blew it out of the nest. All four of its siblings were found dead on other tree branches and the ground. Photograph by Robert Rosenfield.

sites, in each of six concurrent study seasons (Rosenfield *et al.* 2007c). We note that this North Dakota study site was a rural grassland and cropland landscape with scattered, small, highly fragmented woodlands, containing the relatively short trees typical of prairie environments (Rosenfield *et al.* 2002a, 2007c). Some North Dakota nests, however, were successful even in areas where woodland cover was as little as 1% within 1 kilometer (0.6 miles) of nests (Nenneman *et al.* 2003). These results may suggest that regional habitat can influence nest success rates. That said, there appears to be no consistent continental pattern suggesting that urban Cooper's Hawks, who of course breed in highly fragmented settings, have either higher or lower nest success, or reproduction of young, than do exurban birds (Rosenfield *et al.* 2018). Interestingly, Thorton *et al.* (2017) reported that nest success rates were significantly higher (97%) in urban versus rural (81%) sites for another accipiter, the Eurasian Sparrowhawk (*A. nisus*), in Scotland, though I note that both of these nest success rates were relatively high. That there is no general difference in nest success rates among habitat types for Cooper's Hawks contradicts the general suggestion that reproduction is—and theoretically should be—lower in highly fragmented landscapes because fragmented environments tend to have more predators, and those predators find it easier to locate nests in smaller wooded tracts (see review by Faaborg *et al.* 2010). Yet across North America, numerous Cooper's Hawk populations in highly fragmented urban environments exhibit high nest success rates and some of the highest productivity indices known for the species. These demographic outcomes are consistent with apparently healthy breeding populations of Cooper's Hawks (Nenneman *et al.* 2002, Rosenfield *et al.* 2016a, 2018).

It is important to emphasize, once again, that the ecology of nest failure in Cooper's Hawks is poorly understood because a multitude of difficult-to-document natural history factors may cause nest failure. These include deaths of breeding birds that are not replaced within a nesting season; severe weather, including prolonged periods of rain or strong wind; predation of eggs, young, or breeding adults; and perhaps even researcher disturbance. This latter factor is one we are asked perhaps the most about by the public. More specifically, the public often asks whether parent hawks will desert young that we touch. We assure them that this is not the case, as adult raptors do not desert young due to responsibly conducted researcher presence (Rosenfield et al. 2007a). Multiple and repeated sources of our potential disturbance, including, for example, attempts (often successful) to trap adults at all stages of nesting; climbs to nests to count eggs, usually completed in less than 10 minutes; and to band young (less than 30 minutes) all adding up to more than 3,000 visits to 330 Wisconsin nests over three to four months of the year, resulted in only four nests believed to have failed due to researcher disturbance. That's 1.2% across a 14-year period. We have demonstrated that our field research activities, which involved techniques commonly used among raptor biologists, do not adversely influence the breeding biology of our study populations of Cooper's Hawks (Rosenfield et al. 2007a). And almost all of our reproductive output measures represent the highest known marks for the species.

Cooper's Hawks are still illegally shot, perhaps more frequently in urban environs where hawks are less wary of humans. But the extent of this illegal activity is inherently difficult to document. That said, residents in several cities in various U.S. states have admitted to me that they shoot Cooper's Hawks, mostly when birds are near nests or when they are at feeders. They acknowledge a disdain for predators in general, say that Cooper's Hawks have the undesired effect of reducing populations of feeder birds, and complain that Cooper's Hawks are preying upon their favorite birds.

SURVIVAL OF BREEDING ADULTS

Survival is a fundamental natural history attribute in understanding the population ecology of avian species. In fact, population ecologists have convincingly shown that survival of adult individuals is probably the demographic factor with the largest impact on population viability in long-lived animals, including birds (Flaspohler et al. 2001b, Pavón-Jordán et al. 2013). Importantly, mortality rates, or number of deaths per year, may vary or be linked with types of habitat, because landscapes typically vary in quality, that is in their ability to provide adequate resources like food or nesting cover to breeding individuals. So habitat-specific mortality rates of nesting populations may reveal the quality of various habitat types. Unfortunately, early and important studies of survival rates in Cooper's Hawks were based on

Breeding Cooper's Hawks do not generally tolerate predators near their nests, which usually results in chasing them, including egg-eating crows and other species of hawks from the vicinity of their nests. But here the tables are turned as an American Crow (Corvus brachyrhynchos) harasses this adult. Note the oft-pitched similarity in size between these birds.   Photo by Brian Rusnica.

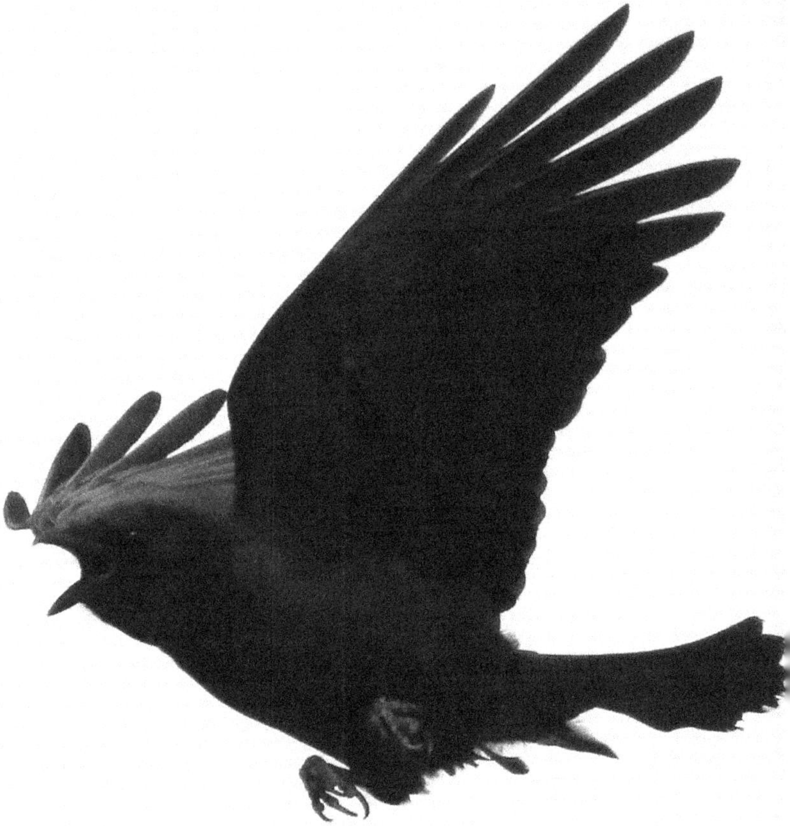

banding data in which geographic affiliations, habitat (changes), and the breeding status of marked individuals were vague or unknown (e.g., Henny and Wight 1972). It is possible that man-made factors in ever-expanding urban environs could render cities less suitable as habitat than exurban sites (Snyder and Snyder 1974a, Sweeney et al. 1997). For example, some researchers claim that mortality rates may be higher for urban birds due to collisions with human obstacles such as windows, electrical utility wires, and cars (Roth et al. 2005, Grimm et al. 2008). Alternatively, the greater abundance of food resources in urban environments (Marzluff et al. 1998) could result in enhanced survival in urban areas. This food-survivorship theme may be particularly pertinent for raptors, because starvation is a predominant source of mortality in birds of prey (Rosenfield et al. 2016c, 2018).

We obtained reliable annual survivorship and longevity estimates of marked breeding male and female Cooper's Hawks across at least four consecutive breeding generations (estimated at six years/generation) in Wisconsin, because we found their nests randomly throughout all representative habitats of the state, including city and rural habitats (Rosenfield et al. 1995a, 2009a, 2016a). Rural nests were those occurring outside municipal limits, in forested tracts of at least 0.16 square kilometers (0.06 square miles), and with no more than three houses within 0.4 km (0.3 miles) of a nest. Thus, our mark-recapture data, including re-sighting of color-banded adults in later years, were unbiased regarding the individuals sampled and the habitats in which they bred. Critically, our rigorous searches of nesting sites for marked breeding adults revealed that males have lifetime nesting-area fidelity and that when males disappeared from a nesting area it was because they were dead (Rosenfield and Bielefeldt 1996). So for males we could, unlike many other researchers, reliably separate death from movement to an unknown locale as possible reasons we didn't detect a particular individual again in a subsequent year. Lifetime fidelity in Wisconsin males meant that the presence of a new male in a nesting area indicated the death of a previous occupant, which in turn allowed for estimates of replacement male survivorship and longevity, and of course the potential to link survivorship to habitat type. Ours was the first, and, at the time of this writing, the only study to determine annual survivorship of breeding adult Cooper's Hawks in urban versus rural habitats (Rosenfield et al. 2009a, 2018).

Before I relay our findings on annual survival rates of breeding birds, which is a common and appropriate practice among population ecologists, allow me, for broader context, to briefly highlight some survival and longevity facts about breeding male and female Cooper's Hawks, mostly in Wisconsin. These data stem from our statewide studies of six consecutive breeding generations, exclusive of the Milwaukee population—the longest such study on Cooper's Hawks in North

Andy Stewart (left front) and the author (right) with a captured mated pair of Cooper's Hawks in Victoria, British Columbia. A live decoy Great Horned Owl tethered to a perch near an almost invisible mist net serves as an excellent trap for nesting adults. Adult Cooper's Hawks stoop readily, if not 'angrily,' at this perceived predator in an attempt to drive it from the vicinity of their nest. But if all goes well for us they become ensnared harmlessly within minutes of attacking the feathered intruder. Upper photo of captured pair by Brad Stewart; other photos by Madeline Hardin.

America. Our oldest breeding birds were 10 and at least 11 years of age for one female and one male, respectively. To my knowledge, the oldest breeding Cooper's Hawk in North America was at least 12 years for a female in British Columbia; the longevity record for the species is 20 years for a migratory male in western North America. It is very rare for breeding birds to attain these older ages, and I estimate that less than 5% of breeding adults of either sex in Wisconsin in a given year attain an age of at least 10 years. I note that there is no difference in age-specific mortality and hence longevity between breeding males and females in Wisconsin (Rosenfield *et al.* 2016c). I further estimate that about 30% of breeding birds in a given year are 5-7 years old, and perhaps 60% of breeders are between 2 and 4 years of age (Rosenfield *et al.* 2009a, 2016c). A male typically enters the breeding population at 2 or 3 years of age, in his third or fourth summer of life, and on average, breeds for 2.7 years and then dies. Given our population age-specific estimates, males on average raised 8.7 young in their lifetimes in Wisconsin (Rosenfield *et al.* 2013).

This latter measure of lifetime production underscores a very important demographic synergy: that among most bird species, including raptors, the minority of individuals who live the longest disproportionately produce the most young (Newton 1989). For example, among 66 male Cooper's Hawks in Wisconsin with documented lifetime production, 15 (23%) produced the most (53%) nestlings from 1980 to 2005 (Rosenfield et al. 2009a). And the greatest lifetime outputs, of 23, 25, 30, and 32 young, were from the longest-lived males, who lived 6–9 years. Two males each produced 23 young, while three other individuals produced 25, 30, and 32 respectively. Thus just five males, representing 8% of all males in the study, produced 24% of 562 young in this analysis. I do not know what privileged these oldest males to live so long, but as discussed in this chapter and elsewhere, we could not link their longevity to their breeding habitat, nor to body size. These oldest males were, in fact, of average-to-below-average size (Rosenfield et al. 2009a, 2013).

Raptor researchers have suggested that longevity in breeding birds may be associated with frequent re-occupancy of high-quality territories, sites often deemed to have greater available food levels (Rosenfield 2018). But we found the greatest longevity in breeding adult male Cooper's Hawks occurred on nesting areas that exhibited comparatively lower re-occupancy by other Cooper's Hawks following the death of the oldest-aged occupants. These results may suggest that nesting area quality was not the primary factor determining longevity and that perhaps intrinsic qualities of the birds (and how their individual abilities manifested use of nesting

This breeding male (named 'Phil') is wearing a standard silver aluminum government leg band, but on his other leg is a color band to allow for individual identification from a distance without having to recapture him. Such marking was necessary in part to ascribe behaviors to known birds. Thus Phil is on his known breeding territory where we first caught him three years earlier, and we too can index his age. His posture, which is similar to components in the bowing display (Chapter 3), shows his svelte build, long legs, and his marked white under-tail coverts. Photos by Madeline Hardin.

area habitat) may explain their longevity, at least in part (Rosenfield 2017, Rosenfield *et al.* 2016a).

We note that conventional analyses of territory quality seem to tacitly assume there is exclusive use of food resources by adults on the site in which they breed. Yet, it may be untenable to assume such exclusive import of food on a site where a female (and perhaps male) Cooper's Hawk nests, because they may acquire some of their food on visits outside their territory during the pre-incubation period, and 'off-site' food could contribute to their eventual reproductive success (Rosenfield *et al.* 2015a, Rosenfield 2017, and see Chapter 3).

It is a bit more challenging to generalize about demographic measures (and their population implications) for females with the same accuracy we have with Wisconsin males, because we estimated that about 23% of breeding females moved annually to a different breeding site. And unfortunately, we had incomplete knowledge of the whereabouts and behavior of these breeding dispersal females for an average of three years before these females were again detected, and then as breeders (Rosenfield *et al.* 2016c, 2013). Indeed, for want of data, it is conceivable that some females may skip a year of breeding (a phenomenon that has been documented in North America for the closely related Northern Goshawk; Reynolds *et al.* 2017). Nevertheless, most Wisconsin females probably begin breeding at 2 or 3 years of age and on average breed for 2-3 years and then die (Rosenfield *et al.* 2013, 2016c, R.N. Rosenfield, unpubl. data). A conservative estimate, therefore, is that a breeding bird of either sex on average lives for about 6 years: about 2-3 years to become a breeder, and then about 2-3 years as a nesting adult. So, as stated earlier, we estimate that one breeding generation averages 6 years in duration in Wisconsin. By comparison, in urban Tucson, Mannan *et al.* (2006) found that most males and females secured a breeding site when they were only 1 or 2 years old. These researchers, as did Millsap (2018) for Albuquerque, NM., noted that more females than males nested in their second summer of life, when these females were only a year-old, and they thus bred at the first possible time in their lives.

Results from Tucson and New Mexico may not be directly comparable to ours, in part because our findings stem from both rural and urban habitats across an entire state. Our larger, statewide scale certainly contains a comparatively greater number of environmental conditions that could potentially influence the Wisconsin study population differently than in Tucson. For example, there is evidence from some areas of North America, including some cities in Wisconsin, that, compared to rural populations, female Cooper's Hawks in larger cities are more likely to enter a breeding population at younger ages, especially as yearlings (Rosenfield *et al.* 2015b, A.C. Stewart, unpubl. data). Indeed, the age-structure of breeding Cooper's

A captured breeding female at one year of age, otherwise known to researchers as a second-year, or SY bird, that is in her second year of life. Most raptors exhibit delayed maturation: they delay breeding until they have gained experience with age. Cooper's Hawks typically enter the breeding population at 2 or 3 years old. But males, not females, are responsible for establishing breeding territories and they almost exclusively hunt prey for the entire family and thus they require comparatively more time than females to gain experience requisite for breeding. Hence 'freed' from these tasks, females, more so than males, can breed as yearlings. Note the marked extent of this female's molt from her brown, first-year plumage, to acquisition of blue-gray feathers. Breeding yearling male and female Cooper's Hawks molt to a greater extent during nesting than do older breeding birds, which may aggravate the physiological 'costs' of breeding when just a year old. Photo by Madeline Hardin.

Hawks in the small (38,000 people) central Wisconsin city of Stevens Point is similar to the age-structure in populations of their rural counterparts outside that city. Collectively, these central Wisconsin habitats annually have relatively few females breeding as yearlings (annual average across years of about 8% of total hens, compared with 16% for the Tucson population [Boal 2001]), and in some years we find no yearling females in either Wisconsin habitat. In Tucson, however, in both the growing population of hawks in metropolitan Milwaukee (1,000,000 people), and in the stable Cooper's Hawk population of Victoria, BC (300,000 people), yearling females are found breeding each year. And these 'teenage' females do so in relatively high numbers, averaging about 25% of all females in both large cities of Milwaukee and Victoria, and even up to 50% of all hens in Victoria in some years (Rosenfield *et al.* 2015b, R.W. Mannan, A.C. Stewart, R.N. Rosenfield, and W.E. Stout, unpubl. data). I do not have an explanation at this time regarding a possible relation between size of city and proportionate population make-up of yearling females. But I am working on it.

Let's return now to the annual survival rates of breeders found across North America. We found no significant difference in annual survivorship rates of adult male Cooper's Hawks breeding in urban (84%) versus rural habitats (79%) of Wisconsin, and no significant variation over a 26-year period in the overall high annual survivorship rates of about 81% in all habitats for nesting males in Wisconsin excluding Milwaukee (Rosenfield *et al.* 2009a, R.N. Rosenfield, unpubl. data). More recently, we reported a similar annual survivorship rate of 75% for breeding females in Wisconsin between 1980 and 2007, a 28-year period that included our long-term study on male breeders (Rosenfield *et al.* 2009a, 2016c). Thus, for either sex, about two out of 10 breeding adults died each year. Interestingly, these survival rates are similar to the rates of 80% reported for both nesting male and female Cooper's Hawks in Tucson (Mannan *et al.* 2008). These measures were also similar to a 75% survival rate for radio-tagged adult male and female Cooper's Hawks over a 110-day interval during winter in rural and urban Indiana (rates not separated by habitat) in one of the few studies that has targeted non-breeding Cooper's Hawks (Roth *et al.* 2005). All these rates are similar to the annual survivorship rates of about 80% for both breeding males and females reported in rural Florida (Millsap *et al.* 2013), and survivorship rates of 82% - 88% for breeding adults in Albuquerque (Millsap 2018). These similar and relatively high survivorship rates from different populations across a large geographical scale of North America are consistent with apparently healthy accipiter nesting populations (Rosenfield *et al.* 2009a, 2018, Mannan *et al.* 2008).

Perhaps the similarity of survival rates suggests that habitat type (or quality?) does not appreciably affect the mortality rate of breeding adults, and that habitat may be less important for survival than acquisition of a nesting area and associated foraging area in this territorial species (Rosenfield et al. 2009a). I note that, despite the relatively food-poor breeding habitat for Cooper's Hawks in rural Florida, which makes for a seemingly lower-quality nesting habitat, adult males and females had relatively high annual survivorship rates there (Millsap et al. 2013). However, we note that our Wisconsin study is the only one to compare urban to rural mortality rates for a population of breeding Cooper's Hawks (i.e., Rosenfield et al. 2009a), so this calls for additional comparative research. Importantly, our survivorship and longevity studies of 26 and 28 years for males and females, respectively, exceed the minimum 10-year mark deemed by researchers as being essential for accurately estimating temporal variation in survival in birds. Long-term data are especially necessary to find a possible link between survival and the effects over time of environmental change (Grosbois et al. 2008, Pavon-Jordan et al. 2013, Reynolds et al. 2017). Most survival studies, including ours, were unable to document many of the causes of mortality, further accentuating an inability to understand or generalize about how habitat type may (or may not) affect how and why Cooper's Hawks die (e.g., Rosenfield et al. 2009a, 2018). That said, and noting that small sample sizes precluded firm conclusions, studies in Indiana (Roth et al. 2005) and in California, (Chaing et al. 2012) suggested that predation on breeding Cooper's Hawks was more common in rural sites than urban ones (see also Boal 1997). Conversely, predation rates did not seem to differ between urban and exurban Cooper's Hawk nests in southeastern Wisconsin (Stout et al. 2007).

I note that the size difference between the sexes within a raptor species, especially in those with extreme reversed size dimorphism, such as the Cooper's Hawk, could potentially result in different survival rates between males and females. Because of their larger size, females theoretically might be expected to have higher annual survival rates because larger individuals can accumulate and store more energy reserves to get them through periods of lower food levels (McNab 2012, Newton et al. 2016). However, our results from Wisconsin breeders, along with the findings of others studying Cooper's Hawks, accord with the conclusion in a recent review article that there is no consistent evidence of differences in survival between the sexes of adult raptors that can be linked to size dimorphism (Rosenfield et al. 2016c, Newton et al. 2016).

Habitat Suitability

Suitability of habitat is generally considered a key factor in the viability of breeding populations of birds (Cody 1985, Flaspohler *et al.* 2001a,b, Andersen *et al.* 2004). Much data suggest there is suitable habitat for breeding Cooper's Hawks continent-wide. Alternatively, many studies, with the vast majority focused on relatively small areas of states or provinces, suggest the species has a marked flexibility to breed successfully in diverse landscapes. Many of North America's landscapes are fragmented, and it seems paradoxical that a species that probably first evolved in forests would not be ill affected by what may be the world's most habitat-altering force, forest fragmentation (Ribon *et al.* 2003, Faaborg *et al.* 2010).

In Wisconsin, we demonstrated with long-term, cross-generational data that Cooper's Hawks nest statewide in a variety of habitats, from sparsely wooded tracts to large continuous forests, including urban and suburban settings (Trexel *et al.* 1999). Further, this hawk does so at relatively high survival rates, and with the highest long-term reproductive indices and nesting densities known for the species in North America (Rosenfield and Bielefeldt 1996, Rosenfield *et al.* 1995a, Rosenfield *et al.* 2016c). We also found numerous Cooper's Hawks nesting in pine plantations (see Chapter 3), which was initially surprising to us, as conifer plantations have been cast as being inferior in quality for breeding birds. Some scientists have characterized pine plantations as 'biological deserts' or 'ornithological deserts,' or biologically desolate habitat (Cody 1985, Rosenfield *et al.* 2000).

Yet pine plantations appear to be important, if not preferred habitat for breeding Cooper's Hawks in some areas of the midwestern United States. In fact, pine plantations appear to be the only habitat across North America documented as preferred breeding habitat for Cooper's Hawks. For example, six of seven Cooper's Hawk nests in southwestern Ohio were found in pine plantations (*Pinus* species), even though this habitat comprised only 1% of the study area (Mutter *et al.* 1984). K.J. Kritz was consistently able to locate Cooper's Hawk nests in Missouri by systematically searching pine plantations (Rosenfield *et al.* 1991b). Murphy *et al.* (1988) reported that 61% of 31 roosts of a telemetered breeding male Cooper's Hawk in Wisconsin occurred in pine plantations, even though this habitat comprised only 10% of its breeding home range. Additionally, we found a total of nine pairs of nesting Cooper's Hawks in pine plantations on a 2,980-hectare (about 12 square miles) study area in rural southeastern Wisconsin in both 1986 and 1992, a time period that represents one breeding generation (Fig. 4.3). I note that all breeding birds in 1986 had been replaced by new breeders in 1992 (Rosenfield *et al.* 1995a). It's likely that plantations were preferred for nesting, as they made up only one-third of available woodland habitat, yet all nests

Figure 4.3. Distribution of Cooper's Hawk nests on a rural 2980-hectare study plot in the Kettle Moraine State Forest in southeastern Wisconsin in 1986, and six years (one breeding generation) later, in 1992. The same number of nests (nine) across years suggests a stable nesting density of 331 hectares per nest, or about 1 pair per 1.3 square miles. This measure ranks among the highest nesting densities reported for the species. Pine plantation habitat was preferred for nesting as it comprised only one-third of available wooded habitat, yet all nests in both years were in plantations (see text). Reproductive output was high in both years, and all breeding adults in 1986 were replaced with new breeders by 1992 (see text). Modified from Rosenfield et al. (1995a).

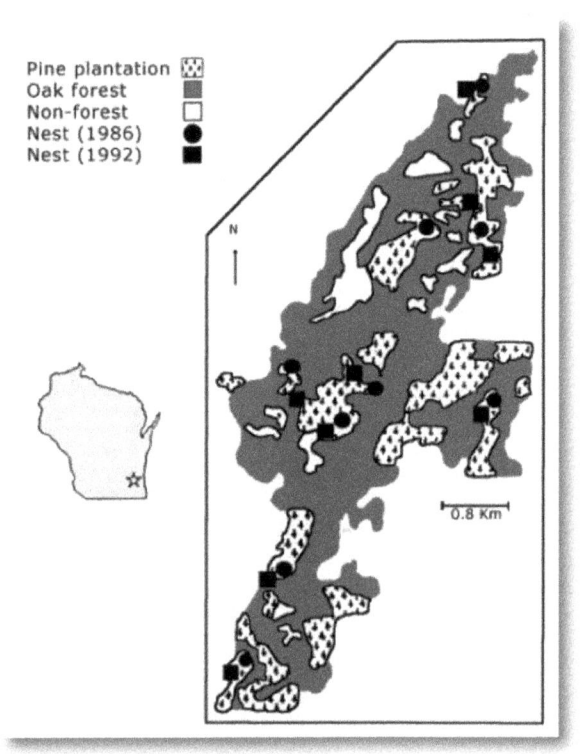

used by different birds a generation removed were in plantations. We highlight that these conifer plantations contained one of the highest nesting densities reported for the species in North America. Conifer plantations also contributed recruits to subsequent breeding generations in proportion to their productivity of bandable nestlings, thereby clearly demonstrating that Wisconsin plantations were high-quality habitat (Rosenfield et al. 2000). We do not know why pine plantations are attractive to breeders. Perhaps birds choose evergreens because they, both as single trees and when closely spaced in plantations, provide concealing, protective cover from predators and inclement weather early in the spring, in contrast to deciduous trees that, in that season, are leafless and lack such seasonal cover (McConnell 2003, Bosakowski et al. 1992).

Another surprising finding since our work began in 1980 was that some of the highest nesting densities of breeding Cooper's Hawks in Wisconsin occurred in highly fragmented urban landscapes, including Stevens Point and metropolitan Milwaukee. This may suggest that urban habitat may be of higher quality than exurban habitat for this raptor, a theme we have addressed earlier in this book. However, and as noted earlier, reproductive output and annual survivorship of breeding males in both cities and rural environments in Wisconsin were among the highest recorded such metrics for Cooper's Hawks across its broad continental distribution (Stout and Rosenfield 2010, Rosenfield et al. 2009a, 2018). Breeding habitat for Cooper's Hawks seems to be of relatively high quality throughout the forest-fragmented landscapes of Wisconsin

(Bielefeldt *et al.* 1998). In fact, it is possible that breeding Cooper's Hawks, like other accipiter hawks and migratory songbirds, have benefited from habitat fragmentation (Hockey and Curtis 2009). The specific mechanisms that might render fragmented habitat suitable for Cooper's Hawks are unclear. It is conceivable that Cooper's Hawks indirectly benefit in part from the higher numbers of insects that occur along a forest edge versus its interior. These invertebrates in turn attract high numbers of songbirds, who in turn provide food for hawks (Keller *et al.* 2009, Terraube *et al.* 2016).

I do, however, wish to highlight one area of concern regarding the suitability of urban habitats. Urbanization can lead to indirect threats to biodiversity via chemical pollution from, for example, heavy metals, rodenticides, and persistent organic pollutants (Elliott *et al.* 2015). These stressors may be most evident in birds of prey because they feed at a high trophic level, where such pollution is biomagnified (Ratcliffe 1980). Samples from Cooper's Hawks in and around Vancouver, BC, from 1999 to 2010 exceeded the highest concentrations of polybrominated diphenyl ethers (or PBDE, a flame retardant used, for example, in household furniture) reported in the literature for any wild bird (Elliott *et al.* 2015). The more urbanized Cooper's Hawks were exposed to a greater concentration than rural birds. Unfortunately, the potential effects of these chemicals to wildlife generally are unknown and under study (Elliott *et al.* 2015, Rosenfield *et al.* 2018). Notably, in a follow-up study on urban Cooper's Hawks in Vancouver, scientists assessed whether various chemical contaminants influenced reproductive success and circulating thyroid hormone levels in individuals. Researchers found several contaminants in the blood of hawks, including polychlorinated biphenyls, flame retardant PBDEs, dieldrin, and DDE, the latter of which is a major breakdown product of the organochlorine DDT. Total thyroxin in adults and nestlings was negatively associated with increases in polychlorinated biphenyls, and exposure to other contaminants, particularly dieldrin, had a negative influence on fledging success. Concentrations of DDE in adult blood were relatively high, with three individuals surpassing a critical threshold associated with reduced eggshell thickness. That said, investigators indicated that Cooper's Hawks have saturated available nesting territories in Vancouver, and they also reported reproductive indices comparable to those in other healthy urban populations (Brogan *et al.* 2017).

Another demographic response that could be related to habitat quality is breeding dispersal, or the between-year movement of experienced breeders to different territories. It appears common for raptor researchers to conclude that breeding dispersal birds tend to move from sites of poorer quality to sites of higher quality habitat, and in so doing improve their reproductive success (e.g., Blakesley *et al.* 2006, Forero *et al.* 1999, Ganey *et al.* 2014, Gutiérrez *et al.* 2011). However, habitat variation *per se* does not generally appear to prompt experienced male and female Cooper's Hawks to change breeding sites in Wisconsin. Indeed, males exhibit career decisions and choose a breeding site only once for their entire lives in both urban and rural sites in Wisconsin (Rosenfield and Bielefeldt 1996, Rosenfield et al. 2009a). Male raptors generally tend to exhibit strong breeding-site fidelity over the years. This is perhaps because the benefits of site-familiarity impart unique 'private value' to males (e.g., as evidenced through routine use of same flight routes, plucking posts, and hunting and nesting sites) that far out-weigh the value of a costly move to and/or fight for another territory of perhaps higher quality (e.g., Piper 2011, Murphy et al. 1988, Stout et al. 2008; see Chapter 3). Notably, the theme of site familiarity is markedly lacking in most theoretical models of habitat selection in birds (Piper 2011). However, inter-year movements by males among breeding territories do occur in other populations of Cooper's Hawks, albeit at small rates (2% of adult males move to other sites in Florida, Millsap et al. 2013; 3% in Arizona, Mannan et al. 2006). Such dispersal, again at small annual rates, also occurs in males of other accipiter hawks (e.g., Eurasian Sparrowhawk, Newton 1986; Northern Goshawk, Detrich and Woodbridge 1994).

In contrast to life-time site fidelity in males, we estimated that 23% of Wisconsin breeding females move annually among nesting areas, for reasons unclear to us (range of detected distance of dispersal is 1-14.6 kilometers [0.6 - 9.0 miles; mean = 4.2 kilometers or 2.6 miles], Rosenfield et al. 2016c, R.N. Rosenfield, unpubl. data). An urban study in Tucson reported a lower, 10% annual rate of breeding dispersal of female Cooper's Hawks (Mannan et al. 2006), while a study in rural Florida reported a much higher annual rate (68%) of dispersal in females (Millsap et al. 2013). Mean breeding dispersal distances were 0.6 kilometers (0.4 miles) and 4.2 kilometers (2.6 miles) for males and females in Florida, respectively. Researchers in Florida suggested that their study area was generally lacking in food resources to the degree that competition for, and thus dispersal by adults to, higher quality nesting sites with greater food resources was widespread each year, especially in females. Conversely, the Tucson site was generally composed of high-quality, food-rich breeding sites, which probably reduced the frequency of (or need for) dispersal (Mannan et al. 2008). Our evidence does not indicate that Wisconsin females become more productive after moving to a different site in a subsequent year, a finding that starkly contrasts with results from many other raptors, whose reproductive output increased following dispersal (Rosenfield et al. 2016a,c). For the 15 females in which we detected such dispersal during the 1980-2007 study, the number of bandable-aged young per nest with nestlings at the initial nesting area were not statistically different from the dispersal site, with means (and medians) of 3.9 (4.0) at the initial nesting area versus 3.5 (4.0) at the second site (Rosenfield et al. 2016a). These productivity metrics are similar to an overall mean of 3.6 and median of 4.0 bandable-aged young per nest for 594 other Wisconsin nests during those years

(Rosenfield *et al.* 2016a). It's difficult to discern an important link between reproductive output (or habitat quality) and dispersal when the productivity of dispersing birds is so similar to the production of the entire sample of other nests in Wisconsin.

However, dispersing females appeared to live longer than non-dispersing birds (interestingly, this result contrasts with Florida, where non-dispersing females actually lived longer). Given that lifetime production correlates with longevity in male Wisconsin Cooper's Hawks (Rosenfield *et al.* 2009a, 2013) and similarly so in both sexes in other raptor species (Rosenfield *et al.* 2016c), it is possible that breeding dispersal in some females may be a favored strategy. Unfortunately, we did not have complete information on every supposed breeding episode of every dispersing female–they are harder to track than non-dispersing birds–and thus we could not accurately and tenably compare the strategies, or advantages of staying put versus moving to another site (Rosenfield *et al.* 2016c). The study of breeding dispersal in birds markedly lacks natural history descriptions of the behavior of individuals when they are vying for sites. Rather, it seems that investigations of dispersal typically use "outcome data," that is, where the bird settled and its production there, rather than producing data that might reveal more completely why females ended up at a site. I suggested in a recent commentary paper that avian ecologists need to up their game with study of the process of movement by individuals among territories, to come to a better understanding of the biology of breeding dispersal in birds (Rosenfield 2017). I wager that this process includes rather complex social interactions that, if revealed, would markedly enhance our understanding of breeding dispersal in Cooper's Hawks (Rosenfield *et al.* 2016c; and see Extra-pair Paternity in Chapter 3).

Natal dispersal is yet another attribute of a population that perhaps could reveal some insight into habitat suitability and/or habitat selection. Natal dispersal is defined as the movement of an individual, also known as a recruit, from its birthplace (natal site) to the site of its first breeding, or more functionally, where the bird is first found breeding (Stout *et al.* 2007). Natal dispersal distances are usually greater than breeding dispersal distances. Among population ecologists, the study of such movement is, along with breeding dispersal, regarded as integral to the study of population dynamics, habitat selection, conservation biology, and other ecological disciplines. This is because moving from one location to another or staying behind can theoretically strongly affect both reproductive and survival rates of populations. That said, the biology of natal dispersal in birds, including raptors, generally is poorly understood, mostly because of the disappointingly few available estimates of dispersal and associated behaviors for natural populations (Macdonald and Johnson 2001, Rosenfield 2017). This lack of data is mostly due to two factors: first, the logistical difficulty of tracking individuals in space and in time, especially the very young, who have relatively high mortality rates in their first year of life; and second, most field studies of Cooper's Hawks span less than six years (Rosenfield *et al.* 2013). These two impediments typically result in very small sample sizes of recruits from restricted time periods, which probably don't cover even one breeding generation. That said, investigators in Tucson did, with large sample sizes across 11 years (92 total recruits; 66 males/26 females), investigate whether recruits would settle in places with similar types of trees and levels of development as their natal sites (Mannan *et al.* 2006). They reported no or limited evidence that natal experience played a role in habitat selection among recruits. Further, they suggested that any small grove of large trees planted in Tucson could be used for nesting, regardless of the level of development surrounding the nest. However, they noted that their study was limited to examining selection within the city, and thus they could not answer the broader question of whether hawks hatched in urban areas choose cities over rural environments. Indeed, if urban habitat was, as suggested earlier, of higher quality, and if we assume that birds choose where to breed based on some urban cues (such as higher prey levels), one might expect a net movement of recruits into cities. In fact, we have evidence, both published and unpublished, from central Wisconsin showing habitat tenacity for recruits of both sexes in both rural and urban sites, and movement of recruits from urban to rural sites and vice versa (Rosenfield *et al.* 1996b, 2000, R.N. Rosenfield unpubl. data). We also have evidence for breeding dispersal in females from rural to urban sites and vice versa in Wisconsin (remember, experienced Wisconsin males do not move, and exhibit lifetime nesting area fidelity). However, we know of no study that can demonstrate that either cities or rural areas disproportionately attract breeding Cooper's Hawks. Regardless, natal and other dispersal data clearly support the general findings that urban environments are indeed high-quality breeding habitat for Cooper's Hawks across North America (Millsap 2018, Sonsthagen *et al.* 2012).

I stress that the researchers in the Tucson study assumed that recruits exercised habitat choice. Pine plantations in the midwestern United States appeared to attract breeders, and these findings also would assume an individual's choice of breeding site. That said, available evidence that demonstrates non-random mating by age in Tucson (Boal 2001) and mass, or body size, in Wisconsin (Rosenfield and Bielefeldt 1999) suggests that factors other than habitat features–that is, intrinsic features of individuals–may also influence where Cooper's Hawks breed. We will tackle this theme of individual competence or quality in the next chapter.

Most studies to date indicate that male birds tend to settle closer to their natal sites than do females; or, to use the technical speak, males are more philopatric to natal sites than are females (Clobert *et al.* 2001). This is generally believed to be because male birds establish breeding territories and thus are, compared to females, more strongly favored to find habitat similar to that in which they were raised. This scenario is accentuated in the Cooper's Hawk and other raptors, because territorial males do most of the hunting for their mates and young on their breeding sites. The few data available suggest that natal dispersal distances of females are greater than those of male Cooper's Hawks. For example, Mannan et al. (2006) reported averages of 9.7 kilometers (6 miles) and 7.4 kilometers (4.6 miles) for females and males, respectively; and maximum natal dispersal distances of 24 kilometers (15 miles) and 18.8 kilometers (12 miles) for females and males, respectively, within Tucson, AZ. Stout et al. (2007) reported averages of 19.9 kilometers (12 miles; maximum of 13 miles) and 4.5 kilometers (2.8 miles; maximum of 3.6 miles) for females and males respectively in Milwaukee, WI. Generally, greater natal dispersal distances are available for combined data from rural and urban habitats in the southern half of Wisconsin, excluding Milwaukee. We found averages of 27.6 kilometers (17 miles; to a maximum of 79 kilometers, or 49 miles) and 7.2 kilometers (4.5 miles; maximum of 35.2 kilometers, or 22 miles), for females and males, respectively (Rosenfield et al.1996a, R.N. Rosenfield, unpubl. data). No recruits in Wisconsin bred on their natal sites. The greater maximum dispersal distances from the much larger study site of southern Wisconsin, compared with the Tucson and Milwaukee sites, seem to accord with the suggestion that size of study area influences the ability to detect dispersers, a well-known potential bias in the study of dispersal in vertebrates (Koenig et al. 1996). That said, after having banded over 3,000 nestling and adult Cooper's Hawks in each of our exclusive study sites of Milwaukee and elsewhere in southern Wisconsin, sites that are as close as 50 kilometers (30 miles) of each other, we have no evidence of recruitment nor movement of breeding adults between these two sites across 35 years. We thus believe that we have reasonably accurate estimates of average natal and breeding dispersal distances for each of these two Wisconsin study sites (Rosenfield et al. 2015b, 2016c, R.N. Rosenfield and W.E. Stout, unpubl. data).

Lastly, habitat fragmentation, or the subdivision of previously large, contiguous tracts of habitat such as forests into smaller stands, often as the result of urbanization and agricultural practices, can isolate wildlife populations. That in turn results in complex demographic dynamics for these populations related to habitat suitability. Interpreting these dynamics is controversial as they relate to fragmentation, and although some of the dynamics may be favorable to a species (as noted above), several appear to cause, or could cause, reduced population viability and are thus of high conservation concern for wildlife biologists throughout the world (Rosenfield et al. 1992b, Blackwell et al. 1995, Faaborg et al. 2010). For example, habitat fragmentation can disrupt movements of individuals (or gene flow), which may result in loss of genetic variability typical of (and perhaps needed for) healthy wildlife populations. It is also conceivable that habitat fragmentation may foster close inbreeding in Cooper's Hawks in isolated woodlands or cities. Close inbreeding involves matings between sibling-sibling or parent-sibling pairs, which may be associated with reduced production due to inbreeding depression, which can result from the union of deleterious genes. Close inbreeding generally is difficult to detect, because it requires long-term monitoring of birds. We discovered a three-year mating of a grandson-grandmother pair of Cooper's Hawks in a fragmented woodland, agricultural landscape of rural southeastern Wisconsin, with some evidence of reduced reproduction, but this pair did produce young. However, this was the only close inbreeding we detected among 70 recruits from over 38 years of Cooper's Hawk research in fragmented environments of Wisconsin (Rosenfield and Bielefeldt 1992, R.N. Rosenfield and W.E. Stout, unpubl. data).

On the other hand, in Victoria, BC, Andy Stewart detected two instances of full-sibling matings of Cooper's Hawks, plus two incidents of recruits breeding on their natal sites across 13 years in their Vancouver Island study site (Stewart *et al.* 2007). Stewart suggested that this insular, urban population may have a higher potential for natal philopatry, and hence inbreeding, because the study site's principal boundaries of ocean water–a form of natural fragmentation–might reduce the extent of suitable habitat for dispersal of recruits to off-city environments. One of these two sibling matings resulted in high production (four nestlings at each nest) comparable to what occurred throughout his study population. The other nest with breeding siblings hatched two or three eggs, but failed at the early nestling stage. Nevertheless, evidence to date, albeit limited, suggests that inbreeding in Cooper's Hawk populations is a rare event across the varied, fragmented landscapes of North America. I note that mating typically is genetically random (that is, not among related individuals) in urban and rural populations of Cooper's Hawks in Wisconsin and in Victoria (Rosenfield *et al.* 2015a, R.N. Rosenfield, S.A. Sonsthagen, and W.E. Stout, unpubl. data). Further, studies of breeding populations of Cooper's Hawks across markedly varied North American landscapes, including Wisconsin, North Dakota, British Columbia, and Arizona, demonstrate favorably high levels of genetic diversity (Sonsthagen *et al.* 2012, Morinha *et al.* 2016).

Chapter Five

INDIVIDUAL TRAITS: THE DESCRIPTIVE CURRENCIES OF
NATURAL HISTORY DYNAMICS

"*Gosh, what a bizarre appearance!*" *we exclaimed as we disentangled the recaptured male from the net in his third successful nesting season at his usual territory in the city of Stevens Point, Wisconsin. He had no tail feathers! I have never seen such a condition in handling hundreds of breeding male and female Cooper's Hawks. In fact, he was similarly unadorned in the next four years. In each of his first two years, he had his full complement of 12 tail feathers, that is, minus some molt of the innermost tail feathers, which is normal among some breeding males in the nestling stage. Regardless of what caused this condition, without tail feathers, how was he able to maneuver with the agility supposedly needed to overcome the evasive tactics of his prey? Further, in his seventh year on his usual territory when he was at least 8 years of age, he had only three full-length, normal talons, two on one foot and one on another. So how could he effectively fight with other males for this territory? It, too, is puzzling why a female–in fact different females in different years–would be attracted to what seemingly appeared to be an inferior or poor quality male. I note that this site did not, on an annual basis, either comparatively out- or under-produce other territories in the city. Alternatively, this 'bad-boy' was apparently some catch, as evidenced by his long life, a trait that reveals a high degree of individual quality in breeding Cooper's Hawks.*"

OVERVIEW

Individuals of species typically vary in their phenotypes, or traits. These traits are in part the outward or 'external' expression of their genes. Phenotypes therefore are the attributes of individuals that engage directly with the physical environment.

Chapter 5

Phenotypes include body size, color, and behavior, and they represent key descriptive currencies of natural history dynamics. Darwin's theory of natural selection is underpinned by the understanding that phenotypes are generally non-randomly distributed, that is, not by chance, throughout a breeding population (Darwin 1859). This non-randomness typically occurs because, in their natural surroundings, some traits make individuals competitively superior, and they will therefore tend to out-survive and/or out-produce their counterparts. That is, some individuals are selectively favored over others, manifesting the powerful biological process of natural selection. Some of these traits have been studied with a focus on their presence in individuals within populations of breeding Cooper's Hawks, but also with research on phenotypes in individuals among different populations. We have done both types of studies with breeding Cooper's Hawks and here will detail some substantive results.

Identifying a possible adaptive or favored phenotype generally involves a use of statistics. As we discuss conceptually below, this usually is done by investigating the correlation or relationship of the measurable extent of a trait in individuals with their productivity and/or their longevity. Recognizing individual variation, a prerequisite for natural selection, at an ecological level is fundamentally required

Adult male, at least 8 years old, who for unknown reason(s) was without a tail for the last five of seven total years he bred at the same urban territory in Stevens Point, WI. He was one of the oldest birds in our study despite his apparent 'inadequacy'; in fact, he successfully fledged young in six seasons. Photo by Robert Rosenfield.

to build a truly integrative approach to evolutionary ecology (Rosenfield 2017), a branch of biology that tries to understand why an individual looks and/or behaves in the manner it does.

The importance of individual variation or individual competence may be particularly pertinent in the ecology of Wisconsin Cooper's Hawks, because in our 38 years of work involving about six consecutive cross-generations of breeding birds, we have found no evidence that habitat (urban or rural, conifer plantation versus non-plantation nests, presumptive site or territory quality, as indexed by consistency of nest use and high breeding density) was related to, or might predict, reproductive success, phenology (calendric timing of nesting), annual adult survival, longevity, or production of breeding recruits from our pool of marked nestlings (Rosenfield and Bielefeldt 1999, Rosenfield et al. 2000, 2009a, 2013, 2016a,c). How unfortunate it is that large volumes (perhaps the majority) of the technical literature regarding the importance of habitat suitability/quality for successful reproduction in birds fails to address the potential role of variation in competence of individuals in their ability to use habitat and/or attract mates (Pulliam 1988, Rosenfield 2017). I further note that the reproductive success of Wisconsin Cooper's Hawks was apparently related, in contrast to findings of many other avian ecology studies, to the intrinsic qualities of individuals (Newton 1986, Milllsap et al. 2013, Rosenfield et al. 2016a,c).

Eye color

For example, although the Cooper's Hawk exhibits little difference in color between the sexes in adult gray plumage (though males tend to have gray-tinted faces, while females' are brown), iris color was generally believed to relate to the individual's age. Indeed, irides change from yellow or light orange in younger birds to shades of orange or red in older birds. These darker eye colors are striking attributes that prompted some researchers to suggest that eye color may be a characteristic or one of several characteristics that signal an individual's age and therefore experience, as shown for instance in its hunting ability. Thus, eye color in male Cooper's Hawks could perhaps offer an opportunity for what is called assortative mating, which is technical speak for non-random mating (Snyder and Snyder 1974b, Boal 2001). That is, those females that tend to select (older) males with darker eyes who supposedly are better food providers may produce relatively more young than if they chose lighter eye-colored males.

However, these hypotheses were based on small or no samples of multi-year data of individually marked birds of known or relative age (Rosenfield et al. 2003).

Besides the usual difference whereby the male's eye (upper bird) in a mated pair is typically darker than that of his mate, this pair also exhibits the typical contrast in plumage color between the sexes in parts of the head and the upper back. Although most adult males have a noticeable gray side to their heads, rather than the brown on the female's head, some males can have brown there too. However, I have never seen an adult female's face colored gray. Photo by Janelle Taylor.

Individual traits such as body mass or size, age, or eye color may be natural history attributes that signal individual competence in birds including Cooper's Hawks. Scientists typically relate the presence or extent of such traits to reproductive output attempting to identify adaptive or favored traits. We use a standard eye color chart to objectively describe the eye color of breeding adults. Eye color generally changes across years from yellow—as in this yearling hawk–to orange or red in older birds and thus eye color can provide a coarse index to age in breeding Cooper's Hawks (see text). To be clear, researchers cannot use eye color to precisely gauge age in Cooper's Hawks. We were unable to demonstrate that variation in eye color was related to reproductive output across several breeding populations (see text). Photo by Madeline Hardin.

These suppositions also were based on the undocumented premise that only (or mostly) females exercise choice of mates, a notion that appears untenable, at least in Wisconsin birds. What's more, there was no published data that related eye color to the reproductive output of individuals for any population of Cooper's Hawks. Remember, the most convincing signal of adaptation is number of descendants.

Fortunately, we were able to investigate these themes with our relatively large samples of birds with known reproductive outcomes in three different populations, including British Columbia, North Dakota, and Wisconsin. In these populations we designated iris color in captured hawks (and recaptured individuals in later years) with different numerical scores pertaining to yellow, light orange, orange, dark orange, or red eyes (these colors follow published standards; Rosenfield *et al.* 1992a). At initial capture we also designated birds as known-age if they were in brown plumage (i.e., yearlings), or if they were birds originally banded by us as nestlings in a known year. Relative-age birds were those who exhibited two generations of gray feathers in the initial year of capture and thus were 2 years or older (i.e., after-second-year, or ASY birds). Recaptures of relative-aged birds were designated A3Y, A4Y, etc., in subsequent years. I remind readers that eye color lightens from a pale blue-gray in nestlings to yellow in post-fledglings. Yellow is the predominant eye color of Cooper's Hawks during their first year of life throughout North America (Rosenfield and Bielefeldt 1993a, Rosenfield *et al.* 2003).

We found that eye color did indeed change from lighter shades of yellow or orange in younger birds to darker shades of orange or red in older birds, in samples of both known-age and recaptured birds of relative age in all study sites. Further, males exhibited a greater mean eye color score (i.e., they had darker eyes) than females of the same relative ages in all three study sites, and between birds of known age in both British Columbia and Wisconsin. However, the pace of color change by age was not the same among populations. For example, ASY adults of both sexes at initial capture had significantly darker eye color categories (dark orange and especially red) in British Columbia and North Dakota than in Wisconsin. Proportions of dark orange and red eyes at initial capture in both ASY males (83%) and females (63%) were much greater in British Columbia and North Dakota than in Wisconsin (49% males, 19% females). In contrast to Wisconsin, where 24% of breeding ASY adults of both sexes had yellow or light orange eyes at initial capture, less than 2% (only two individuals) had these lighter shades in British Columbia and North Dakota.

Further, in comparison to Wisconsin birds, known-age male and female hawks in British Columbia also appeared to show quicker and more frequent changes to darker eyes. In general, our samples of known-age males demonstrated that dark orange or red eyes were acquired by the minimum age of 2 years in British Columbia and by a minimum age of 3 or 4 in Wisconsin. Six (29%) of 21 females captured or recaptured in British Columbia had dark orange eyes at ages 2-7, while all nine females of the same age captured and recaptured in Wisconsin had eyes that were orange or lighter (Rosenfield *et al.* 2003). Regarding the darkest eye color in ASY birds, red-eyed males were relatively common in British Columbia and North Dakota (about 45% of all ASY males at initial capture), but uncommon at initial capture in Wisconsin (17%). In ASY females, red-eyed birds were uncommon in British Columbia and North Dakota (about 10%), and rare in Wisconsin (1%).

We have no definitive explanation for the disparity in eye color proportions in breeding birds among the three different breeding populations. However, we do not believe that genetic differences explain the variation, because British Columbia birds are separable genetically from both North Dakota and Wisconsin hawks (Sonsthagen *et al.* 2012), and British Columbia and North Dakota populations exhibited similar proportions of eye color. We believe that it is possible that the disparity in eye color between populations is related in part to metabolic rates by body size, as smaller birds generally exhibit higher metabolic rates (per gram body mass) relative to larger birds (McNab 2012), which may produce the quicker changes in eye color of the smaller British Columbia and North Dakota birds. Indeed, these three breeding populations are separable by mass, as the British Columbia and North Dakota birds are similar to each other but both have birds on average smaller than

Wisconsin birds. Also, males, who are the smaller sex in this species, acquire dark orange or red eyes quicker than females in all our study populations. Interestingly, males are proportionately smaller than females to the same extent in all these populations; we found no difference in indices of reversed size dimorphism among populations (Rosenfield *et al.* 2010).

Still, some suggest it is conceivable that eye color is adaptive and that it serves as one, or one of many, honest cues to females that the potential mate is an older male with experience and individual competence, capable of enhanced food-provisioning skills (Boal 2001). If this line of logic is true, then nests with males of darker-colored eyes should have greater productivity (egg and brood counts) compared to nests where males have lighter colored eyes (Rosenfield *et al.* 2003). Again, a sound measure of adaptive or evolutionary success is number of descendants produced. Alternatively, eye color may not be adaptive and it is simply an age-related phenomenon (like, perhaps, the apparent non-adaptive progressive loss of head hair in aging human males!). It is also possible that human perception of colors, a fundamental basis for these investigations of eye color, does not correspond to that of birds, including raptors, who can see color (Mahler and Kempenaers 2002). Further, some bird species, including raptors, are sensitive to near-ultraviolet wavelengths (Hunt *et al.* 2015; Viitala *et al.* 1995). However, we stress that it is unclear how raptors use color or ultraviolet vision (Lind *et al.* 2013). Regardless, using human perception in eye color analyses, prompted by prior propositions of other researchers that assortative mating may occur on the basis of age and eye color in Cooper's Hawks (Snyder and Snyder 1974, Boal 2001), we did not detect any relationship between male eye color and their clutch or brood counts among three North American populations (Rosenfield *et al.* 2003). Underscoring these conclusions, Rosenfield and Bielefeldt (1997) reported that younger Wisconsin males with light orange eyes had mean brood sizes (four young) that were as large or slightly larger than older orange or dark orange-eyed males (about 3.5). Light-orange-eyed males had mean brood sizes essentially the same as red-eyed males (3.9 young), even though the lighter-eyed males were likely to be two years younger.

Thus, despite the variation in pace of eye color change and the varied proportion of darker irides among three populations of Cooper's Hawks, we could not detect any selective benefits to potential pairing based on eye color *per se*. We note that others have cautioned that ecological settings and behaviors, in combination with single sexual traits, may be involved in mate choice in birds (Rosenfield *et al.* 2003). These combinations, to our knowledge, have not been explored regarding eye color in breeding Cooper's Hawks.

We further note that although iris color changes with age in both sexes, some breeding birds of the same age showed variation in eye color (for example, we recorded 2-year-old Wisconsin males with either light orange, orange, or dark orange eyes). In addition, nesting individuals of the same eye color category showed variation in known or relative ages (for example, some orange-eyed females in Wisconsin were 2, 3, or 4 years old). In fact, many Wisconsin females never attained the darkest eyes–dark orange or red–no matter what age they reached. Because of these types of variation we, when asked, advised the U.S. Geological Survey's Bird Banding Laboratory that eye color could not be used by their licensed banders to accurately age a given individual Cooper's Hawk (Rosenfield *et al.* 2003). However, we did suggest that birds with lighter and darker extremes of eye color could be regarded by ecologists as younger and older individuals, respectively, especially when an adequate sample for the population became available. In fact, two studies used lighter and darker extremes of eye color as coarse surrogates for younger and older ages, respectively, in studies of the possible influence of age (or experience) in between-year movements of females among different nesting areas in Cooper's Hawk populations in Florida (Millsap *et al.* 2013) and Wisconsin (Rosenfield *et al.* 2016c).

Body Mass

Although we were unable with our research design to show that an individual's eye color was related to fitness, or number of young produced, this was not the case with another intrinsic trait in breeding Cooper's Hawks. For example, body mass, or breeding adult weight in grams during the nestling stage, a measure that reliably indicates body size of Cooper's Hawks 2 years or older in both sexes, is a strong factor in the nesting ecology of several northern populations of this species (Rosenfield and Bielefeldt 1999, Rosenfield *et al.* 2010, Sonsthagen *et al.* 2012). Recall, for example, that body size correlates with the size of prey among northern populations of breeding Cooper's Hawks. Body size is an important factor in the ecology of raptors because larger size generally allows for a greater accumulation of body reserves, which in turn could enhance survival, thanks in part to the increased ability to withstand periods of food deprivation. Starvation is a predominant reason for death in raptors (Newton 1979, Sunde 2002).

It should be stressed that a reliable index to body size in breeding Cooper's Hawks is their mass during the nestling stage. Mass varies in both male and female Wisconsin breeders across the pre-incubation, incubation, and nestling stages, so you cannot, for example, tenably compare masses of different individuals if their weights are obtained at different stages of the breeding season. Both sexes significantly lose mass during the breeding season, from its highest mark at pre-laying to its lowest, or lean body mass, measure at the nestling stage (Rosenfield and Bielefeldt 1999, Sonsthagen et al. 2012). The proportionate loss of mass across the three breeding stages averages about 6% for males and 9% for females. This loss makes sense from the standpoint that birds may be most active and therefore using more energy at the nestling stage, when they are protecting and feeding young (mostly by adult females) and gathering food (almost exclusively by males) for several growing nestlings. Interestingly, the proportionate loss of mass in Cooper's Hawks was not linked to habitat type or size of breeding birds in either sex. Some of these findings contrasted with results from the few other similar studies of raptors. For example, Eurasian Sparrowhawks (Newton et al. 1983), Barn Owls (*Tyto alba*; Marti 1990), Prairie Falcons (*F. mexicanus*; Steenhof and McKinley 2006), and Boreal Owls (Korpimäki 1990) exhibited a qualitatively similar decline in mass over the course of the nesting season for breeding females but not for breeding males. Newton et al. (1983) found no significant change in male mass over the breeding season of the ecologically similar accipiter, the Eurasian Sparrowhawk. By contrast, we demonstrated a seasonal and significant decline in the mass of breeding male Cooper's Hawks. Clearly, generalizations made by others (e.g., Newton et al. 1983, Korpimäki 1990, Steenhof and McKinley 2006) about within-year trends in mass of male raptors, and the behavioral and physiological factors that may affect these trends, should be made with caution. Contextually it is worth remembering that during the nesting season adult male raptors in general capture food they do not eat, and adult females eat food they do not catch. These disparities occur over several months during the nesting season. These disparate natural histories between the sexes are typical among most breeding raptors, and thus these differences would seem to influence and perhaps even explain some of the difference over time in their masses. Yet the similar division in sex roles among breeding raptors of various species, including Cooper's Hawks, do not seem to affect in a similar way the change in mass between sexes in the Cooper's Hawk. At least not in our study populations. Why not? I do not know.

Importantly, we have found that the mass of breeding Cooper's Hawks in Wisconsin was unrelated to the type of nesting area habitat. Body size was instead a heritable trait and positively correlated with annual clutch and brood counts, and with the number of detected recruits. Larger birds also tended to breed seasonally earlier in a given year than smaller ones (Rosenfield and Bielefeldt 1999). However, longevity was more important than body mass in determining lifetime reproduction of male Cooper's Hawks in our Wisconsin study areas (Rosenfield et *al.* 2009a). Similarly, longevity strongly correlates with lifetime reproduction for several other raptor species, including the Eurasian Sparrowhawk (Newton 1986), the Eastern Screech-Owl (Gehlbach 1989), the Osprey (Postupalsky 1989), and the Barn Owl (Marti 1997). However, we also found that body mass in breeding male and female Cooper's Hawks in Wisconsin was unrelated to longevity (Rosenfield *et al.* 2009a, 2016c), a finding different from several other studies of accipiters (Newton 1986, Sunde 2002, Kenward 2006). In fact, the longest-lived breeding male Cooper's Hawks in Wisconsin (aged 8-11 years) were of average to below-average size. Thus, other unknown factors, apparently unrelated to habitat or their body size *per se*, influenced their long lives (Rosenfield *et al.* 2009a, R.N. Rosenfield, unpubl. data).

Variation in size of individual breeding hawks within our Wisconsin population offered the opportunity for non-random (or assortative) mating with respect to body mass. Mueller (1986) speculated that the reverse size difference between the sexes (females larger than males), and hence the potential for non-random pairing, probably evolved in raptors because of the advantage of female dominance over males during pair formation, which could result in greater reproductive output. Indeed, male birds of prey, including Cooper's Hawks, often seem intimidated by or reluctant to approach their larger mates (Wrege and Cade 1977, Snyder and Wiley 1976, Newton 1986; see "Vocalizations" in Chapter 3). Perhaps larger females can more readily than smaller females influence the behavior of male mates, such as demanding food provisioning. Mueller's hypothesis therefore predicts that large females should pair preferentially with small males, and smaller females should avoid mating with larger males because these bigger males may be difficult to dominate. Findings from several studies were unable to support this claim and instead have reported random mating with respect to size in raptors (e.g., Newton *et al.* 1983, Bowman 1987, Marti 1990). However, one study using wing chord length (distance from wrist to longest flight feather in a folded wing) as an index to body size of paired birds, demonstrated positive assortative mating in the Peregrine Falcon, Brown Falcon (*F. berigora*), and the Nankeen Kestrel (*F. cenchroides*) in Australia. That is, larger females paired with larger males (Olsen *et al.* 1998). These authors offered no natural history basis for the non-random pairing they detected in these falcons and encouraged further investigation of the apparently complex relationship between mating and reverse size dimorphism in raptors. Warkentin *et al.* (1992) found non-random mating in tail length (a morphological or body form positively correlated with wing length) in a population of the Merlin and suggested that longer-tailed birds may be more agile and better hunters of the agile small birds they prey upon. However, they indicated that body characteristics probably played only a minimal role in choice of partners in their study population. Moreover, none of these studies demonstrated increased reproduction due to assortative pairing by body size *per se*, or that non-random mating was linked to recruitment.

By contrast, our results from an 18-year study of 104 mated pairs of Wisconsin Cooper's Hawks were the first to demonstrate non-random pairing in raptors based on mass *per se* (as well as wing chord). Birds at the extremes of size and mass (small/large) appeared to avoid mating with each other (contra to what Mueller [1986] predicted), whereas birds of relatively similar size (medium/medium) seemed more likely to form pairs (Rosenfield and Bielefeldt 1999). We suggested that enhanced reproductive benefits (we reiterate that body mass was positively correlated with annual reproductive output) provided a basis for non-random pairing. Because bigger birds produced more young, there would seemingly be a basis, or, to use the language of evolutionary ecologists, a selective pressure to pair with a larger mate. Thus, larger birds should avoid pairing with smaller birds, and birds of medium or small size would pair more by default. We also found that larger pairs produced a disproportionate share of recruits to subsequent breeding generations. To our knowledge, ours was the first study to show a link between non-random pairing and recruitment in raptors.

One might logically conclude that, given the heritability of body size, and the positive relation between body size and recruitment that we demonstrated in Wisconsin breeding Cooper's Hawks, that the state's population would evolve into one of larger birds. However, we have reported that body size has not changed across our long-term study of Wisconsin breeding Cooper's Hawks (Rosenfield *et al.* 2013, 2016c, and see Chapter 2). We reiterate that there was no relationship between body size and longevity in either sex of breeding birds in Wisconsin, and males with the greatest longevity, and thus with the greatest lifetime reproductive output, were of smaller-than-average size. Also, there was no difference in body size between females that exhibited nest-site fidelity versus those exhibiting breeding dispersal. However, breeding dispersal females may have lived longer than those that remained on nest sites across years.

Our study design did not allow us to investigate the possible adaptive value of body size in breeders outside the breeding season. Nor do we know of any other such reports concerning the seasonal adaptive value of body size (or variation in body size) in any other known breeding population of Cooper's Hawks. Some researchers have shown or suggested that, within a population, smaller size in males has an advantage under particular environmental conditions in some raptor species. But the possible adaptive role of smaller size, or what maintains smaller size in our or other breeding populations of raptors, is a controversial and a challenging field of raptor science (see Deshler and Murphy 2012, Perez-Camacho *et al.* 2015). Clearly, our understanding of the potential liabilities or advantages of variation in body size within a population are yet other areas of raptor biology that require additional natural history investigations.

Unlike other studies that investigated mating dynamics based on body size, our Wisconsin study population, excluding Milwaukee, was composed predominantly of adults 2 years or older (in gray plumage). Yearling (brown plumage) breeders were uncommon, and we have only one record of a pairing of a yearling male with a yearling female over the 38 years of study (Rosenfield *et al.* 2013, 2016a, R.N. Rosenfield, unpubl. data). Thus, our analyses, unlike those of others, were not complicated with pairings involving yearling birds, who by virtue of their inexperience generally exhibit lower reproductive output (Boal 2001, Warkentin *et al.* 1992). Non-random pairing of similar-aged birds, including Cooper's Hawks (e.g., yearling/yearling and adult/adult pairings, Boal 2001), is not uncommon in birds; indeed assortative mating by age has been found in many varieties of birds, including falcons, gulls, jays, and geese (see review in Warkentin *et al.* 1992).

However, it's important to note that, while statistics show that breeding male and female Cooper's Hawks exhibited a choice of social partners, we, like others, do not know the behavioral dynamics that led to non-random mating. Is it possible that large males exhibit choice by opting to only courtship-feed larger females? Our understanding of the social dynamics involved in pairing and the consequent demographics of productivity is clouded with the unexpected and mostly unexplored role that extra-pair paternity contributes to the potential correlations between pairing of mates and reproductive output in Cooper's Hawks. Because a substantial number of nests include extra-pair nestlings, it can't be assumed, for example, that just because the tending male raises the young, all were sired by him.

We do not know the short- or long-term individual reproductive ramifications nor the population consequences of extra-pair behavior in the ecology of the Cooper's Hawk. And we surely need to explore how prevalent extra-pair paternity may be in different populations. That said, we did suggest that males, despite the high risk of being cuckolded in our Milwaukee population (34% of nests had at least one extra-pair young; see Chapter 3), did not seem to reduce their parental investment, because productivity indices of this population were among the highest for Cooper's Hawks in North America (Rosenfield *et al.* 1991b, 2015a, Stout and Rosenfield 2010). In some species of birds, males reduce their parental investment, perhaps as a form of retaliation toward females, after being cuckolded (Petrie and Kempenaers 1998, Westneat and Stewart 2003, Li *et al.* 2014, Smith *et al.* 2016). Similar to what possibly happens in owls (e.g., Koopman *et al.* 2007), male Cooper's Hawks could potentially reduce their feeding of promiscuous mates and/

or the (possibly extra-pair) young to adaptively withhold their parental investment. However, assuming that a male cannot identify his genetic young, perhaps it is better for a male to deliver as much food to the entire brood as possible, to ensure that one or more of his genetic young will fledge and later become a breeder. Such a strategy, if adaptive, might suggest a difference in the eventual breeding fitness of his own young (higher) compared with the fitness of extra-pair young (lower). It would also seem that his mate should not be involved in extra-pair reproduction if her own survival or future fitness is compromised by raising extra-pair young.

We know of only one avian study that attempted to determine if extra-pair young showed greater fitness as breeding adults compared to that of within-pair young who became breeders. In fact, there was no difference in the reproductive success of extra-pair versus within-pair young, measured as their lifetime number of hatched offspring, recruited offspring, and hatched grand-offspring in a 17-year genetic parentage study of the Song Sparrow (*Melospiza melodia*; Sardell *et al.* 2012). Despite the fact that extra-pair reproduction can substantially influence physiology, behavior, and the dynamics of mating systems, the forces driving extra-pair reproduction by socially monogamous female birds remain unclear (Sardell *et al.* 2012). Avian ecologists have a daunting task to identify and understand these forces.

Similarly, we are currently investigating further the role of extra-pair behavior in the natural history of mating systems in several separate populations of the Cooper's Hawk. Such studies, including ours, would do well to also identify the traits and possible role of floaters in these dynamics. Indeed, studies of phenotype expression are markedly and unsurprisingly skewed toward research on territorial birds because these birds are predictably present and thus relatively easily observed at a nest. But the import of such traits may be difficult to interpret without considering the range of traits in floaters, the sexually mature birds in a population that are unable to obtain a territory (Moreno 2016, Rosenfield 2017). We note that we could not identify the sires of 89% of extra-pair young in our Milwaukee study of extra-pair paternity of Cooper's Hawks, and we therefore suggested that male floaters may be a factor in the occurrence and frequency of EPP in that population (Rosenfield *et al.* 2015a).

Chapter Six

The Meaning and Implication of Natural History Variation

Some biologists, as the renowned animal physiologist Brian McNab (2012) suggests, appear to be seduced by the successes of theoretical physicists in finding the, or at least, an equation that will describe or explain a broad range of phenomena. Thus, he continues, if one could find the proper equation it might adequately explain some dynamic of nature. It is conceivable that such a calculus could guide biologists toward making meaningful observations, maybe even predictions, about species and their demographic responses (and conservation risks) to changes in an ever-changing environment (Hockey and Curtis 2009). Yet an appreciable and likely important amount of variation occurs in biological phenomena. For example, in complete clutches some Cooper's Hawks lay two eggs, some four, and yet others five. This variation reflects in part the ability of an individual (or a species) to flex its natural history in response to ecological challenges or opportunities. Recall from Chapter 4 that the North Dakota population of Cooper's Hawks laid on average comparatively smaller clutches than those in other northern populations, perhaps because of trade-offs between migration and energy reserves requisite for egg production in that prairie population.

Species, of course, are not morphological or ecological constants that exhibit invariant natural histories across space and time, most especially if a species, like the Cooper's Hawk, is distributed across a large geographical area rich with environmental variation, including different stressors that surely influence the ecology and evolutionary trajectory of different breeding populations of this predator (Rosenfield et al. 2010). Thus, deriving average or mean mathematical values from collated samples to describe, say, the typical number of eggs produced by breeding Cooper's Hawks, may obscure important variations in environmental pressures that could cause differences in clutch counts both within and across populations of the species. Similarly, variations in natural history across breeding populations of Cooper's Hawks may suggest that inferring population-specific relationships, say to habitat in one region, may not adequately predict that relationship in another region. This of course doesn't mean that an average measure cannot be useful. For instance, an average or 'general' measure can sometimes establish a standard against which to evaluate individual or population performance, as we have done throughout this text.

In fact, only when we have a thorough account of biological variation in natural histories across a geographic range of a species can we begin to accurately understand a species' niche. Variation allows for detecting patterns that become hypotheses and theories that serve as portals into meaningful interpretations of nature. Following McNab further, without comprehensive natural history accounts of where a species lives, how it behaves, and what it eats, a species is simply a dot on a graph. Hence, variations in natural histories covered in this book are essential to our understanding of the breeding biology of the Cooper's Hawk.

Accordingly, I challenged the reader at the book's outset to tally the variations of the breeding natural histories of the Cooper's Hawk presented here. Now it's time to see how well you did. Let's start with variations primarily among different populations of Cooper's Hawks, with a little attention to selective context.

Natural history variation among populations of breeding Cooper's Hawks

The physical form or morphology of Cooper's Hawks clearly varies across different breeding populations, which likely reflects differences in habitat and foraging and migratory behavior among different populations. Sedentary adult hawks in Victoria, BC tended to have shorter wings than their more migratory counterparts in Wisconsin and North Dakota. In addition, tails in the Wisconsin and British Columbia birds were longer than breeders in the sparsely scattered woodlands of North Dakota. These disparities may reflect the energetic advantages to lift that longer wings provide to long-distance, migrating birds, and the greater agility that a longer tail may provide to Cooper's Hawks hunting densely wooded landscapes (Chapters 1 and 2).

We also documented overall body-size differences among several northern populations, differences consistent with a well-documented relationship in carnivore ecology, which indicates that a predator's size tracks the size of its prey. In fact, smaller and similar-sized breeding birds in British Columbia and western North Dakota took small avian prey, while eastern North Dakota hawks, who took larger prey, were larger than Cooper's Hawks in western North Dakota and British Columbia. The largest hawks occurred in Wisconsin, where even larger and comparatively more mammalian prey was taken. We note that these northern populations differed genetically, with birds in western and eastern North Dakota and in Wisconsin being genetically similar. However, these three populations were genetically different from that in British Columbia. Interestingly, although overall body size differed among some of these populations, we found little evidence that the extent of size dimorphism between males and females varied among these populations. In all these northern populations and elsewhere in North America, breeding Cooper's Hawks hunt primarily ground- and shrub-oriented avian prey; however, researchers in Florida reported a 'heavy reliance' on nestling songbirds taken from tree canopy nests (Chapters 1 and 2).

Breeding adult Cooper's Hawks vocalized less during feeding activities in urban than in rural environments in and around Tucson, AZ Females in the food-rich city were less likely to give calls at urban nests, apparently because of lower food stress compared to rural sites where food was more limited (Chapter 3).

There were several differences in demographics among breeding populations of Cooper's Hawks. Nesting densities of Cooper's Hawks varied 18-fold across the continent, with the highest and least varying density metrics occurring in and among cities, respectively. These data seem to suggest that cities are of higher nesting habitat quality (perhaps due to large numbers of avian prey) than are rural environments. In fact, production of young in some urban sites in Arizona and California was higher than productivity in surrounding rural landscapes. However, production of young was comparable in both urban and exurban environments in Wisconsin. Nesting birds in Tucson, AZ, initiated nesting about two weeks earlier than their counterparts in that city's rural surroundings, but there was no difference in calendric timing of breeding between urban and rural landscapes in Wisconsin. Production of eggs and young was significantly lower in a prairie nesting population in North Dakota compared with other northern breeding populations of Cooper's Hawks (see above, this chapter), but the breeding habitat in North Dakota was suitable and in fact that prairie population was increasing (Chapter 4).

Nest success, or the proportion of nests with eggs producing at least one young to an advanced age, varied significantly, and it concorded with nest height among three northern populations of Cooper's Hawks in British Columbia (highest nest height), North Dakota (lowest nest height), and Wisconsin (intermediate nest height). Lower nests in North Dakota may have been more susceptible to ground predators, suggesting regional differences in habitat quality. That said, research across North America generally has not demonstrated preferred breeding habitat for Cooper's

Hawks, that is, a net movement to (or disproportionate use of) one habitat rather than others. However, pine plantations in some areas of the Midwestern United States appear to be preferred habitat for nesting Cooper's Hawks (Chapter 4).

Sex ratios differed between two populations of breeding Cooper's Hawks in Wisconsin. The increasing population in Milwaukee adjusted its sex ratio toward a greater number of female young compared to the stable population outside the city. Given that offspring sex ratios in Cooper's Hawks tend to be skewed toward males outside Milwaukee, an adult Milwaukee female was more likely to have her female offspring enter this growing population, where breeding sites were still available. Offspring sex ratios also differed between Wisconsin and New Mexico populations (Chapter 4).

The majority of rarely breeding yearling, or SY, males were paired with older ASY females in Wisconsin, whereas SY males in Arizona were paired with SY females (Chapter 4).

The proportion of experienced breeding females who dispersed to different territories each year was relatively low in food-rich areas of Arizona and Wisconsin, but much higher in a limited-food study area in Florida. Dispersing females in Wisconsin appeared to live longer than non-dispersing females, whereas in Florida females who were faithful to their territory appeared to live longer than non-dispersing females (Chapter 4).

The distance that matured young traveled to their breeding sites was relatively short in an urban population of breeding Cooper's Hawks in Victoria, BC. This may have led to inbreeding, in a few rare instances, involving matings between siblings, and between parents and their siblings. The study site's principal boundary of ocean water may have restricted off-island, out-of-city movements, thereby increasing the incidence of shorter dispersal movements and a greater chance for close inbreeding (Chapter 4).

Some relatively large cities in Arizona, Wisconsin, and British Columbia tended to have a higher proportion and a consistent annual presence of yearling female breeders in their populations, compared with populations of Cooper's Hawks in smaller cities and some rural areas. It is unknown what causes this apparent difference in age-structure of female breeders among populations. This topic needs further investigation (Chapter 4).

Urban populations of Cooper's Hawks exhibited several other natural histories, either undocumented or occurring more frequently than those seen in rural populations of the species, including presence of the diseases trichomoniasis, West Nile Virus, and avian pox. These diseases may be more likely to occur in cities because urban birds used as prey by Cooper's Hawks serve as hosts for disease-causing agents, and such prey birds are present in higher densities, especially around bird feeders. Thus feeders may increase the probability of disease transmission. However, despite studies in several northern populations of breeding and migratory Cooper's Hawks in which trichomoniasis occurred at low levels and produced no deaths, the disease occurred at a relatively high prevalence and caused significant nestling mortality in Tucson, AZ, and Albuquerque, NM. Notably, higher disease rates occurred in urban settings than rural ones in these southwestern states. Trichomoniasis more likely occurs in Cooper's Hawk populations that consume relatively high numbers of doves, which are hosts for the disease-causing organism. West Nile Virus was detected in Milwaukee, WI, but no adverse effects were detected on its breeding population of Cooper's Hawks. Unfortunately, few bird feeder studies exist in North America or elsewhere around the world, and it is thus unclear how feeders affect avian infection risk dynamics in cities (Chapter 4).

Samples of Cooper's Hawks in and around Vancouver, BC, exceeded the highest concentrations of polybrominated diphenyl ethers (a flame retardant) reported in the literature for wild birds. The more urbanized Cooper's Hawks were exposed to a greater concentration of this chemical than rural birds, and some evidence indicated that other contaminants like polychlorinated biphenyls and dieldrin adversely influenced the physiology of some birds and their reproductive output. However, nesting territories were saturated in Vancouver, and overall reproduction was at comparably high levels. Unfortunately, the potential effects of flame retardants and many other modern chemical pollutants to urban wildlife are unknown and under study. The paucity of disease-related investigations concerning Cooper's Hawks and other wildlife in cities is concerning (Chapters 2 and 4).

We also showed that eye color varied among breeding birds in British Columbia, North Dakota, and Wisconsin. Cooper's Hawks in British Columbia and North Dakota acquired darker orange or red eyes more frequently and more quickly than their counterparts at known and relative ages in Wisconsin. Females in all these study sites were slower and less likely than males to acquire the darkest eye colors. Individual hawks of a given eye color in both sexes displayed variation in known and relative ages in British Columbia and Wisconsin, and thus eye color was not a reliable indicator of age in individual birds. There was no significant relationship between eye color of males and their brood sizes in any of these three populations, and therefore no discernible support for the oft-pitched premise that male eye color *per se* signals male fitness, or functions as a sexual trait for mate choice in this species. We do not know what specifically causes the variation in eye color by age between the sexes, nor do we know what causes the variation in eye color among different populations of the breeding Cooper's Hawks we studied. The relationships between eye color, age, sex, and reproductive output are unreported natural histories for Cooper's Hawk populations elsewhere in North America (Chapter 5).

And now, let's briefly overview contrasts in the natural history of breeding Cooper's Hawks versus that in other nesting raptors.

Variation in breeding natural histories between Cooper's Hawks and other raptors

The Cooper's Hawk exhibits one of the highest degrees of reversed sexual size dimorphism among the world's raptors, with females about a third larger than males, and some breeding males half the size of some females. Unlike many raptors, non-random mating occurred by size, with Wisconsin birds of like sizes (e.g., large female/large male) more likely to pair. Such non-random mating led to increased recruitment by larger paired individuals (Chapters 1 and 5).

The first documented cases of successful polygyny (one male mated simultaneously to two females) in the genus *Accipiter* occurred in Cooper's Hawks (at urban nests; Chapter 2).

Unlike some raptor species that use artificial substrates for nests in cities, Cooper's Hawks use only trees (Chapter 2).

Molt in male Cooper's Hawks begins about the same time as in females in Wisconsin, during the mid-incubation period, whereas in some other raptors, males begin molt later than females, during egg-hatching and the early nestling stage (Chapter 3).

In contrast with other raptors, the body size of breeding birds, as indexed by mass of adults at the nestling stage, was not associated in Wisconsin breeders with survivorship or related to habitat type, or possible territory quality (Chapters 4 and 5). Body mass of breeding males declined significantly during the nesting season, in contrast to males of other nesting raptor species, where it did not (Chapter 5).

Cooper's Hawks may be the most abundant breeding diurnal raptor across the broad array of natural and human-altered landscapes on the continent. They exhibit high nesting densities in all sizes of cities and towns, but also commonly nest in prairies and larger forested habitats. Thus, the Cooper's Hawk shows remarkable behavioral flexibility in its use of varied habitat types. It surely is the most common backyard breeding raptor, and likely the most prevalent beneficiary of bird feeding of all the nesting raptors throughout North America. This is to a large degree because bird feeders generally attract the size of birds preyed upon by this raptor: small to medium-sized songbirds and doves (Chapters 1, 2, and 4). Likewise, other important prey, such as the American Robin and chipmunks, are species commonly found on residential lawns and surrounding landscapes.

The productivity of Cooper's Hawks increased with increasing breeding density in Milwaukee, WI, unlike many other raptors (Chapter 4).

Also unlike other raptors, productivity was unrelated to habitat type in Wisconsin Cooper's Hawks. Similarly, breeding females did not improve their reproductive output by moving to different territories (Chapter 4).

One of the most notable natural history events is that females typically copulate after the male Cooper's Hawk delivers prey. In other raptors, there is little or no association between courtship feeding and copulations (Chapter 2). This behavior may provide a means by which females trade copulations for food with extra-pair males and thus maximize their energy intake needed for egg production. Such trades provide a possible explanation for why the Cooper's Hawk, unlike all other raptors studied to date, exhibits a high rate of extra-pair paternity (Chapter 3). These breeding dynamics suggest a complex social system among breeding Cooper's Hawks. Indeed, the Cooper's Hawk exhibits three successful breeding strategies: monogamy, extra-pair paternity, and polygyny. The role that sociality plays in influencing these strategies, non-random mating, nesting densities, natal and breeding dispersal, and other population attributes is unclear, if not unknown (Chapters 3, 4, and 5).

Final thoughts

Throughout the research described in this book, we have seen that the breeding natural history of the Cooper's Hawk has commonalities throughout North America. Annual adult survivorship rates are similar in virtually all study populations, for example, and birds are the primary prey throughout most of the continent. But we've also found much variation in the species' biology among nesting populations. There are also marked differences in the breeding biology of Cooper's Hawks from that of other raptors. The rich detail we have learned reveals much about the species' ecology and provides substantial insight into the breadth of its niche. I believe that the natural history of breeding Cooper's Hawks provides ample fascinating phenomena for the public to marvel at and ponder, to better understand and possibly heighten their appreciation of this winged, apex predator.

Behind this fascinating array of natural history facts lies a significant societal, conservation context. That is, the ability of species to adapt to the massive alterations in habitat being imposed by humans on our planet, and how or what our species will do to enhance (or not) the viability of biodiversity in the face of such forces. A key component of preserving biodiversity may be the identifying of factors that

The Cooper's Hawk's broad and abundant presence in and near cities across North America readily affords the opportunity for researchers to directly engage the general public with the natural history of breeding Cooper's Hawks. Citizens of all ages enjoy seeing birds up close and seem insatiable in their desire to know all they can about their winged neighborhood predators and why this bird is of interest to scientists. Photos by Madeline Hardin.

potentially threaten a species' very existence. Given the current fast pace of habitat change, there is no way to avoid disappearance of some populations and extinction of species (Piersma and van Gils 2011).

What a profound but pleasant irony, therefore, that a species traditionally thought of as a forest raptor heading toward extinction in the last century, in part because of woodland loss, has now become perhaps the most common backyard breeding raptor in cities throughout North America (Rosenfield *et al.* 2018). Who would have guessed, as my colleagues and I have speculated, that city planners and the urban bird-feeding public perhaps unwittingly contributed to the recovery of this red-eyed, blue-backed predator, which is so boldly tolerant of the vast array of human activities (Rosenfield *et al.* 2018)? Surely, remarkable behavioral and habitat flexibility have helped the Cooper's Hawk maintain high survival rates, nesting densities, and reproductive success throughout the continent, thus ensuring its population viability, at least for the immediate future.

Species that persist in the face of habitat alteration tend to show a large geographic distribution and considerable phenotypic and natural history variation, including broad tolerances for varying environmental conditions throughout their ranges (Brown 1995, Gaston 2003). As we have shown, these are strong attributes of breeding Cooper's Hawks in North America. But much work yet remains for researchers, particularly as to predicting the long-term effects of both urbanization and climate change on breeding birds. More information is needed to better understand and disseminate natural history knowledge of breeding Cooper's Hawks. Such knowledge may be the most powerful tool overall for engaging society with nature, and my hope is that this text contributes to that connection.

the meaning & implication of natural history variation

What a grand irony that Cooper's Hawks, once thought of as birds that required large, undisturbed forests for successful nesting, now show some of the highest production in some of the most congested human settings. This adult female is poised to fledge five young from a nest on the campus of Bowling Green State University in Ohio. Photo by Tom Muir.

REFERENCES

Alcock, J. 2009. Animal behavior, ninth edition. Sinauer Publishers, Sunderland, MA.

Alonso-Alvarez, C. 2006. Manipulation of primary sex ratio: an updated review. Avian and Poultry Biology Review 17: 1-20.

Andersen, D.E., S. DeStefano, M.I. Goldstein, K. Titus, D.C. Crocker-Bedford, J.J. Keane, R.G. Anthony, and R.N. Rosenfield. 2004. The status of Northern Goshawks in the western United States. Technical Review 04-1, The Wildlife Society, Bethesda, MA.

Arnott, G. and R.W. Elwood. 2009. Assessment of fighting ability in animal contests. Animal Behaviour 77: 991-1004.

Bednarz, J., D. Klem, L.J. Goodrich, and S.E. Senner. 1990. Migration counts of raptors at Hawk Mountain, Pennsylvania, as indicators of population trends, 1934-1986. Auk 107: 96-109.

Beehler, B.M. 2010. The forgotten science: a role for natural history in the twenty-first century? Journal of Field Ornithology 81: 1-4.

Bennett, P.M. and I.P.F. Owens. 2002. Evolutionary ecology of birds. Oxford University Press, New York, NY.

Bent, A.C. 1937. Life histories of North American birds of prey. Part 1. Smithsonian Institution United States National Museum Bulletin Number 167, Dover Publications, New York, NY.

Bielefeldt, J. and R.N. Rosenfield. 1997. Reexamination of cowbird parasitism and edge effects in Wisconsin forests. Journal of Wildlife Management 61: 1222-1226.

Bielefeldt, J. and R.N. Rosenfield. 2000. Comment: comparative breeding ecology of Cooper's Hawks in urban vs. exurban areas of southeastern Arizona. Journal of Wildlife Management 64: 599-600.

Bielefeldt, J., R.N. Rosenfield, and J.M. Papp. 1992. Unfounded assumptions about diet of the Cooper's Hawk. Condor 94: 427-436.

Bielefeldt, J., R.N. Rosenfield, W.E. Stout, and S.M. Vos. 1998. The Cooper's Hawk in Wisconsin: a review of its breeding biology and status. Passenger Pigeon 60: 111-121.

Bird, D.M., D.E. Varland, and J.J. Negro. 1996. Raptors in human landscapes: adaptations to built and cultivated environments. Academic Press, New York, NY.

Bird, D.M., R.N. Rosenfield, G. Septon, M.A. Gahbauer, J.H. Barclay, and J.L. Lincer. 2018. Management and conservation of urban raptors. Pages 258-272 In C.W. Boal and C.R. Dykstra (Eds.), Urban raptors: ecology and conservation of birds of prey in cities. Island Press, Washington, DC.

Birkhead, T.R. and C.M. Lessels. 1988. Copulation behavior in the Osprey. Animal Behaviour 36: 1672-1682.

Birkhead, T.R. and A.P. Møller. 1992. Sperm competition in birds: evolutionary causes and consequences. Academic Press, London, U.K.

Birkhead, T.R., L. Atkin, and A.P. Møller. 1987. Copulation behavior of birds. Behaviour 101: 101-138.

Blakesley, J.A., D.R. Anderson, and B.R. Noon. 2006. Breeding dispersal in the California Spotted Owl. Condor 108: 71-81.

Blackwell, B.F., P.D. Doerr, J. Michael Reed, and J.R. Walters. 1995. Inbreeding rate and effective population size: a comparison of estimates from pedigree analysis and a demographic model. Biological Conservation 71: 299-304.

Bloom, P.H., M.D. McCrary, J.M. Papp, and S.E. Thomas. 2017. Banding reveals potential northward migration of Cooper's Hawks from southern California. Journal of Raptor Research 51: 409-416.

Boal, C.W. 1997. An urban environment as an ecological trap for Cooper's Hawks. P.hD. dissertation, University of Arizona, Tucson, AZ.

Boal, C.W. 2001. Nonrandom mating and productivity of adult and subadult Cooper's Hawks. Condor 103: 381-386.

Boal, C.W. and R.W. Mannan. 1998. Nest-site selection by Cooper's Hawks in an urban environment. Journal of Wildlife Management 62: 864-871.

Boal, C.W. and R.W. Mannan. 1999. Comparative breeding ecology of Cooper's Hawks in urban and exurban areas of southeastern Arizona. Journal of Wildlife Management 63: 77-84.

Boal, C.W. and R.L. Spaulding. 2000. Helping at a Cooper's Hawk nest. Wilson Bulletin 112: 275-277.

Boal, C.W., R.W. Mannan, and K.S. Hedelson. 1998. Trichomoniasis in Cooper's Hawks from Arizona. Journal of Wildlife Diseases 34: 590-593.

Boggie, M.A. and R.W. Mannan. 2014. Examining seasonal patterns of space use to gauge how an accipiter responds to urbanization. Landscape and Urban Planning. 124: 34-42.

Bosakowski, T., D.G. Smith, and R. Speiser. 1992. Nest sites and habitat selected by Cooper's Hawks, Accipiter cooperii, in northern New Jersey and southeastern New York. Canadian Field-Naturalist 106: 474-479.

Bosakowski, T., R. Speiser, D.G. Smith, and L.J. Niles. 1993. Loss of Cooper's hawk nesting habitat to suburban development: inadequate protection for a state-endangered species. Journal of Raptor Research 27: 26-30.

Bowman, R. 1987. Size dimorphism in mated pairs of American Kestrels. Wilson Bulletin 99: 465-467.

Bradley, C.A. and S. Altizer. 2007. Urbanization and the ecology of wildlife diseases. Trends in Ecology and Evolution 22: 95-102.

Bradley, N.L., A.C. Leopold, J. Ross, and W. Huffaker. 1999. Phenological changes reflect climate change in Wisconsin. Proceedings of National Academy of Science, USA 96: 9701-9704.

Brogan, J.M., D.J. Green, F. Maisonneuve, and J.E. Elliott. 2017. An assessment of exposure and effects of persistent organic pollutants in an urban Cooper's hawk (Accipiter cooperii) population. Ecotoxicology 26: 32-45.

Brown, J.H. 1995. Macroecology. University of Chicago Press, Chicago, IL.

Caballero, I.C., J.M. Bates, M. Hennen, and M.V. Ashley. 2016. Sex in the city: breeding behavior of urban Peregrine Falcons in the Midwestern US. PLosOne 11: e015905.

References

Cade, T.J., J.H. Enderson, C.G. Thelander, and C.M. White. 1988. Peregrine Falcon populations: their management and recovery. The Peregrine Fund, Inc., Boise, ID.

Carson, R. 1962. Silent spring. Houghton Mifflin Company, Boston, MA.

Cartron, J.-L.E., P.L. Kennedy, R. Yaksich, and S.H. Stoleson. 2010. Cooper's Hawk (Accipiter cooperii). Pages 177-193 In J.-L.E. Cartron (Ed.), Raptors of New Mexico. University of New Mexico, University of New Mexico Press, Albuquerque, NM.

Caughley, G. 1977. Analysis of vertebrate populations. John Wiley and Sons. New York, NY.

Cava, J., A.C. Stewart, and R.N. Rosenfield. 2012. Introduced species dominate the diet of breeding Cooper's Hawks in British Columbia. Wilson Journal of Ornithology 124: 775-782.

Chamberlain, D.E., A.R. Cannon, M.P. Toms, D.I. Leech, B.J. Hatchwell, and K.J. Gaston. 2009. Avian productivity in urban landscapes: a review and meta-analyses. Ibis 151: 1-18.

Chiang, S.N., P.H. Bloom, A.M. Bartuszevige, and S.E. Thomas. 2012. Home range and habitat use of Cooper's Hawks in urban and natural areas. Pages 1-16 In C.A. Lepczyk and P.S. Warren (Eds.), Urban bird ecology and conservation. Studies in Avian Biology No. 45. University of California Press, Berkeley, CA.

Clobert, J., E. Danchin, A.A. Dhondt, and J.D. Nichols (Eds). 2001. Dispersal. Oxford University Press, New York, NY.

Clutton-Brock, T. and B.C .Sheldon. 2010. Individuals and populations: the role of long-term, individual-based studies of animals in ecology and evolutionary biology. Trends in Ecology and Evolution 25: 562-573.

Cody, M.L. 1985. An introduction to habitat selection in birds. Pages 3-56 (M.L. Cody, Ed.) In Habitat selection in birds. Academic Press, San Diego, CA.

Conrads, D.J. 1997. Nesting status of the Cooper's Hawk in Iowa: 1988-1996. Journal of Iowa Academy of Science 104: 82-84.

Craighead, J.J., and F.C. Craighead. 1956. Hawks, owls and wildlife. Stackpole Co. and Wildlife Management Inst., New York, NY.

Curtis, O.E., R.N. Rosenfield, and J. Bielefeldt. 2006. Cooper's Hawk (Accipiter cooperii). In A. Poole (Ed.), The birds of North America Online. Cornell Lab of Ornithology, Ithaca, NY.

Darwin, C. 1859. On the origin of species by means of natural selection or the preservation of favoured races in the struggle for life. J. Murray, London, U.K.

Deal, E., J. Bettesworth, and M. Muller. 2017. Two records of female Cooper's Hawks courting two different males in neighboring urban territories. Journal of Raptor Research 51: 83-84.

Deshler, J.F. and M.T. Murphy. 2012. The breeding biology of the Northern Pygmy-Owl: do the smallest of the small have an advantage? Condor 114: 314-322.

Detrich, P.J. and B. Woodbridge. 1994. Territory fidelity, mate fidelity, and movements of color-marked Northern Goshawks in the Southern Cascades of California. Pages 130-132 In W.M. Block, M.L. Morrison, and M.H. Reiser (Eds.), The Northern Goshawk: ecology and management. Studies in Avian Biology No. 16.

Donald, P.F. 2007. Adult sex ratios in wild bird populations. Ibis 149: 671-692.

Driscoll, T.G. and R.N. Rosenfield. 2015. Polygyny leads to disproportionate recruitment to urban Cooper's Hawks (Accipiter cooperii). Journal of Raptor Research 49: 344-346.

Dunn, E.H. and D.L. Tessaglia. 1994. Predation of birds at feeders in winter. Journal of Field Ornithology 65: 8-16.

Elliott, J.E., J.M. Brogan, S.L. Lee, K.G. Drouillard, and K.H. Elliott. 2015. PBDEs and other POPs in urban birds of prey partly explained by trophic level and carbon source. Science of the Total Environment 524-525: 157-165.

Errington, P.L. 1933. Food habits of southern Wisconsin raptors. Part 2. Hawks. Condor 35: 19-29.

Estes, W.A. and R.W. Mannan. 2003. Feeding behavior of Cooper's Hawks at urban and rural nests in southeastern Arizona. Condor 105: 107-116.

Evans, D.L. 1982. Status reports on twelve raptors. U.S. Department of the Interior Fish and Wildlife Service, Special Scientific Report – Wildlife No. 238. Washington, DC.

Faaborg, J., R.T. Holmes, A.D. Anders, K.L. Bildstein, K.M. Dugger, S.A. Gauthreaux, Jr., P. Heglund, K.A. Hobson, A.E. Jahn, D.H. Johnson, S.C. Latta, D.J. Levey, P.P. Marra, C.L. Merkord, E. Nol, S.I. Rothstein, T.W. Sherry, T.S. Sillett, F.R. Thompson III, and N. Warnock. 2010. Recent advances in understanding migration systems of New World land birds. Ecological Monographs 80: 3-48.

Fidino, M. and S.B. Magle. 2017. Trends in long-term urban bird research. Pages 161-184 In E. Murgui and M. Hedblom (Eds.), Ecology and conservation of birds in urban environments. Springer International Publishing, Chicago, IL.

Fischer, D.L. 1986. Daily activity patterns and habitat use of coexisting Accipiter hawks in Utah. Ph.D. dissertation, Brigham Young University, Provo, UT.

Fisher, A.K. 1893. The hawks and owls of the United States in their relation to agriculture. U.S. Department of Agriculture, Division of Ornithology and Mammalogy, Bulletin No. 8, Washington, DC.

Fitch, H.S., B. Glading, and V. House. 1946. Observations on Cooper's Hawk nesting and predation. California Department Fish and Game 32: 144-154.

Flaspohler, D.J., S.A. Temple, and R.N. Rosenfield. 2001a. Species-specific effects on nest success and breeding bird density in a forested landscape. Ecological Applications 11: 32-46.

Flaspohler, D.J., S.A. Temple, and R.N. Rosenfield. 2001b. Effects of forest edges on Ovenbird demography in a managed forest landscape. Conservation Biology 15: 173-183.

Forero, M.G., J.A. Donázar, J. Blas, and F. Hiraldo. 1999. Causes and consequences of territory change and breeding dispersal distance in the Black Kite. Ecology 80: 1298-1310.

Ganey, J.L., D.L. Apprill, S.C. Kyle, T.A. Rawlinson, R.S. Jones, and J.P. Ward, Jr. 2014. Breeding dispersal of Mexican Spotted Owls in the Sacramento Mountains, New Mexico. Wilson Journal of Ornithology 126: 516-524.

Gaston, K.J. 2003. The structure and dynamics of geographic ranges. Oxford University Press, New York, NY.

References

Gavin, T.A., R.T. Reynolds, S.M. Joy, D. Leslie, and B. May. 1998. Genetic evidence for low frequency of extra-pair fertilizations in northern Goshawks. Condor 100: 556-560.

Gehlbach, F.R. 1989. Screech-Owl. Pages 315-326 In I. Newton (Ed.), Lifetime reproduction in birds. Academic Press, San Diego, CA.

González-Oreja, J.A., I. Zuberogoita, and F.J. Jiménez-Moreno. 2019. First record of Cooper's Hawk (Accipiter cooperii) breeding in Puebla, Mexico. Journal of Raptor Research 53. In press.

Greene, H.W. 2005. Organisms in nature as a central focus for biology. Trends in Ecology and Evolution 20: 23-27.

Grier, J.W. 1982. Ban of DDT and subsequent recovery of reproduction in Bald Eagles. Science 218: 1232-1235.

Grimm, N.B., S.H. Faeth, N.E. Golubiewski, C.L. Redman, J. Wu, X. Bai, and J.M. Briggs. 2008. Global change and the ecology of cities. Science 319: 756-760.

Grosbois, V., O. Gimenez, J.M. Gaillard, R. Pradel, C. Barbraud, J. Clobert, A.P. Møller, and H. Weimerskirch. 2008. Assessing the impact of climate variation on survival in vertebrate populations. Biological Review 83: 357-399.

Gutiérrez, R.J., W.S. Lahaye, and G.S. Zimmerman. 2011. Breeding dispersal in an isolated population of Spotted Owls Strix occidentalis: evidence for improved reproductive output. Ibis 153: 592-600.

Hamerstrom, F.N., Jr. and F. Hamerstrom. 1951. Food of young raptors on the Edwin S. George Reserve. Wilson Bulletin 63: 16-25.

Hannon, S.J., S. Wilson, and C.A. McCallum. 2009. Does cowbird parasitism increase predation risk to American Redstart nests? Oikos 118: 1035-1043.

Haughey, C.L., A. Nelson, P. Napier, R.N. Rosenfield, S.A. Sonsthagen, and S.A. Talbot. 2019. Genetic confirmation of a natural hybrid between a Northern Goshawk (Accipiter gentilis) and a Cooper's Hawk (A. cooperii). Wilson Journal of Ornithology 131. In press.

Hedenström, A. and S. Sunada. 1999. On the aerodynamics of molt gaps in birds. Journal of Experimental Biology 202: 67-76.

Henny, C.J. and H.M. Wight. 1972. Population ecology and environmental pollution: Red-tailed and Cooper's Hawks. Pages 229-250 In Population ecology of migratory birds: a symposium. U.S. Fish and Wildlife Service Report 2. Washington, DC.

Hockey, P.A.R. and O.E. Curtis. 2009. Use of basic biological information for rapid prediction of response of species to habitat loss. Conservation Biology 23:64-71.

Howe, H.F. 1977. Sex-ratio adjustment in the Common Grackle. Science 198: 744-746.

Hunt, W.G. 1998. Raptor floaters at Moffat's equilibrium. Oikos 82: 191-197.

Hunt, W.G., C.J.W. McClure, and T.D. Allison. 2015. Do raptors react to ultraviolet light? Journal of Raptor Research 49: 342-343.

Janik, C.A. and J.A. Mosher. 1982. Breeding biology of raptors in the central Appalachians. Raptor Research 16: 18-24.

Jetz, W., C.H. Sekercioglu, and K. Bohning-Gaese. 2008. The worldwide variation in avian clutch size across species and space. PLoS Biology 6: 2650-2657.

Johnsgard, P.A. 1990. Hawks, eagles, and falcons of North America. Smithsonian Institution Press, Washington, DC.

Keller, G.S., B.D. Ross, D.S. Klute, and R.H. Yahner. 2009. Temporal changes in migratory bird use of edges during spring and fall seasons in Pennsylvania. Northeastern Naturalist 16: 535-552.

Kelly, E.J. and P.L. Kennedy. 1993. A dynamic state variable model of mate desertion in Cooper's Hawks. Ecology 74: 351-366.

Kennedy, P.L. 1980. Prey size selection patterns of nesting male and female Cooper's Hawks (Accipiter cooperii). M.S. thesis, University of Idaho, Moscow, ID.

Kennedy, P.L. 1989. The nesting ecology of Cooper's Hawks and Northern Goshawks in the Jemez Mountains, NM: a summary of results, 1984-1988. Sante Fe, New Mexico: U.S. Department of Agriculture, Forest Service, Santa Fe National Forest.

Kennedy, P.L. 1991. Reproductive strategies of Northern Goshawks and Cooper's Hawks during brood rearing in north-central New Mexico. Ph.D. dissertation, Utah State University, Logan, UT.

Kennedy, P.L. and D.R. Johnson. 1986. Prey-size selection in nesting male and female Cooper's Hawks. Wilson Bulletin 98: 110-115.

Kenward, R.E. 2006. The goshawk. T. and A.D. Poyser, London, U.K.

Kenward, R.E., S.S. Walls, K.H. Hodder, M. Pahkala, S.N. Freeman, and V.R. Simpson. 2000. The prevalence of non-breeders in raptor populations: evidence from rings, radio-tags and transect surveys. Oikos 91: 271-279.

Kettel, E.F., L.K. Gentle, J.L. Quinn, and R.W. Yarnell. 2017. The breeding performance of raptors in urban landscapes: a review and metanalysis. Journal of Ornithology 159: 1-18.

Kilpatrick, A.M. 2011. Globalization, land use, and the invasion of West Nile virus. Science 334: 323-3237.

Kilpatrick, A.M., L.D. Kramer, M.J. Jones, P.P. Marra, and P. Daszak. 2006. West Nile virus epidemics in North America are driven by shifts in mosquito feeding behaviors. PLoS Biology 4: e82.

Koenig, W.D., D. Van Vuren, and P.N. Hooge. 1996. Detectability, philopatry, and the distribution of dispersal distances in vertebrates. Trends in Ecology and Evolution 11: 514-517.

Koopman, M.E., D.B. McDonald, and G.D. Hayward. 2007. Microsatellite analysis reveals genetic monogamy among female Boreal Owls. Journal of Raptor Research 41: 314-318.

Korpimäki, E. 1988. Factors promoting polygyny in European birds of prey: a hypothesis. Oecologia 77: 278-285.

Korpimäki, E. 1990. Body mass of breeding Tengmalm's Owls Aegolius funereus: seasonal, between-year, site and age-related variation. Ornis Scandinavica 21: 169-178.

Krebs, C.J. 1994. Ecology: the experimental analysis of distribution and abundance. HarperCollins College Publishers, New York, NY.

References

Kroodsma, D. 1996. *Ecology and evolution of acoustic communication in birds*. 2 volumes. Academic Press, New York, NY.

Krüger, O. and A.N. Radford. 2008. Doomed to die? Predicting extinction risk in the true hawks Accipitridae. *Animal Conservation* 11: 83-91.

Lack, D.L. 1968. *Ecological adaptations for breeding in birds*. Methuen and Company, London, U.K.

Langham, G.M., J.G. Schuetz, T. Distler, C.U. Soykan, and C. Wilsey. 2015. Conservation status of North American Birds in the face of future climate change. *PLosOne* 10: 0135350.

LeFranc, M.N. and B.A. Millsap. 1984. A summary of state and federal agency raptor management programs. *Wildlife Society Bulletin* 12: 272-282.

Li, J., Y. Liu, Y. Wong, and Z. Zhang. 2014. Extra-pair paternity in two sympatric Aegithalos tits: patterns and implications. *Journal of Ornithology* 155: 83-90.

Lien, L.A., B.A. Millsap, K. Madden, and G.W. Roemer. 2015. Male brood provisioning rates provide evidence for inter-age competition for mates in female Cooper's Hawks *Accipiter cooperii*. *Ibis* 157: 860-870.

Lind, O., M. Mindaugas, P. Olsson, and A. Kelber. 2013. Ultraviolet sensitivity and colour vision in raptor foraging. *Journal of Experimental Biology* 216: 1819-1826.

Macdonald, D.W. and D.D.P. Johnson. 2001. Dispersal in theory and practice: consequences for conservation biology. Pages 358-372 In J. Clobert, E. Danchin, A.A. Dhondt, and J.D. Nichols (Eds.), *Dispersal*. Oxford University Press, New York, NY.

Mack, R.N., D. Simberloff, W.M. Lonsdale, H. Evans, M. Clout, and F. Bazzaz. 2000. Biotic invasions: causes, epidemiology, global consequences and control. *Issues in Ecology* 5: 1-22.

Madden, K. 2011. Factors influencing nest site defense toward humans by Cooper's Hawks in the Albuquerque area. M.A. thesis, Prescott College of Environmental Studies, Prescott, AZ.

Mahler, B. and B. Kempenaers. 2002. Objective assessment of sexual plumage dichromatism in the Picui Dove. *Condor* 104: 248-254.

Mannan, R.W. and C.W. Boal. 2000. Home range characteristics of male Cooper's Hawks in an urban environment. *Wilson Bulletin* 112: 21-27.

Mannan, R.W., R.J. Steidl, and C.W. Boal. 2008. Identifying habitat sinks: a case of Cooper's Hawks in an urban environment. *Urban Ecosystem* 11: 141-148.

Mannan, R.W., W.A. Shaw, W.A. Estes, M. Alnen, and C.W. Boal. 2004. A preliminary assessment of the attitudes of people towards Cooper's Hawks nesting in an urban environment. Pages 87-92 In W.W. Shaw, L.K. Harris, and L. Vandruff (Eds.), *Proceedings of the 4th international symposium on urban wildlife conservation*. School of Natural Resources, College of Agriculture and Life Sciences, University of Arizona, Tucson, AZ. http//:cals.arizona.edu/pubs/adjunct/snr0704

Mannan, R.W., R.N. Mannan, C.A. Schmidt, W.A. Estes-Zumpf, and C.W. Boal. 2006. Influence of natal experience on nest-site selection by urban-nesting Cooper's Hawks. *Journal of Wildlife Management* 71: 64-68.

Marti, C.D. 1990. *Sex and age dimorphism in the Barn Owl and a test of mate choice.* Auk 107: 246-254.

Marti, C.D. 1997. *Lifetime reproductive success in Barn Owls near the limit of the species' range.* Auk 114: 581-592.

Marti, C.D., M. Bechard, and F.M. Jaksic. 2007. *Food habits.* Pages 129-149 In D.M. Bird and K.L. Bildstein (Eds.), Raptor research and management techniques. Hancock House Publishers, Surrey, BC.

Martin, L.B., and M. Boruta. 2014. *The impacts of urbanization on avian disease transmission and emergence.* Pages 116-128 In D. Gill and H. Brumm (Eds.), Avian urban ecology, behavioral and physiological adaptations. Oxford University Press, Oxford, U.K.

Marzluff, J.M. 2016. *A decadal review of urban ornithology and a prospectus for the future.* Ibis 159: 1-13.

Marzluff, J.M., F.R. Gehlbach, and D.A. Manuwal. 1998. *Urban environments: influences on avifauna and challenges for the avian conservationist.* Pages 283-299 In J.M. Marzluff and R. Sallabanks (Eds.), Avian conservation: research and management. Island Press, Washington, DC.

McCallum, H., N. Barlow, and J. Hone. 2001. *How should pathogen transmission be modeled.* Trends Ecology and Evolution 16: 295-300.

McConnell, S. 2003. *Nest site vegetation characteristics of Cooper's Hawks in Pennsylvania.* Journal of the Pennsylvania Academy of Science 76: 72-76.

McNab, B.K. 2012. *Extreme measures: the ecological energetics of birds and mammals.* University of Chicago Press, Chicago, IL.

Meehan, T.D., C.A. Lott, Z.D. Sharp, R.B. Smith, R.N. Rosenfield, A.C. Stewart, and R.K. Murphy. 2001. *Using hydrogen stable-isotope geochemistry to estimate the natal latitudes of immature Cooper's Hawks migrating through the Florida Keys.* Condor 103: 11-20.

Meehan, T.D., R.N. Rosenfield, V.N. Atudorei, J. Bielefeldt, L.J. Rosenfield, A.C. Stewart, W.E. Stout, and M.A. Bozek. 2003. *Variation in hydrogen stable-isotope ratios between adult and nestling Cooper's Hawks.* Condor 105: 567-572.

Meiri, S. and Y. Yom-Tov. 2004. *Ontogeny of large birds: migrants do it faster.* Condor 106: 540-548.

Meng, H.K. 1951. *Cooper's Hawk Accipiter cooperii (Bonaparte).* Ph.D. dissertation, Cornell University, Ithaca, NY.

Meng, H.K. 1959. *Food habits of nesting Cooper's Hawks and Goshawks in New York and Pennsylvania.* Wilson Bulletin 71: 169-174.

Meng, H.K. and R.N. Rosenfield. 1988. *Cooper's Hawk: reproduction.* Pages 331-349 In R.S. Palmer (Ed.), Handbook of North American birds, Volume 4, part 1: diurnal raptors. Yale University Press, New Haven, CT.

Miller, J.R. 2005. *Biodiversity conservation and the extinction of experience.* Trends in Ecology and Evolution 20: 430-434.

References

Millsap, B.A. 2018. Demography and metapopulation dynamics of an urban Cooper's Hawk subpopulation. Condor 120: 63-80.

Millsap, B.A., T.F. Breen, and L.M. Phillips. 2013. Ecology of the Cooper's Hawk in north Florida. North American Fauna 78: 1-58.

Moore, K.R. and C.J. Henny. 1984. Age-specific productivity and nest site characteristics of Cooper's Hawks (Accipiter cooperii). Northwest Science 58: 290-299.

Moreno, J. 2016. The unknown life of floaters: the hidden face of sexual selection. Ardeola 63: 49-77.

Morinha, F., P.S. Ramos, S. Gomes, R.W. Mannan, H. Guedes-Pinto, and E. Bastos. 2016. Microsatellite markers suggest high genetic diversity in an urban population of Cooper's Hawks (Accipiter cooperii). Journal of Genetics 95: 19-24.

Morrow, J., L. Morrow, and T.G. Driscoll. 2015. Aberrant plumages in Cooper's Hawks. Journal of Raptor Research 49: 501-505.

Mougeot, F. 2004. Breeding density, cuckoldry risk and copulation behaviour during the fertile period in raptors: a comparative analysis. Animal Behaviour 67: 1067-1076.

Mueller, B. 1989. The effects of hawks and owls on bobwhite quail. Quail Unlimited 8: 8-12.

Mueller, H.C. 1986. The evolution of reversed size dimorphism in owls: an empirical analysis of possible selective factors. Wilson Bulletin 98: 387-406.

Murphy, R.K. 1993. History, nesting biology, and predation ecology of raptors in the Missouri Coteau of northwestern North Dakota. Ph.D. dissertation, Montana State University, Bozeman, MT.

Murphy, R.K., M.W. Gratson, and R.N. Rosenfield. 1988. Activity and habitat use by a breeding male Cooper's Hawk in a suburban area. Journal of Raptor Research 22: 97-100.

Mutter, D., D. Nolin, and A. Shartle. 1984. Raptor populations on selected park reserves in Montgomery County, Ohio. Ohio Academy of Science 84: 29-32.

Negro, J.J., M. Villarroel, J.L. Tella, U. Kuhnlein, F. Hiraldo, J.A. Donazar, and D.M. Bird. 1996. DNA fingerprinting reveals a low incidence of extra-pair fertilizations in the Lesser Kestrel. Animal Behaviour 51: 935-943.

Nenneman, M.P., R.K. Murphy, and T.A. Grant. 2002. Cooper's Hawks, Accipiter cooperii, successfully nest and at high densities in the northern Great Plains. Canadian Field-Naturalist 116: 580-584.

Nenneman, M.P., T.A. Grant, M.L. Sondreal, and R.K. Murphy. 2003. Nesting habitat of Cooper's Hawks in northern Great Plains woodlands. Journal of Raptor Research 37: 246-252.

Neudorf, D.L.H. 2004. Extrapair paternity in birds: understanding variation among species. Auk 121: 302-307.

Newton, I. 1979. Population ecology of raptors. Buteo Books, Vermillion, SD.

Newton, I. 1986. The Sparrowhawk. T. and A.D. Poyser, Berkhamsted, U.K.

Newton, I. 1989. Lifetime reproduction in birds. Academic Press, New York, NY.

Newton, I., M. Marquiss, and A. Village. 1983. Weights, breeding, and survival in European Sparrowhawks. Auk 100: 344-354.

Newton, I., M.J. McGrady, and M.K. Oli. 2016. A review of survival estimates for raptors and owls. Ibis 158: 227-248.

Nicewander, J. and R.N. Rosenfield. 2006. Behavior of a brood of post-fledging Cooper's Hawks: non-independence of sibling movements. Passenger Pigeon 68: 321-343.

Olsen, P. 1995. Australian birds of prey. The John Hopkins University Press, Baltimore, MD.

Olsen, P., S. Barry, G.B. Baker, N. Mooney, and G. Cam. 1998. Assortative mating in falcons: do big females pair with big males? Journal of Avian Biology 29: 197-200.

Partners in Flight. 2017. Avian conservation and assessment database [Online]. http://pif.birdconservancy.org

Pavón-Jordán, D., P. Karell, K. Ahola, H. Kolunen, H. Pietiäninen, T. Karstinen, and J.E. Brommer. 2013. Environmental correlates of annual survival differ between two ecologically similar and congeneric owls. Ibis 155: 823-834.

Paxton, E.H., R.J. Camp, P.M. Marcos Gorresen, L.H. Crampton, D.L. Leonard, Jr., and E.A. VanderWerf. 2016. Collapsing avian community on a Hawaiian island. Science Advances 2: 1-8.

Pérez-Comacho, L., G. García-Salgado, S. Rebollo, S. Martinez-Hesterkamp, and J.M. Fernández-Pereira. 2015. Higher reproductive success of small males and greater recruitment of large females may explain strong reversed sexual dimorphism (RSD) in the Northern Goshawk. Oecologia 177: 379-387.

Peterson, D.J. and R.K. Murphy. 1992. Prey delivered to two Cooper's Hawk, Accipiter cooperii, nests in northern mixed grass prairie. Canadian Field-Naturalist 106: 385-386.

Petrie, M. and B. Kempenaers. 1998. Extra-pair paternity in birds: explaining variation between species and populations. Trends in Ecology and Evolution 13: 52-58.

Piersma, T. and J.A. van Gils. 2011. The flexible phenotype: a body-centred integration of ecology, physiology, and behavior. Oxford University Press, New York, NY.

Pike, T.W. and M. Petrie. 2003. Potential mechansims of avian sex manipulation. Biological Reviews 78: 553-574.

Piper, W.H. 2011. Making habitat selection more "familiar": a review. Behavioral Ecology and Sociobiology 65: 1329-1351.

Postupalsky, S. 1989. Osprey. Pages 441-469 In I. Newton (Ed.), Lifetime reproduction in birds. Academic Press, New York, NY.

Pulliam, H.R. 1988. Sources, sinks, and population regulation. American Naturalist 132: 652-661.

Ratcliffe, D. 1980. The Peregrine Falcon. Poyser, Calton, U.K.

Reynolds, R.T. and E.C. Meslow. 1984. Partitioning of food and niche characteristics of coexisting Accipiter during breeding. Auk 101: 761-779.

Reynolds, R.T. and H.M. Wight. 1978. Distribution, density, and productivity of accipiter hawks breeding in Oregon. Wilson Bulletin 90: 182-196.

Reynolds, R.T., E.C. Meslow, and H.M. Wight. 1982. Nesting habitat of coexisting Accipiter in Oregon. Journal of Wildlife Management 46: 124-138.

References

Reynolds, R.T., J.S. Lambert, C.H. Flather, G.C. White, B.J. Bird, L.Scott Baggett, C. Lambert, and S. Bayard De Volo. 2017. Long-term demography of the Northern Goshawk in a variable environment. Wildlife Monographs 197: 1-40.

Ribon, R., J.E. Simon, and G.T. de Mattos. 2003. Bird extinctions in Atlantic forest fragments of the Vicosa Region, southeastern Brazil. Conservation Biology 17: 1827-1839.

Robb, G.N., A. McDonald, R.A. Chamberlain, and S. Bearhop. 2008. Food for thought: supplementary feeding as a driver of ecological change in avian populations. Frontiers in Ecology and Environment 6: 476-484.

Robertson, B.A. and R.L. Hutto. 2006. A framework for understanding ecological traps and an evaluation of existing evidence. Ecology 87: 1075-1086.

Robinson, S.K. 1991. Effects of habitat fragmentation on midwestern raptors. Pages 195-202 In B.E. Pendleton and D.L. Krahe (Eds.), Proceedings midwest raptor management symposium and workshop. National Wildlife Federation Scientific Technical Series 15. Washington, DC.

Rollins, D. and J.P. Carrol. 2001. Impacts of predation on northern bobwhite quail. Wildlife Society Bulletin 29: 39-51.

Rosenfield, R.N. 1988. Cooper's Hawk: food. Pages 353-354 In R.S. Palmer (Ed.), Handbook of North American birds, Volume 4, part 1: diurnal raptors. Yale University Press, New Haven, CT.

Rosenfield, R.N. 1990. Pre-incubation behavior and paternity assurance in the Cooper's Hawk (Accipiter cooperii [Bonaparte]). Ph.D. dissertation, North Dakota State University, Fargo, ND.

Rosenfield, R.N. 2017. Moffat's anticipation of 21st century bird population dynamics theory: is variation in site quality exclusively the core tenant? Ibis 159: 703-706.

Rosenfield, R.N. and J.M. Papp. 1988. Subadult intrusion and probable infanticide at a Cooper's Hawk nest. Wilson Bulletin 100: 506-507.

Rosenfield, R.N. and J. Bielefeldt. 1991a. Vocalizations of Cooper's Hawks during the pre-incubation stage. Condor 93: 659-665.

Rosenfield, R.N. and J. Bielefeldt. 1991b. Reproductive investment and anti-predator behavior in Cooper's Hawks during the pre-laying period. Journal of Raptor Research 25: 113-115.

Rosenfield, R.N. and J. Bielefeldt. 1991c. Undescribed bowing display in the Cooper's Hawk. Condor 93: 191-193.

Rosenfield, R.N. and J. Bielefeldt. 1992. Natal dispersal and inbreeding in the Cooper's Hawk. Wilson Bulletin 104: 124-126.

Rosenfield, R.N. and J. Bielefeldt. 1993a. Cooper's Hawk (Accipiter cooperii). In A. Poole and F. Gill (Eds.), The birds of North America, No. 75. The Academy of Natural Sciences, Philadelphia, PA, and the American Ornithologists' Union, Washington, DC.

Rosenfield, R.N. and J. Bielefeldt. 1993b. Trapping techniques for breeding Cooper's Hawks: two modifications. Journal of Raptor Research 27: 170-171.

Rosenfield, R.N. and J. Bielefeldt. 1996. Lifetime nesting area fidelity in male Cooper's Hawks in Wisconsin. Condor 98: 165-167.

Rosenfield, R.N. and J. Bielefeldt. 1997. Reanalysis of relationships among eye color, age, and sex in the Cooper's Hawk. Journal of Raptor Research 31: 313-316.

Rosenfield, R.N. and J. Bielefeldt. 1999. Body mass, reproductive biology, and nonrandom pairing in Cooper's Hawks. Auk 116: 830-835.

Rosenfield, R.N. and J. Bielefeldt. 2006. Cooper's Hawk (Accipiter cooperii). Pages 162-163 In N.J. Cutright, B.R. Harriman, and R.W. Howe (Eds.), Atlas of the breeding birds of Wisconsin. Wisconsin Society for Ornithology, Madison, WI.

Rosenfield, R.N. and L.E. Sobolik. 2014. Proning behavior in Cooper's Hawks (Accipiter cooperii). Journal of Raptor Research 48: 294-297.

Rosenfield, R.N. and R.K. Anderson. 2016. Wisconsin endangered resources report 8: status of the Cooper's Hawk in Wisconsin. Passenger Pigeon 78: 171-189.

Rosenfield, R.N. and L.E. Sobolik. 2017. Unusual timing of alternative nest building by an urban Cooper's Hawk (Accipiter cooperii). Journal of Raptor Research 51: 483-484.

Rosenfield, R.N., M.W. Gratson, and L.B. Carson. 1984. Food brought by Broad-winged Hawks to a Wisconsin nest. Journal of Field Ornithology 55: 246-247.

Rosenfield, R.N., J. Bielefeldt, and R.K. Anderson. 1988. Effectiveness of broadcast calls for detecting breeding Cooper's Hawks. Wildlife Society Bulletin 16: 210-212.

Rosenfield, R.N., J. Bielefeldt, and J. Cary. 1991a. Copulatory and other pre-incubation behaviors of Cooper's Hawks. Wilson Bulletin 103: 656-660.

Rosenfield, R.N., J. Bielefeldt, and K.R. Nolte. 1992a. Eye color of Cooper's Hawks breeding in Wisconsin. Journal of Raptor Research 26: 189-191.

Rosenfield, R.N., J. Bielefeldt, and S.M. Vos. 1996a. Skewed sex ratios in Cooper's Hawk offspring. Auk 113: 957-960.

Rosenfield, R.N., J.W. Grier, and R.W. Fyfe. 2007a. Reducing management and research disturbance. Pages 351-364 In D.M. Bird and K.L. Bildstein (Eds.), Raptor Research and management techniques. Hancock House, Blaine, WA.

Rosenfield, R.N., R.W. Mannan, and B.A. Millsap. 2018. Cooper's Hawks: the bold backyard hunters. Pages 93-109 In C.W. Boal and C.R. Dykstra (Eds.), Urban raptors: ecology and conservation of birds of prey in cities. Island Press, Washington DC.

Rosenfield, R.N., J. Bielefeldt, R.K. Anderson, and J.M. Papp. 1991b. Status reports: accipiters. Pages 42-49 In B.E. Pendleton and D.L. Krahe (Eds.), Proceedings midwest raptor management symposium and workshop. National Wildlife Federation Scientific Technical Service 15, Washington, DC.

Rosenfield, R.N., C.M. Morasky, J. Bielefeldt, and W.L. Loope. 1992b. Forest fragmentation and island biogeography: a summary and bibliography. U.S. National Park Service Technical Report NPS/NRUW/NRTR 92/08.

Rosenfield, R.N., J. Bielefeldt, J.L. Affeldt, and D.J. Beckmann. 1995a. Nesting density, nest area reoccupancy, and monitoring implications for Cooper's Hawks in Wisconsin. Journal of Raptor Research 29: 1-4.

References

Rosenfield, R.N., J.W. Schneider, J.M. Papp, W.S. Seegar. 1995b. Prey of Peregrine Falcons breeding in West Greenland. Condor 97: 763-770.

Rosenfield, R.N., J. Bielefeldt, J.L. Affeldt, and D.J. Beckmann. 1996b. Urban nesting biology of Cooper's Hawks in Wisconsin. Pages 41-44 In D.M. Bird, D.E. Varland, and J.J. Negro (Eds.), Raptors in human landscapes. Academic Press, London, U.K.

Rosenfield, R.N., J. Bielefeldt, D.R. Trexel, and T.C.J. Doolittle. 1998. Breeding distribution and nest-site habitat of Northern Goshawks in Wisconsin. Journal of Raptor Research 32: 189-194.

Rosenfield, R.N., J. Bielefeldt, S.A. Sonsthagen, and T.L. Booms. 2000. Comparable reproductive success at conifer plantation and non-plantation nest sites for Cooper's Hawks in Wisconsin. Wilson Bulletin 112: 417-421.

Rosenfield, R.N., S.A. Sonsthagen, W.E. Stout, and S.L. Talbot. 2015a. High frequency of extra-pair paternity in an urban population of Cooper's Hawks. Journal of Field Ornithology 86: 144-152.

Rosenfield, R.N., M.G. Hardin, J. Bielefeldt, and R.K. Anderson. 2016a. Status of the Cooper's Hawk in Wisconsin. Wisconsin Endangered Resources Report Number 8: with selective retrospective and interpretations. Passenger Pigeon 78: 191-200.

Rosenfield, R.N., M.G. Hardin, J. Bielefeldt, and E.R. Keyel. 2016b. Are life history events of a northern breeding population of Cooper's Hawks influenced by changing climate? Ecology and Evolution 7: 399-408.

Rosenfield, R.N., J. Bielefeldt, L.J. Rosenfield, T.L. Booms, and M.A. Bozek. 2009a. Survival rates and lifetime reproduction of breeding male Cooper's Hawks in Wisconsin, 1980-2005. Wilson Journal of Ornithology 121: 610-617.

Rosenfield, R.N., D. Lamers, D.L. Evans, M. Evans, and J.A. Cava. 2011. Shift to later timing by autumnal migrating Sharp-shinned Hawks. Wilson Journal of Ornithology 123: 154-158

Rosenfield, R.N., J. Bielefeldt, T.L. Booms, J.A. Cava, and M.A. Bozek. 2013. Life-history trade-offs of breeding in one-year-old male Cooper's Hawks. Condor 115: 306-315.

Rosenfield, R.N., J. Bielefeldt, L.J. Rosenfield, R.K. Murphy, M.A. Bozek, and D.A. Grosshuesch. 2002a. The status of Merlin and Cooper's Hawk populations on the Little Missouri National Grassland in western North Dakota. USDA, Forest Service. Final Report. Minot, ND.

Rosenfield, R.N., J. Bielefeldt, L.J. Rosenfield, S.J. Taft, R.K. Murphy, and A.C. Stewart. 2002b. Prevalence of Trichomonas gallinae in nestling Cooper's Hawks among three North American populations. Wilson Bulletin 114: 145-147.

Rosenfield, R.N., T.G. Driscoll, R.P. Franckowiak, L.J. Rosenfield, B.L. Sloss, and M.A. Bozek. 2007b. Genetic analysis confirms first record of polygyny in Cooper's Hawks. Journal of Raptor Research 41: 230-234.

Rosenfield, R.N., S.J. Taft, W.E. Stout, T.G. Driscoll, D.L. Evans, and M.A. Bozek. 2009b. Low prevalence of Trichomonas gallinae in urban and migratory Cooper's Hawks in north central North America. Wilson Journal of Ornithology 121: 641-644.

Rosenfield, R.N., J. Bielefeldt, T.G. Haynes, M.G. Hardin, F.J. Glassen, and T.L. Booms. 2016c. Body mass of female Cooper's Hawks is unrelated to longevity and breeding dispersal: implications for the study of breeding dispersal. Journal of Raptor Research 50: 305-312.

Rosenfield, R.N., J. Bielefeldt, L.J. Rosenfield, A.C. Stewart, R.K. Murphy, D.A. Grosshuesch, and M.A. Bozek. 2003. Comparative relationships among eye color, age, and sex in three North American populations of Cooper's Hawks. Wilson Bulletin 115: 225-230.

Rosenfield, R.N., J. Bielefeldt, L.J. Rosenfield, A.C. Stewart, M.P. Nenneman, R.K. Murphy, and M.A. Bozek. 2007c. Variation in reproductive indices in three populations of Cooper's Hawks. Wilson Journal of Ornithology 119: 181-188.

Rosenfield, R.N., W.E. Stout, M.D. Giovanni, N.H. Levine, J.A. Cava, M.G. Hardin, and T.G. Haynes. 2015b. Does breeding population trajectory influence disparate nestling sex ratios in two populations of Cooper's Hawks? Ecology and Evolution 5: 4037-4048.

Rosenfield, R.N., L.J. Rosenfield, J. Bielefeldt, R.K. Murphy, A.C. Stewart, W.E. Stout, T.G. Driscoll, and M.A. Bozek. 2010. Comparative morphology of northern populations of breeding Cooper's Hawks. Condor 112: 347-355.

Roth, T.C., and S.L. Lima. 2003. Hunting behavior and diet of Cooper's Hawks: an urban view of the small-bird-in-winter paradigm. Condor 105: 474-483.

Roth, T.C., S.L. Lima, and W.E. Vetter. 2005. Survival and causes of mortality in wintering Sharp-shinned Hawks and Cooper's Hawks. Wilson Bulletin 117: 237-244.

Roth, T.C., W.E. Vetter, and S.L. Lima. 2008. Spatial ecology of wintering Accipiter hawks: home range, habitat use, and the influence of bird feeders. Condor 110: 260-268.

Rutz, C.R. 2008. The establishment of an urban bird population. Journal of Animal Ecology 77: 1008-1019.

Sanchez, C. 2007. How much do raptors vocalize: generalities, importance, and the need for song studies. Pages 210-219 In K.L. Bildstein, D.R. Barber, and A. Zimmerman (Eds), Neotropical raptors: proceedings of the second neotropical raptor conference, Iguazú, Argentina, 2006. Raptor Conservation Science Series No. 1. Hawk Mountain Sanctuary, Orwigsburg, PA.

Sardell, R.J., P. Arcese, L.F. Keller, and J.M. Reid. 2012. Are there fitness benefits of female extra-pair reproduction? Lifetime reproductive success of within-pair and extra-pair offspring. American Naturalist 179: 779-793.

Scott, J.D., J.F. Anderson, and L.A. Durden. 2013. First detection of Lyme disease spirochete Borrelia burgdorferi in ticks collected from a raptor in Canada. Journal of Veterinary Science & Medical Diagnosis 2:1-4.

Siders, M.S. and P.L. Kennedy. 1994. Nesting of Accipiter hawks: is body size a consistent predictor of nest site characteristics? Studies in Avian Biology 16: 92-96.

References

Siders, M.S. and P.L. Kennedy. 1996. Forest structural characteristics of accipiter nesting habitat: is there an allometric relationship? Condor 98: 123-132.

Smith, G.D., O.E. Murillo-Garcia, J.A. Hostetler, R. Mearns, I. Newton, M.J. McGrady, and M.K. Oli. 2015. Demography of population recovery: survival and fidelity of Peregrine Falcons at various stages of population recovery. Oecologia 178: 391-401.

Smith, S.B., J.E. McKay, M.T. Murphy, and D.A. Duffield. 2016. Spatial patterns of extra-pair paternity for Spotted Towhees Pipilo maculatus in urban parks. Journal of Avian Biology 47: 815-823.

Snyder, H.A. and N.F. R. Snyder. 1974a. Increased mortality of Cooper's Hawks accustomed to man. Condor 76: 215-216.

Snyder, N.F.R. and H.A. Snyder. 1974b. Function of eye coloration in North American accipiters. Condor 76: 219-222.

Snyder, N.F.R. and J.W. Wiley. 1976. Sexual size dimorphism in hawks and owls of North America. American Ornithologists' Union Monograph No. 20.

Snyder, N.F.R., H.A. Snyder, J.L. Lincer, and R.T. Reynolds. 1973. Organochlorines, heavy metals, and the biology of North American accipiters. Bioscience 23: 300-305.

Sonsthagen, S.A., R.N. Rosenfield, J. Bielefeldt, R.K. Murphy, A.C. Stewart, W.E. Stout, T.G. Driscoll, M.A. Bozek, B.L. Sloss, and S.L. Talbot. 2012. Genetic and morphological divergence among Cooper's Hawk (Accipiter cooperii) populations breeding in north-central and western North America. Auk 129: 427-437.

Squires, J.R. and R.T. Reynolds. 1997. Northern Goshawk (Accipiter gentilis). In A. Poole and F. Gill (Eds.), The birds of North America, No. 298. The Academy of Natural Sciences, Philadelphia, PA, and the American Ornithologists' Union, Washington, D.C.

Steenhof, K. and J.O. McKinley. 2006. Size dimorphism, molt status, and body mass variation of Prairie Falcons nesting in the Snake River Birds of Prey National Conservation Area. Journal of Raptor Research 40: 71-75.

Stewart, A.C. 2003. Observations of nest predation by Cooper's Hawks on Vancouver Island, British Columbia. British Columbia Birds 13: 7-8.

Stewart, A.C., R.W. Campbell, and S. Dickin. 1996. Use of dawn vocalizations for detecting breeding Cooper's Hawks in an urban environment. Wildlife Society Bulletin 24: 291-293.

Stewart, A.C., R.N. Rosenfield, and M.A. Nyhof. 2007. Close inbreeding and related observations in Cooper's Hawks. Journal of Raptor Research 41: 227-230.

Stewart, A.C., R.N. Rosenfield, and I.I. Stewart. 2009. Non-breeding observations of a marked population of urban-nesting Cooper's Hawks. Abstract. Raptor Research Foundation, Inc., Annual Conference, 29 September - 4 October 2009, Pitlochry, Scotland.

Stout, W.E. 2009. First documented eight-egg clutch for Cooper's Hawks. Journal of Raptor Research 43: 75-76.

Stout, W.E. and R.N. Rosenfield. 2010. Colonization, growth, and density of a pioneer Cooper's Hawk population in a large metropolitan environment. Journal of Raptor Research 44: 255-267.

Stout, W.E., R.N. Rosenfield, and J. Bielefeldt. 2008. Wintering location of a Wisconsin Cooper's Hawk and the impact of digital photography on wildlife research. Passenger Pigeon 70: 373-379.

Stout, W.E., R.N. Rosenfield, W.G. Holton, and J. Bielefeldt. 2007. Nesting biology of urban Cooper's Hawks in Milwaukee, Wisconsin. Journal of Wildlife Management 71: 366-375.

Stout, W.E., A.G. Cassini, J.K. Meece, J.M. Papp, R.N. Rosenfield, and K.D. Reed. 2005. Serologic evidence of West Nile virus infection in three wild raptor populations. Avian Diseases 49: 371-375.

Stutchbury, B.J.M. and E.S. Morton. 2008. Recent advances in the behavioral ecology of tropical birds. Wilson Journal of Ornithology 120: 26-37.

Sullivan, A.R., D.J. Flaspohler, R.E. Froese, and D. Ford. 2016. Climatic variability and the timing of spring raptor migration in eastern North America. Journal of Avian Biology 47: 208-218.

Sunde, P. 2002. Starvation mortality and body condition of goshawks Accipiter gentilis along a latitudinal gradient in Norway. Ibis 144: 301-310.

Sweeney, S.J., P.T. Redig, and H.B. Tordoff. 1997. Morbidity, survival, and productivity of rehabilitated Peregrine Falcons in upper midwestern U.S. Journal of Raptor Research 31: 347-352.

Taft, S.J., R.N. Rosenfield, and J. Bielefeldt. 1994. Avian hematozoa of adult and nestling Cooper's Hawks (Accipiter cooperii) in Wisconsin. Journal of Helminthological Society of Washington 61: 146-148.

Taft, S.J., R.N. Rosenfield, and D.L. Evans. 1996. Hematozoa in autumnal migrant raptors from Hawk Ridge Nature Reserve, Duluth, Minnesota. Journal of Helminthological Society of Washington 63: 141-143.

Terraube, J., F. Archaux, M. Deconchat, I. van Halder, H. Jactel, and L. Barbaro. 2016. Forest edges have high conservation value for bird communities in mosaic landscapes. Ecology and Evolution 6: 5178-5189.

Thorton, M., I. Todd, and S. Roos. 2017. Breeding success and productivity of urban and rural Eurasian Sparrowhawks Accipiter nisus in Scotland. Ecoscience 2017: 1-12. DOI: 10.1374322.

Trexel, D.R., R.N. Rosenfield, J. Bielefeldt, and E.G. Jacobs. 1999. Comparative nest site habitats in Sharp-shinned and Cooper's Hawks in Wisconsin. Wilson Bulletin 111: 7-14.

Trivers, R.L. 1972. Parental investment and sexual selection. Pages 136-179 In B. Campbell (Ed.), Sexual selection and the descent of man, 1871-1971. Aldine-Atherton, Chicago, IL.

Urban, E.H. and R.W. Mannan. 2014. The potential role of oral pH in the persistence of Trichomonas gallinae in Cooper's Hawks (Accipiter cooperii). Journal of Wildlife Diseases 50: 50-55.

U.S. Fish and Wildlife Service. 2012. 2011 National survey of fishing, hunting, and wildlife-associated recreation - National Overview, http://wsfrprogram.fws.gov/Subpages/NationalSurvey/National_Survey.htm

References

Viverette, C.B., S. Struve, L.J. Goodrich, and K.L. Bildstein. 1996. Decreases in migrating Sharp-shinned Hawks (Accipiter striatus) at traditional raptor-migration watch sites in eastern North America. Auk 113: 32-40.

Villarroel, M., D.M. Bird, and U. Kuhnlein. 1998. Copulatory behavior and paternity in the American Kestrel: the adaptive significance of frequent copulations. Animal Behaviour 56: 289-299.

Viitala, J., E. Korpimäki, P. Palokangas, and M. Koivula. 1995. Attraction of kestrels to vole scent marks visible in ultraviolet light. Nature 373: 425-427.

Warkentin, I.G., P.C. James, L.W. Oliphant. 1992. Assortative mating in urban-breeding Merlins. Condor 94: 418-426.

Warkentin, I.G., A.D. Curzon, R.E. Carter, J.H. Wetton, P.C. James, L.W. Oliphant, and D.T. Parkin. 1994. No evidence for extra-pair fertilizations in the Merlin revealed by DNA fingerprinting. Molecular Ecology 3: 229-234.

Wattel, J. 1973. Geographical differentiation in the genus Accipiter. Publication of the Nuttall Ornithological Club, No. 13. Cambridge, MA.

West, S.A. and B.C. Sheldon. 2002. Constraints in the evolution of sex ratio adjustment. Science 295: 1685-1688.

Westneat, D.F. and P.W. Sherman. 1997. Density and extra-pair fertilizations in birds: a comparative analysis. Behavioral Ecology and Sociobiology 41: 205-215.

Westneat, D.F. and I.R.K Stewart. 2003. Extra-pair paternity in birds: causes, correlates, and conflict. Annual Review Ecology and Evolutionary Systematics 34: 365-396.

Whaley, W.H. and C.M. White. 1994. Trends in geographic variation of Cooper's Hawk and Northern Goshawk in North America: a multivariate analysis. Proceedings of the Western Foundation of Vertebrate Zoology 5: 160-209.

Wiggers, E.P. and K.J. Kritz. 1991. Comparison of nesting habitat of coexisting Sharp-shinned and Cooper's hawks in Missouri. Wilson Bulletin 103: 568-577.

Wiggers, E.P. and K.J. Kritz. 1994. Productivity and nesting chronology of the Cooper's Hawk and Sharp-shinned Hawk in Missouri. Raptor Research 28:1-3.

Wilcoxen, T.E., D.J. Horn, B.M. Hogan, C.N. Hubble, S.J. Huber, J. Flamm, M. Knott, L. Lundstrom, F. Salik, S.J. Wassenhove, and E.R. Wrobel. 2015. Effects of bird-feeding activities on the health of wild birds. Conservation Physiology 3: 1-13.

Wrege, P.H. and T.J. Cade. 1977. Courtship behavior of large falcons in captivity. Raptor Research 11: 1-27.

Wrobel, E.R., T.E. Wilcoxen, J.T. Nuzzo, and J. Seitz. 2016. Seroprevalence of avian pox and Mycoplasma gallisepticum in raptors in central Illinois. Journal of Raptor Research 50: 289-294.

INDEX

Accipiter cooperii	13
A. striatus	19
A. gentilis	19
A. nisus	100
Aegolius funereus	69
age-structure	88, 90, 92, 107, 109, 135
Alaska Science Center	72
alternative nests	84
American beech	57
American Crow	102
American Kestrel	11
American Robin	21, 31, 33, 35, 47, 83, 138
assortative mating	121, 125, 128, 130
ASY bird	74, 75, 92, 123, 124
aspergillosis	41
Avian pox	41, 135
bacterium	46
bark flakes	53
Barn Owl	127, 128
Belted Kingfisher	31
blue darter	18
biodiversity	15, 113, 138
bird feeder	9, 26, 29, 39-42, 47, 136, 137
blood parasites	42
Blue Jay	29-32
body mass	22, 67, 123, 124, 126-129, 137
body size	20-21, 23, 28, 48, 72, 76, 106, 116, 126-130, 133, 134, 137
Boreal Owl	69, 127
Borrelia burgdorferi	46
bowing display	60, 61, 63, 67, 106
brancher	91
breeding dispersal	43, 107, 113-117, 129, 138
breeding density	40, 79, 81, 87, 88, 121, 138
British Columbia	21, 23, 40, 46, 56, 57, 67, 94, 95, 98, 105, 118, 123-124, 133-136
Broad-winged Hawk	34, 81
brood counts	48, 92-96, 125, 127
brood parasitism	73
Brown Falcon	128
Bubo virginianus	14
Bubulcus ibis	32
Buteo buteo	75
B. platypterus	34
B. jamaicensis	57
cak-cak-cak calls	66, 77
Cardinalis cardinalis	33
Cattle Egret	32, 36
cheep call	68
chemical pollutants	136
chicken	32
chicken hawk	24
chirrp call	68
Chordeiles minor	58
Circus cyaneus	69
cities	9, 19, 33, 42, 45, 47, 49, 61, 94, 96, 98, 101, 104, 107, 116-117, 135-139
climate change	47-49, 93, 140

Index

clutch counts	93, 95-96, 132	*Eutamias*	34
Cnemidophorus tesselatus	37	extra-pair fertilization	57, 68-72
columbid	42	extra-pair paternity	57, 68-72, 131
Colinus virginianus	28	exurban environment	26, 48, 87, 134
Columba livia	23	eye color	21, 99, 121-126
Columbina inca	42	evolution	21, 48, 121, 125, 129, 132
Common Buzzard	75		
Common Grackle	31	*Fagus grandifolia*	57
Common Nighthawk	58	*Falco berigora*	128
conjunctivitis	41	*F. cenchroides*	128
Cooper's Hawk	13, 18-26	*F. columbarius*	71
copulation	63-65, 68-76, 84, 138	*F. mexicanus*	127
		F. naumanni	73
copulation calls	68	*F. peregrinus*	34
Corvus brachyrhynchos	102	*F. sparverius*	71
courtship	58-59, 61-66, 72, 74, 130, 138	fitness	68, 131
		flame retardant	113
courtship feeding	39, 72, 74, 138	fledging	92
cuckolded	68, 71, 130	fledgling	91
Culex sp.	46	floaters	75, 131
Cyanocitta cristata	29	Florida	18, 32, 33, 35, 38, 57, 85, 95, 110, 114-115
DDT	24, 28, 87, 113		
DDE	113		
demographics	78, 134	food habits	29
dieldrin	113, 136	food habits study	29-39
disease	29, 39, 40-42, 46-47, 95-96, 135-136	foraging behavior	28, 29, 38
		forest fragmentation	25, 111
dispersal	43, 79	*Fraxinus pennsylvanica*	57
Douglas-fir	56-57	gene flow	117
Eastern Chipmunk	23, 31, 34, 41	geographic distribution	20, 23-24, 140
Eastern Cottontail Rabbit	23, 32	grasslands	24, 85
Eastern Screech-Owl	42, 128	*Gallus gallus*	32
eeeeeeee call	68	Gray Squirrel	23, 27
eeeeeeee-oo call	68	Great Horned Owl	14, 98, 105
ecological trap	43, 46	green ash	57
Eurasian Sparrowhawk	54, 100, 114, 127, 128	ground squirrel	36
		habitat fragmentation	113, 117
European Starling	33, 35, 87, 98	habitat suitability	79, 95, 111-121

Haemoproteus	42	nest	14, 33, 50-57
Haemorhous mexicanus	31	nest building	50-57
home range	38-39, 95	nesting density	74, 78, 80-81, 85-88, 112
House Sparrow	23, 33, 35, 36, 87		
hybrid (COHA x GOHA)	49	nestling	18, 68, 71-73, 78, 88-90, 97-98
inbreeding	117-118, 135		
Inca Dove	42	nest finding	77, 79-84
individual fitness	131	nesting phenology	82, 95-96
Juniperus scopulorum	57	nest-site fidelity	104, 113-117
Kettle Moraine State Forest	112	nest success	78, 98-100, 134
ki-ki-ki calls	66	nest tree	57
kik calls	30, 58, 62, 66-67	niche	13, 24, 133
Lesser Kestrel	73	non-random mating *see* assortative mating	
Leucocytozoan toddi	42	North Dakota	21, 23, 46, 57, 85-87, 99, 123-124
lifetime reproduction	127-128		
longevity	91, 104-106, 110, 115, 120, 127-129	Northern Bobwhite	28, 35
		Northern Cardinal	33
Lyme disease	46	Northern Goshawk	19, 20, 27, 49, 71, 87, 90, 114
mate guarding	70-71		
maternity	61, 68	Northern Great Plains	85-86
Megascops asio	42	Northern Harrier	69
Megaceryle alcyon	31	Northern Mockingbird	33
Merlin	71, 128	oak	57
metapopulation	43	organochlorines	9, 113
Milwaukee	25, 46, 70-75, 85, 88-90, 109, 117, 135-136	Osprey	71, 128
		Pandion haliaetus	71
		parental investment	89, 130-131
Mimus polyglottis	33	*Passer domesticus*	21
monogamy	57, 69, 138	paternity *see* extra-pair paternity	
Mourning Dove	31, 34, 83	pellets	29
mortality	42-43, 46, 78, 89, 94-95, 101, 104-105, 110	Peregrine Falcon	34, 57, 74, 128
		phenology	121
		phenotypes	119-120
mosquito	46	phenotypic plasticity	23
Nankeen Kestrel	128	philopatric	116
natal dispersal	43, 115, 117	pine plantations	57, 78, 80, 111-112, 116
natural history	13-17, 76, 82, 100, 130, 132, 138		
		Pine Siskin	31

Index

Pinus strobus	57	*Sciurus carolinenesis*	23
plasticity	23	sex ratios	78, 88-90, 93
plucking post	29-31, 66, 82-83, 114	Sharp-shinned Hawk	19, 20, 34, 40
		sibling mating	118
polybrominated diphenyl ethers	113	Silent Spring	24
polychlorinated biphenyls	113	*speeeeeeeeo* call	68
polygyny	69-70, 137	sperm competition	71
population sink	43	*Spermophilus*	36
population source	43	*Sphyrapicus varius*	31
population trajectory	87-88, 90	*Spinus pinus*	31
Populus tremuloides	57	starling	30, 33, 35, 45, 87-98
prairie	18, 23, 43, 86, 94-95, 100		
		Stevens Point	25, 70, 85, 97, 112
Prairie Falcon	127	*Sturnus vulgaris*	33
preferred habitat	111-112	survivorship	90, 104
preferred prey	36-37	SY bird	72, 90, 92, 108-110
pre-incubation	30, 39, 47, 54, 57, 61, 63, 65, 70-71, 82-83, 107	*Sylvilagus floridanus*	23
		Tamais striatus	23
		taped calls, broadcasts	77-78
prey	18, 20-21, 23, 28-34	threatened status	13
		thyroxin	113
prey remains	29, 83 and *see* prey	traits	20, 48, 119-120, 123, 125, 131
productivity	78, 92-101	trembling aspen	57
Pseudotsuga menziesii	57	*Trichomonas gallinae*	43
quadrat sampling	80-82	trichomoniasis	41, 42, 46, 96, 135-136
Quercus	57		
Quiscalus quiscula	31	Tucson, Arizona	25, 32, 38, 42, 43, 46, 85, 96, 107, 109, 114, 136
raccoon	98		
Rachel Carson	24		
Red Junglefowl	32	*Turdus migratorius*	21
Red-tailed Hawk	57, 75, 98	Victoria, British Columbia	21, 23, 56, 57, 67, 94, 95, 98, 123-124, 133-136
reproductive output	76, 78, 92-98, 123, 129		
reversed sexual size dimorphism	20, 65, 137	urban habitat	13-17, 24-26, 28-29, 34-50, 69-70, 74-75, 79-80, 85-
Rock Pigeon	10, 23, 32		
Rocky Mountain Juniper	57		
salmonellosis	41		

	88, 96, 98-104, 109-118, 134-136
urbanization	26, 47, 113, 140
vocalizations	50, 64-68, 77, 82-83
West Nile virus	46, 135-136
whaa calls	14, 30, 65-68
Whiptail Lizard	37
white pine	57, 77
whitewash	31, 81-83
White-winged Dove	42
Wisconsin	20-23, 29-34, 53, 85, 92, 112
yearling	37, 75-76, 90-92, 94, 107-109, 123, 130, 135
Yellow-bellied Sapsucker	31
Zenaida macroura	31
Z. asiatica	42

other ornithology titles by Hancock House Publishers

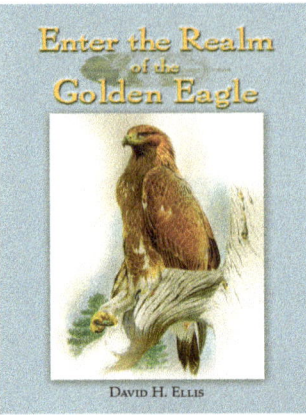

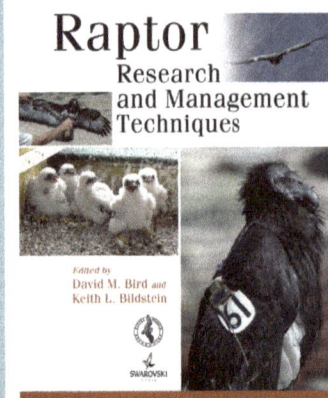

Behavior of the Golden Eagle: an illustrated ethogram
David Ellis, 2017
ISBN 978-0-88839-078-3 Trade SC
102pp, 88 illustrations, 8½ x 11

Enter the Realm of the Golden Eagle
David Ellis, 2013
ISBN 978-0-88839-704-1 Trade HC
ISBN 978-0-88839-705-8 Lim Ed. HC
496pp, 329 photos, 8½ x 11

Raptor Research & Management Techniques
David Bird & Keith Bildstein, 2007
ISBN 978-0-88839-639-6 SC
464pp, 66 photos, 8½ x 11

Hunting Tactics of Peregrines and other Falcons
Dick Dekker, 2009
ISBN 978-0-88839-683-9 Trade SC
200pp, 15 photos, 6 x 9

Bald Eagles in Alaska
Bruce Wright, Phil Schempf, 2010
ISBN 978-0-88839-695-2 Trade SC
440pp, 83 photos, 8½ x 11

North American Ducks, Geese & Swans: identification guide
Frank S. Todd, 2018
ISBN 978-088839-093-6 Trade SC
208pp, 5000+ photos, 6½ x 9

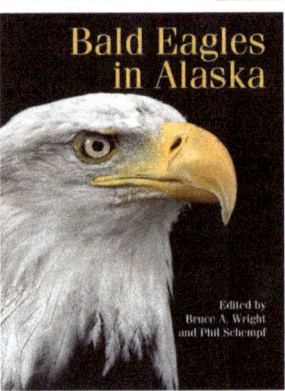

Hancock House Publishers
19313 0 Ave, Surrey, BC V3Z 9R9
www.hancockhouse.com
sales@hancockhouse.com
1-800-938-1114

www.ingramcontent.com/pod-product-compliance
Lightning Source LLC
LaVergne TN
LVHW060741300125
802520LV00006B/19